IMAGES
of America

ORRVILLE

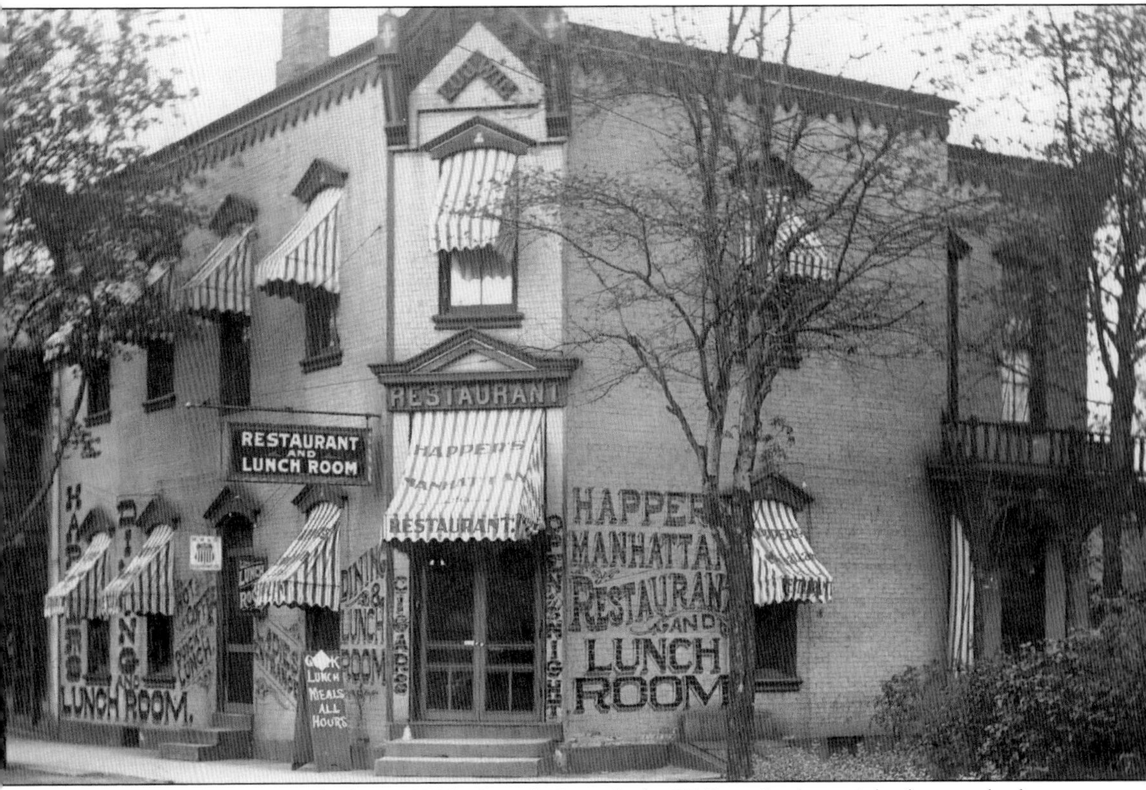

The Manhattan was built in 1872 by Joseph Snavely for William Ludwig. A bathroom, bedrooms, and living quarters were located on the second floor, and a saloon operated on the first floor. The upstairs rooms were later rented out to travelers on the railroad and men who worked the rail lines. In 1908, Howard Happer took over the Manhattan, turning it into a restaurant. Offering home-cooked meals daily and later famous for its pies, the Manhattan remained a restaurant until 1994. The building is currently owned by the Orrville Historical Society and houses its museum. A vast collection of items pertaining to Orrville history can be seen on display throughout the year. (Courtesy of Wayne Liechty.)

On the Cover: Pictured is the interior of Fouch's Meat Market, located on North Main Street in the downtown business district. Later, the Fouch family owned and operated Fouch's IGA on the corner of South Main and Chestnut Streets. That building then housed Smith's Grocery, and today, it is home to Bob Snyder's Auto Exchange. In the center of the photograph are Bob Simon (left) and Johnny Fouch; the others are unidentified. (Courtesy of Alison Wagner.)

IMAGES
of America

ORRVILLE

Mollie B. Curie on behalf of
the Orrville Historical Society

ARCADIA
PUBLISHING

ISBN 978-0-7385-9384-5

Published by Arcadia Publishing
Charleston, South Carolina

Printed in the United States of America

Library of Congress Control Number: 2012930210

For all general information, please contact Arcadia Publishing:
Telephone 843-853-2070
Fax 843-853-0044
E-mail sales@arcadiapublishing.com
For customer service and orders:
Toll-Free 1-888-313-2665

Visit us on the Internet at www.arcadiapublishing.com

*To Josh: Thank you for tolerating my stacks of photographs,
binders, and papers littering our dining room table.
Your support means everything. I love you.*

Contents

ACKNOWLEDGMENTS

When driving straight through Orrville on Ohio State Route 57, it is very obvious that history is ever present. The town has grown, all the while embracing and holding fast to much of the architecture that makes Orrville what it is. Thank you to all the people who read my *Orrviews* articles and responded with photographs and memories of our great city.

Putting this together on behalf of the Orrville Historical Society has been an amazing opportunity, and I thank you all for allowing me to do so and trusting in my work. Thank you to my family, lifetime residents of "O-town," for sharing all of their stories and memories and answering my many random questions to help guide this book to completion."

Our collection of photographs is extensive at the Orrville Historical Museum and much of it exists thanks to Harold Bowman. Harold, a lifetime resident of Orrville, collected and saved photographs and memorabilia throughout his lifetime, and upon his passing, he donated that collection to the society.

L.O. Weiss, a longtime member of the society, compiled images, clippings, and timelines in a number of volumes and donated them to the museum. "Depicting the village of the past and the city of today, Orrville, Wayne County, Ohio," a series of binders filled with clippings and writings collected by the original museum curator, was helpful during my research for information on people, businesses, and day-to-day life of the past.

Thanks goes to Wayne Liechty for allowing me to borrow his Orrville photograph and postcard collections. Just looking through them offered a better look at a simpler time. A number of Wayne's photographs can be seen throughout the book.

And to those who came before us: learning your ways of life was something special. I enjoyed every step of the way and know that every face in every photograph means something. I am thankful for all you did in helping bring our town to where it is today.

Unless otherwise specified, all photographs in the book are in possession of the Orrville Historical Museum archives. If an image was submitted by someone other than the museum, it will be specified at the end of the caption.

Introduction

Often, when people think of Orrville, a small northeastern Ohio city, they think of Smucker's Jelly, Bob Knight, and vast farmland; however, those of us who live here know that it is so much more.

Baughman and Green Townships, where Orrville sits, became authorized townships in 1816 and 1817, respectively. Inhabited by Native American tribes, the land was covered by swamps, lakes, and dense forest that was also home to a number of wild animals. Known as "the great swamp" or "dismal swamp," hickory, beech, oak, chestnut, walnut, and maple trees emerged, creating unlivable land. Deer, fox, wolves, elk, rattlesnakes, bear, wildcats, and wild turkeys roamed the land. These animals destroyed crops and farmland, making survival for the earliest settlers very difficult. Guns were carried at all times to ward off these everyday threats on crops and human life.

Among the dangers of living in the area were winters, which were especially difficult with nearly two feet of snow covering most of the area from December to April. Homes had bare dirt floors, and the howling winds blew snow through the space between the rafters, bringing the outside hazards in. Having to survive on what was produced that year because travel into the nearest town was impossible, many went hungry. If a doctor was needed, he would make a house call if the elements allowed him to do so; otherwise, ailments were dealt with to the best of one's ability.

After the Revolutionary War, Irishman James Taggart was given an opportunity to claim land in Ohio. In 1814, he picked his plot of land but did not want to relocate, so he went back to Pennsylvania, and his sons Samuel and Robert came to Ohio to settle the land instead. Samuel Taggart built the first home in Orrville in 1828. Then, Irish immigrant Smith Orr moved to the area in 1821. Orr came to America in 1801 with his family, and they settled in Applecreek in 1812. After he was married and his father passed away, he moved to the Orrville area. In 1825, he bought 160 acres of farmland on the southern end of town. In 1854, he moved his family into town and purchased the Christian Horst home and property on West Market Street.

Orrville was beginning to come together. The first school, a 20-foot-by-20-foot, one-room building on North Mill Street, was built in 1851. The first church, the Union Church, was erected in 1854 on the southeast corner of Mill and Church Streets. Meanwhile, Smith Orr worked with the railroad companies to bring their lines through Orrville. He and William Gailey established a sawmill and began to saw out the ties that would be used to build the railroad. Then, in 1852, the first line, the Pennsylvania Railroad, went through the village, running east and west. Smith Orr became justice of the peace and surveyor for the area due to his knowledge of the land. Then, a north-and-south line was added: the Cleveland, Zanesville & Cincinnati Railroad.

By 1855, there were 20 businesses, 50 homes, and 250 residents. Orrville was incorporated on May 9, 1864, near the end of the Civil War, and named on behalf of Judge Smith Orr, acknowledging the huge part he played in bringing the railroad through the area and developing the village. Orr's business partner, William Gailey, became the first mayor, D.G. Horst was the clerk, and T.D. McFarland was acting treasurer. Almost one year later, on April 23, 1865, Smith Orr passed away.

By 1870, the village boasted some 40 businesses, 200 homes, two doctors, two dentists, two pharmacists, three attorneys, five hotels, three churches, a mill, a school, a number of restaurants, and six saloons. The amount of saloons far outweighed anything else in town, and Orrville had many transient travelers and guests, with a Saturday night shooting or brawl not out of the ordinary after attending a local "girlie show." Then, in 1872, the unthinkable happened: the Central Ohio Fair was closing for the day, and some rowdy fairgoers had a brush with the law. It is said that after the incident, the group went downtown and set a building on fire. Later known as the great fire of 1872, it leveled the downtown area. The only building to survive was the two-story brick block on the northeast corner of the square. Thus, most of the original architecture was lost and had to be rebuilt. In late 1872, the Orrville Fire Department was officially formed.

Slowly but surely, Orrville was becoming a mark on the map. The Winkler Horse Traders had become known as one of the largest traders in the Midwest. In 1881, the first class graduated two students from Orrville High School. Business downtown was in full swing, mostly centering on the railroads. Then, in 1897, Jerome Smucker bought his first apple cider press, beginning his incredible business journey. H.C. Auble opened his furniture shop and undertaking business in 1906. The year 1928 was when Orrville gained national attention for the sudden disappearance of four-year-old Melvin Horst. The crime was never solved, and the boy was never found.

Some 20 passenger trains and 40 freight trains passed through Orrville daily, making it one of the largest stops between Pittsburgh and Chicago. When the market crashed in 1929, the Great Depression began, but by 1930, Orrville was still growing with a population of 4,427. In the early 1930s, railroading slowed down, and the village turned into an area of diversification and industry. In 1950, Orrville became a city and was no longer considered a village. A huge citywide celebration was held in 1964 for its centennial. Everyone took part in the 100th anniversary of the town, dressing up and reenacting what life was like as a pioneer in Orrville.

Over the next nearly 50 years, many things changed, but many things also stayed the same. If you are from Orrville, you know the sound of a train whistle and locomotive clanking over the tracks through the center of town. This is a daily reminder of where we came from and of all the people who came before us, some of whom worked toward goals that they knew they would never see come to fruition in their lifetimes. Their selfless dedication to make a life for themselves and their families has benefited us all.

Ask around, and you'll find that longtime residents agree: life here is pretty simple, as it always was, and we like it that way.

One

The Village

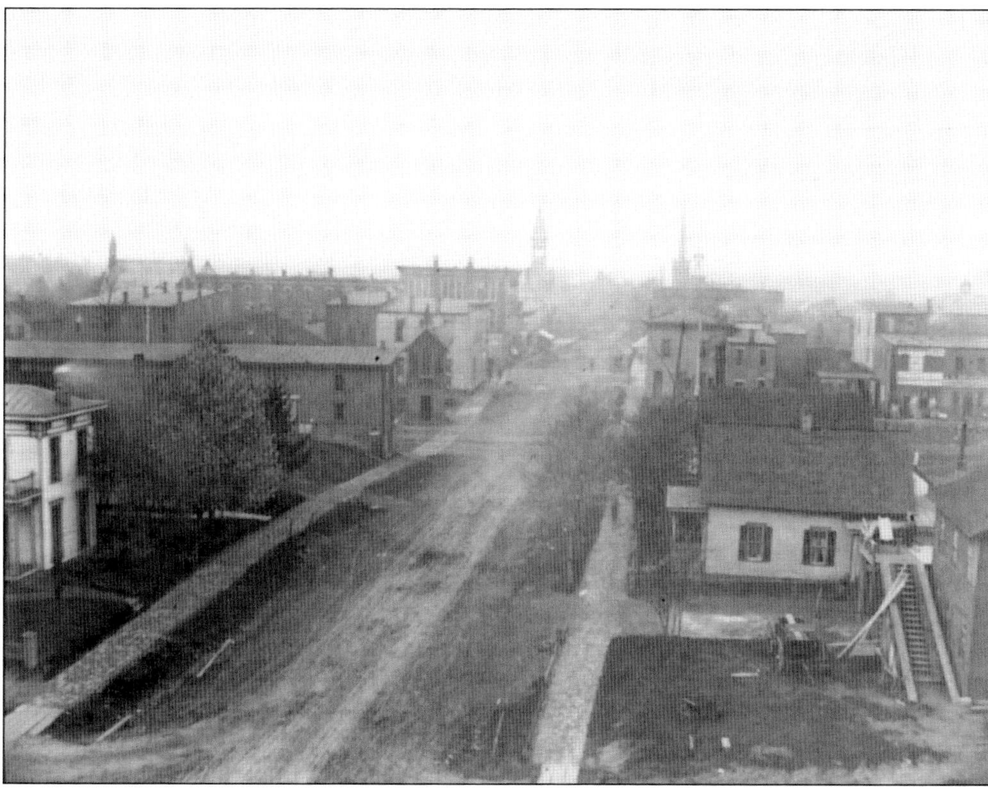

Taken in the late 1880s, this is a view of downtown looking north on Main Street. Seen here are the tracks that cross Main Street; the Pennsylvania Line was first run through town in 1852. Orrville stood out at the time, not for being a cattle town or a gold rush town but for being a railroad town.

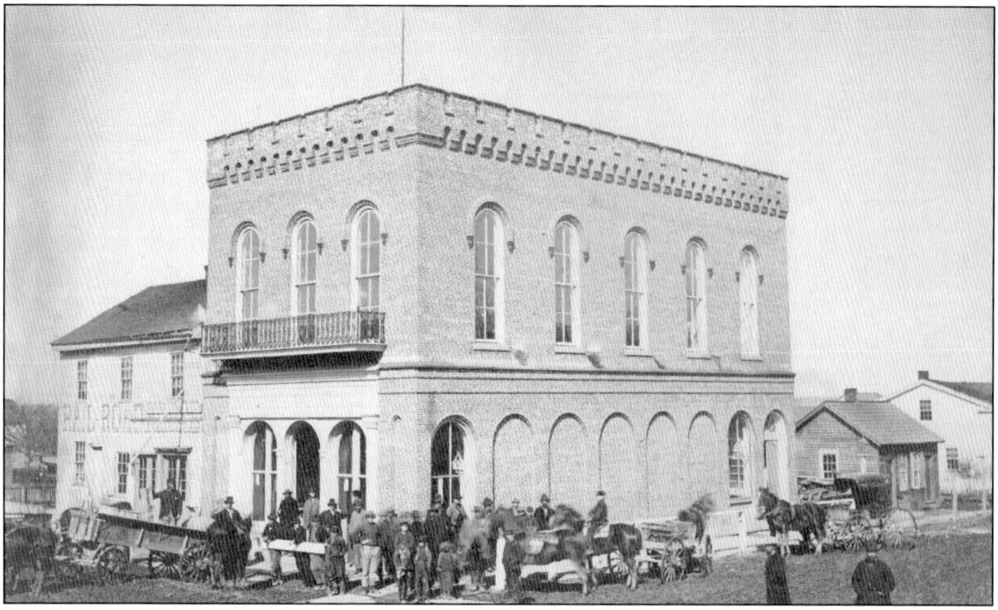

Built in 1866, the Metropolitan Building, or Evans' Hall, stood on the northeast corner of North Main and East Market Streets, known today as the "square" in downtown. It was dedicated with a Thanksgiving ball that year, held on the second floor of the building. Theodore Latimer took this photograph, which includes owner D.G. Evans, on March 15, 1867. The building to the left, with the words "RailRoad House," was the first hotel in Orrville, built by Henry Seas. The small building directly on the right of Evans' Hall was a meat market, constructed and owned by Sam Clark. The Metropolitan Building was crushed by the falling walls of the three-story brick block that was just north of it when it was destroyed in the fire of 1872.

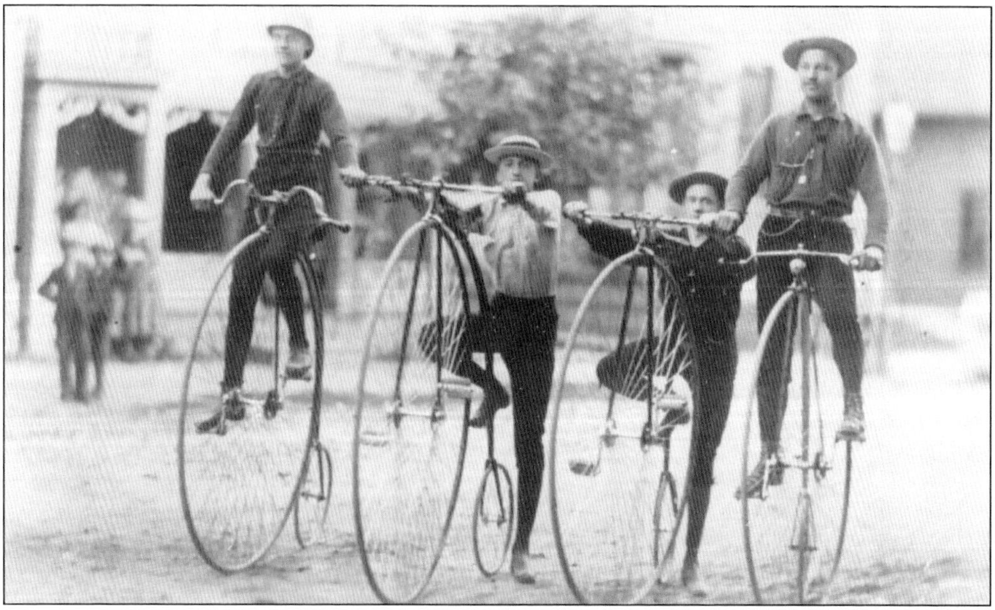

Boneshaker bikes are being ridden in the downtown area in 1884. Taken at the corner of Main and Water Streets, the boys from left to right are Andy Brenneman, Chas Bowman, Ernie Fisher, and Proctor Seas.

The downtown area looks much the same as it did in 1885. This photograph looks north on the business district on the east side of North Main Street. Most of the buildings were destroyed in the fire of 1872, leaving none of the original structures of Orrville standing.

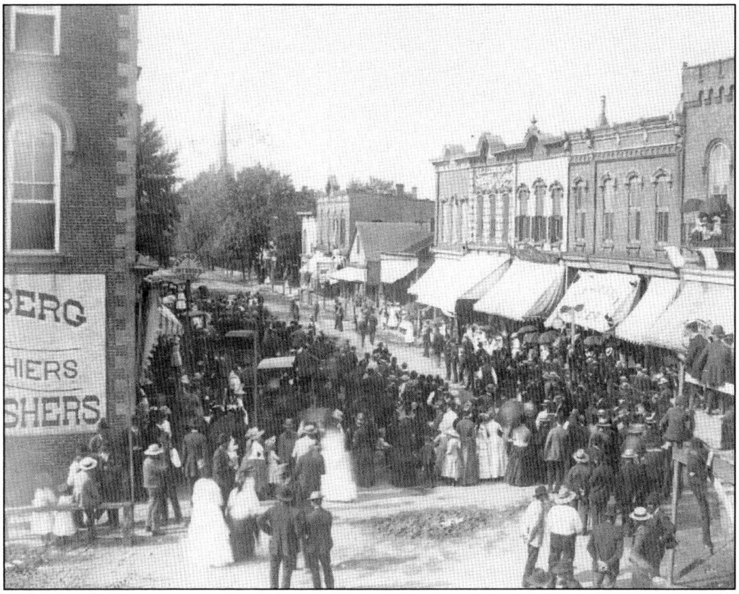

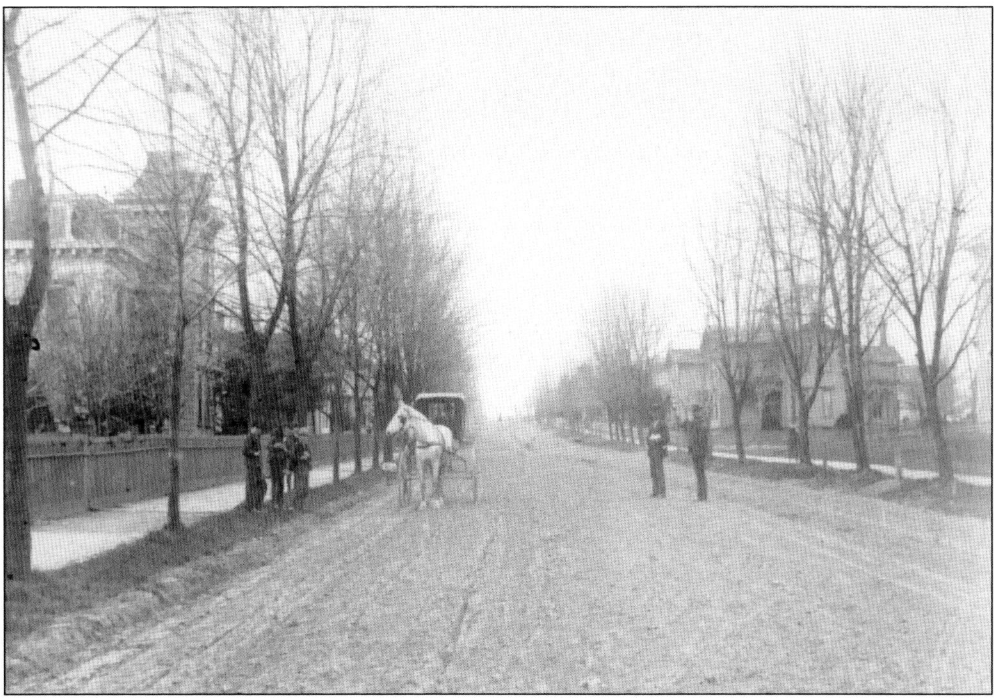

As the town grew, so did the population. The residential parts of town began to spread out into the country. Up until this time, most residences were located right around the downtown area, surrounding the railroad and depot. This 1885 photograph was taken on South Main Street, looking north from Paradise Street. Many of these homes are gone, but a handful of them still stand today, like a historical corridor when entering Orrville.

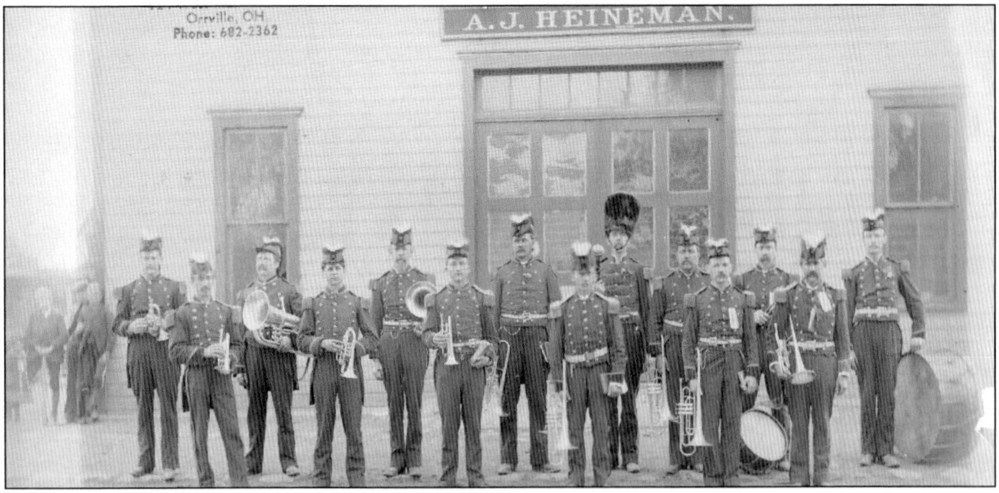

The Orrville Band in 1885 included, from left to right, bandleader Frank Harbaugh, Jonnie Boiggrain, John Sommer, Will Dayley, John Frank, Charles Bowman, Donald Thorn, Jonnie Beals, Jake Heffelman, Will Brown, Frank Herr, Fred Speilman, Elli Aultman, and John Speilman.

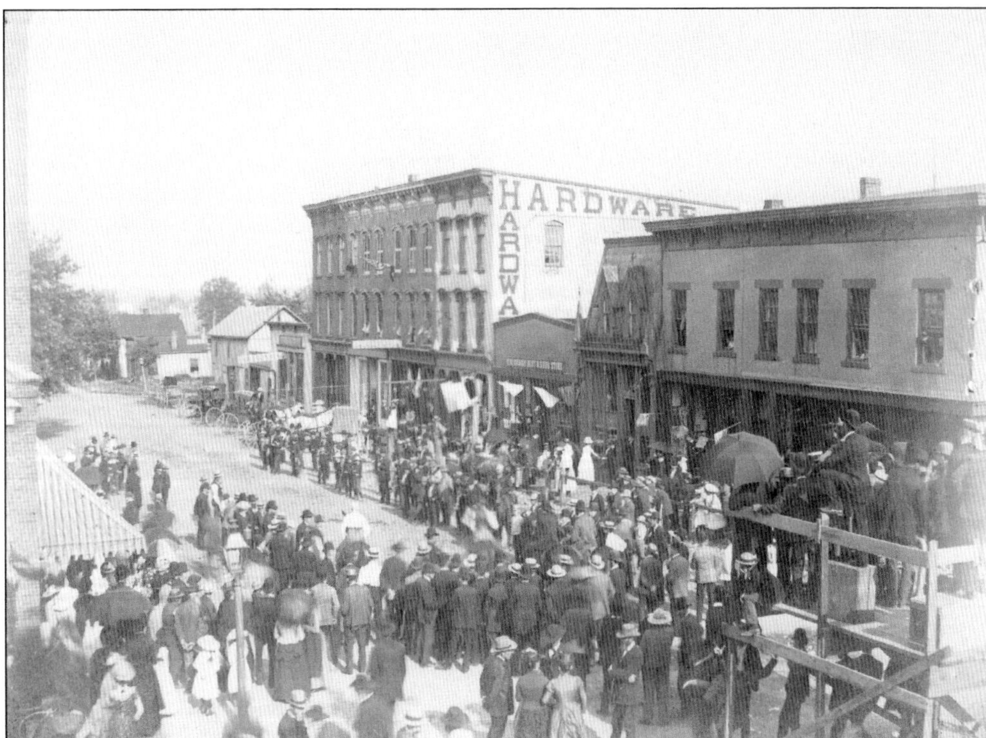

Facing east on Market Street, this photograph shows part of the business district as it was in 1885. Looking at the south side of the street, the building on the far right is where Ming-Hing Chinese restaurant is located today.

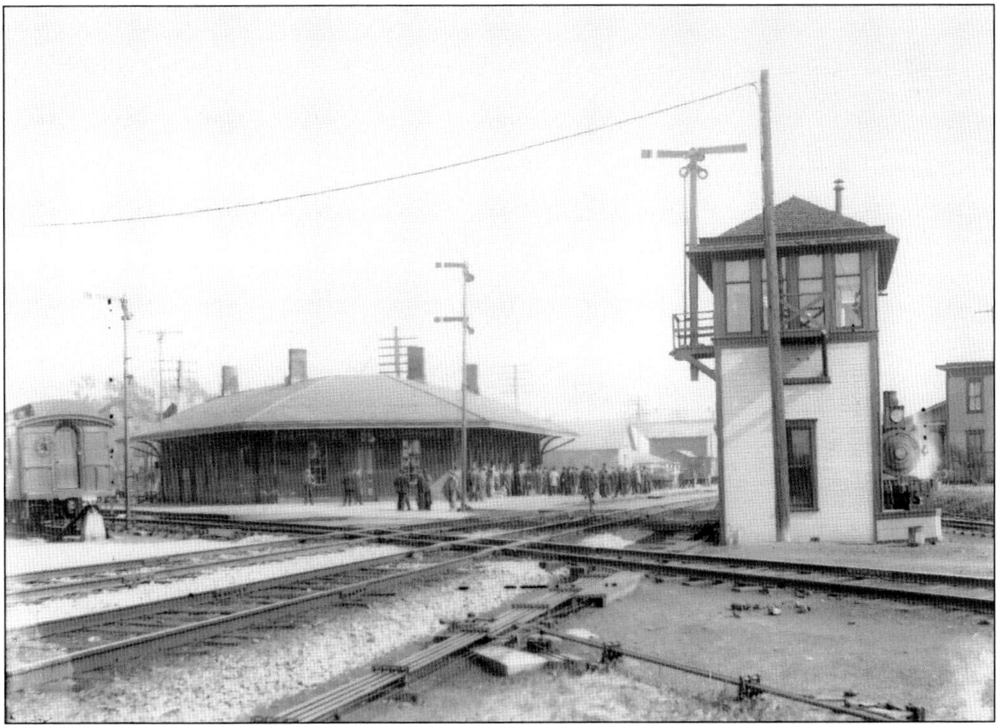

The Union Depot, the center for all the railroads that ran through Orrville, has seen many people pass through, including Harry Houdini, Eleanor Roosevelt, and President Taft. During the boom of the railroad, Orrville became one of the largest stops between Pittsburgh and Chicago, serving 40 passenger trains daily. (Courtesy of Wayne Liechty.)

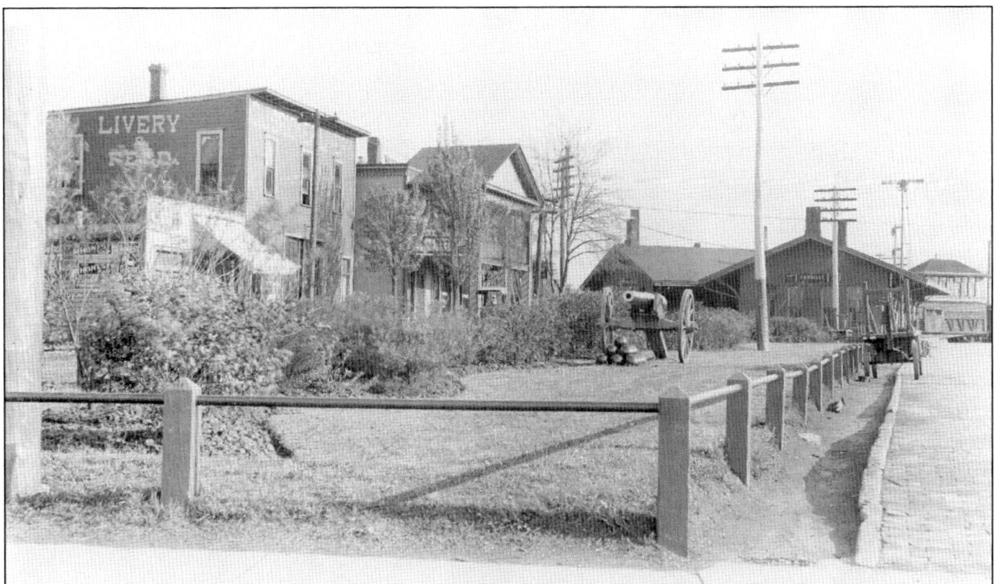

The area seen here, known today as Depot Street, Railroad Park, is located just off of West Market Street. In the background is the Union Depot; the businesses to the left include C.J. Bricker Livery and Houser's Saloon. The cannon in this photograph was used during the Civil War.

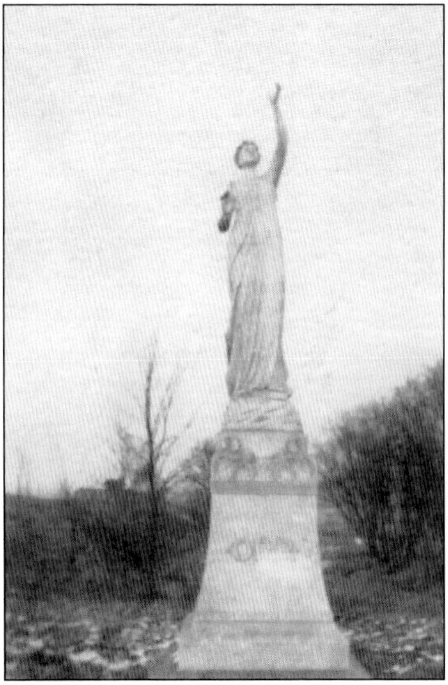

The statue at the old cemetery on East Church Street stands in the exact same place today as it did then; however, the female statue is missing both of her hands, with one missing piece extending most of the way up her arm today. The land for the cemetery was given to the city by Robert Taggart in 1861. The first person to be buried there was Isaac Hamilton, and the first Civil War veteran buried was Lt. Thomas McGill in 1862. The founding Orr family is entombed here, as well as a number of other settlers. Owned and maintained by the city, the cemetery is full of history and open year-round from dawn to dusk.

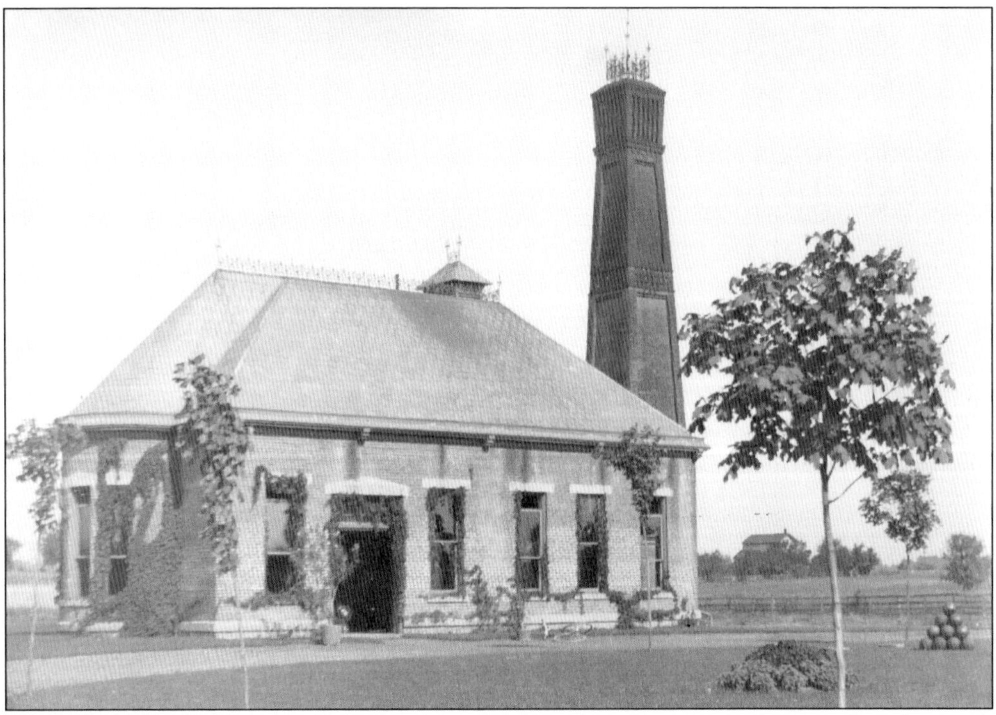

Pictured here is the original Orrville Water Works Building in 1894. It was located on the north end of town near the land that Orr Park sits on today, but it was not too far from where most of Orrville utilities buildings are currently located. The stack of Civil War cannonballs in the photograph is no more; it is said they were slowly stolen one by one over time. Unfortunately, this unique building no longer exists.

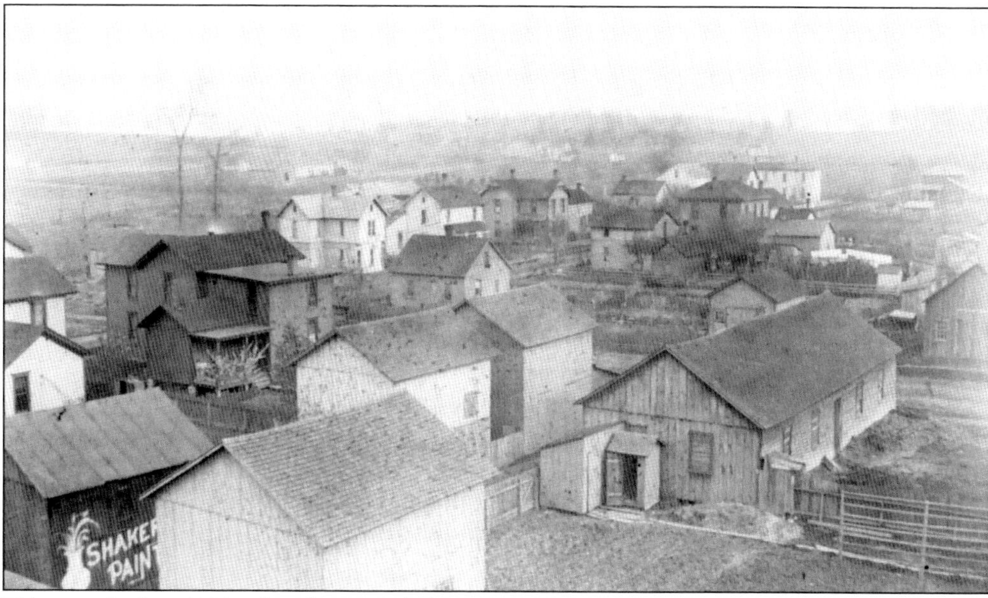

Taken in the late 1890s, this photograph shows some of the homes and farms that were located in Orrville. By 1893, the population of Orrville was 1,800, complete with four hotels, five churches, one school, one bank, one funeral parlor, four doctors, two dentists, three lawyers, and 11 saloons. It is said that a number of men passing through town would spend time in the saloons and then retire to the sleeping quarters of these establishments with professional members of the opposite sex.

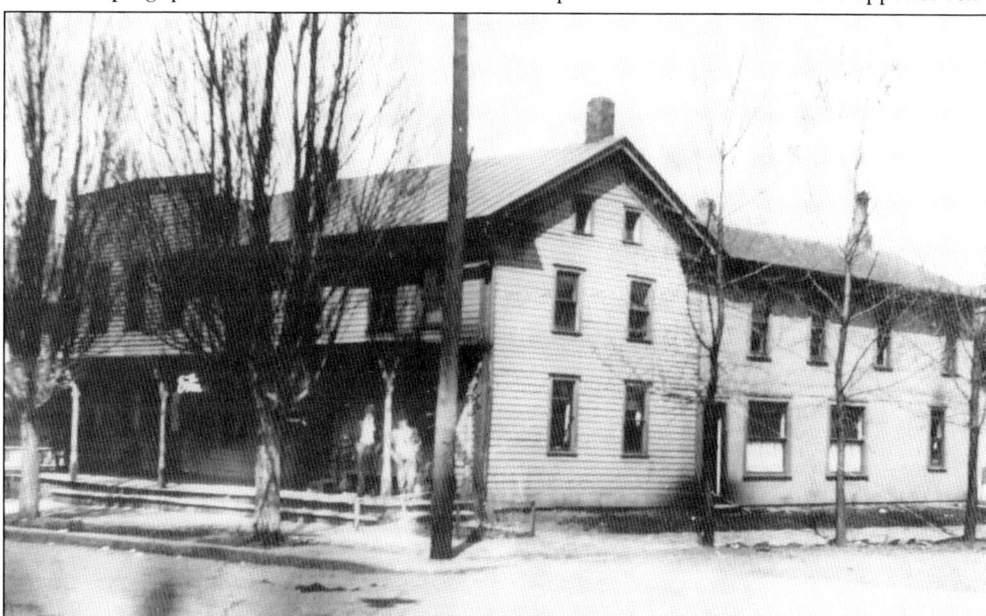

The Mansion House, built in 1854 by Smith Orr, was one of the first hotels in Orrville. It was located on the northwest corner of West Market and North Vine Streets and boasted 32 rooms, an office, sample room, parlor, dining room, full kitchen, pantry, attic, and front and back porches. Owned by Absalom and Maria Sponhour, it was just a three-minute walk from the Union Depot. An 1885 ad lists room rates from $1 to $1.50 per day. It was torn down in May 1913 to erect the Standard Oil station. Today, the site is the location of Cornerstone Park.

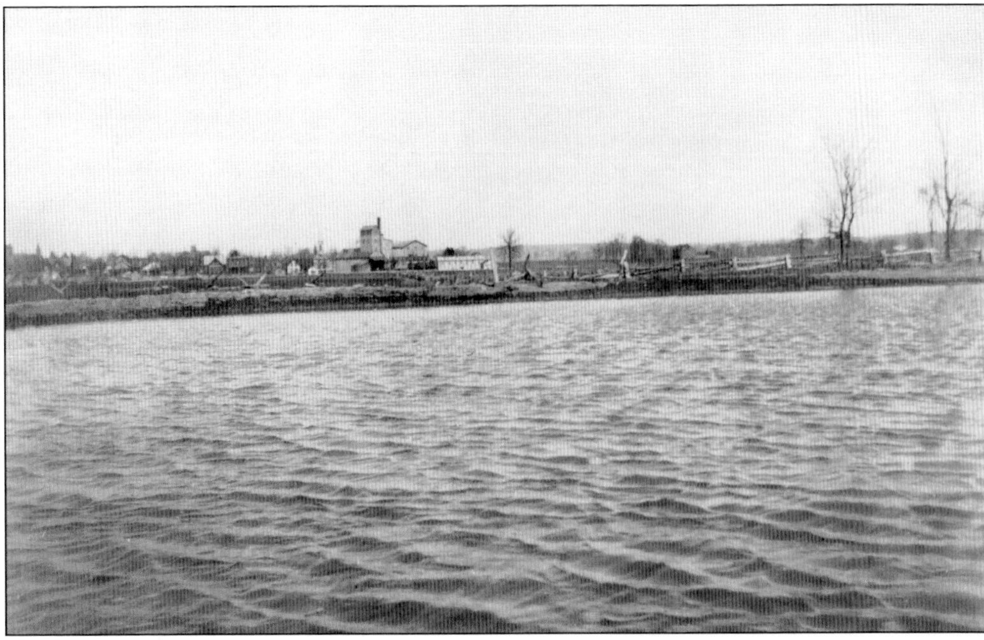

This photograph of Griffith's Pond was taken in 1898. The shallow body of water was located on land that is now a residential neighborhood on East Paradise Street. One of the structures seen in the background is the Orrville Flour Mill.

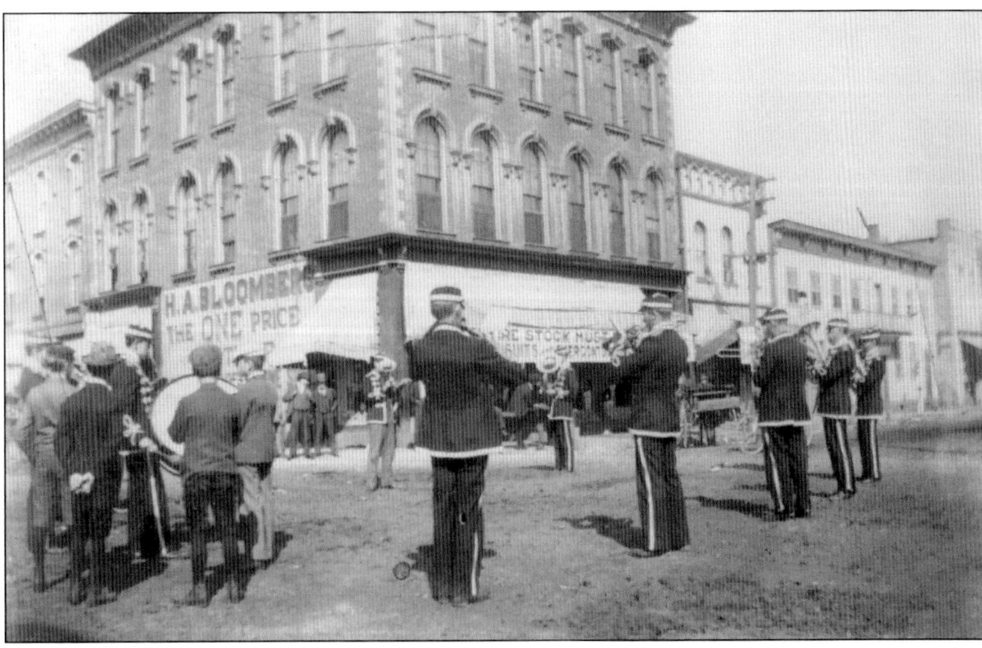

The Orrville Citizens Band is pictured at the corner of North Main and Market Streets in 1900. The building seen in the background is Bloomberg's; it was later the Orrville Savings Bank, and today, it is the home of PNC Bank.

This is city hall as it appeared in the late 1800s and early 1900s. Constructed in 1882 and razed in 1929 after being condemned, the building housed both the police and fire departments. The clock from the tower was refurbished in 1995 and is currently located inside the Municipal Building. The clock was originally given to the city by J.B. Stuffer in 1913.

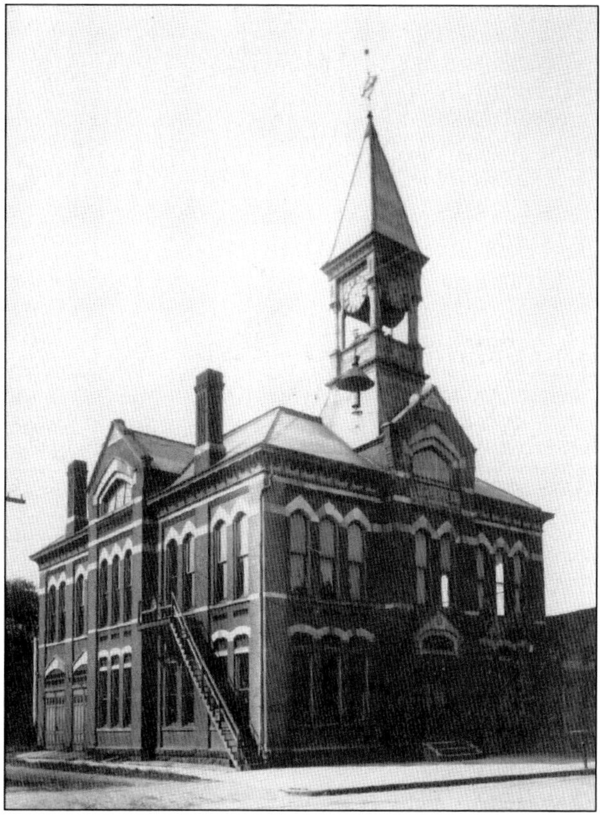

Pictured here are some unidentified rail yard workers on the Pennsylvania Railroad line. The men posed for a quick photograph along the tracks on the west side of Orrville, past the depot, heading toward Wooster.

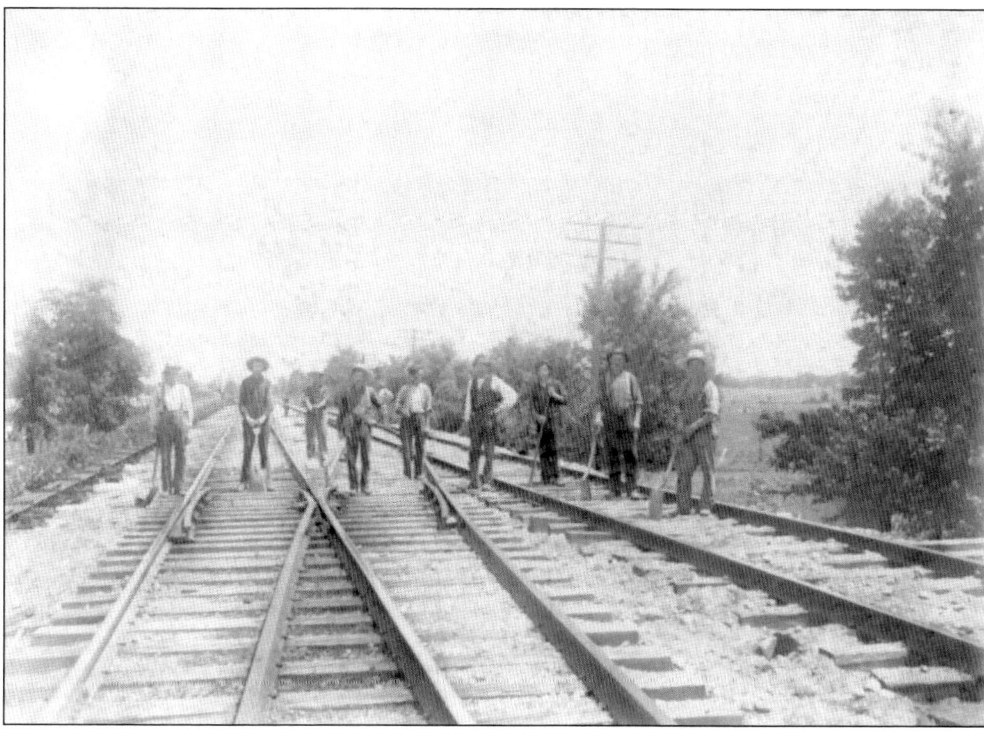

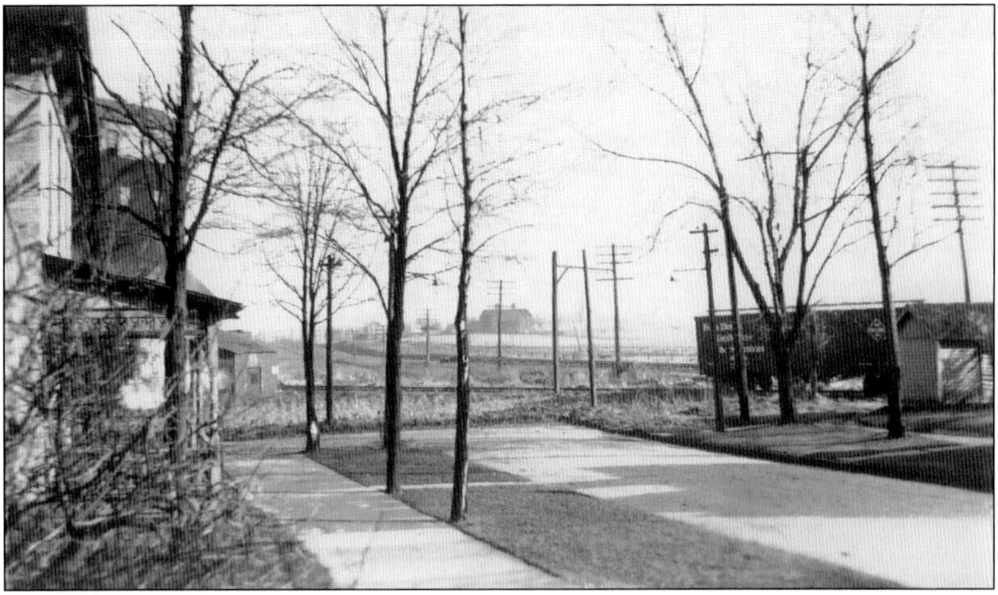

This is a photograph of the end of East Market Street; the street halted and opened up into the lush farmland that was just on the eastern outskirts of town. The street now dead-ends into the Imhoff Construction Company's building. Long before the overpass was on Walnut Street, East Market Street was lined with grand homes owned by some of Orrville's first residents.

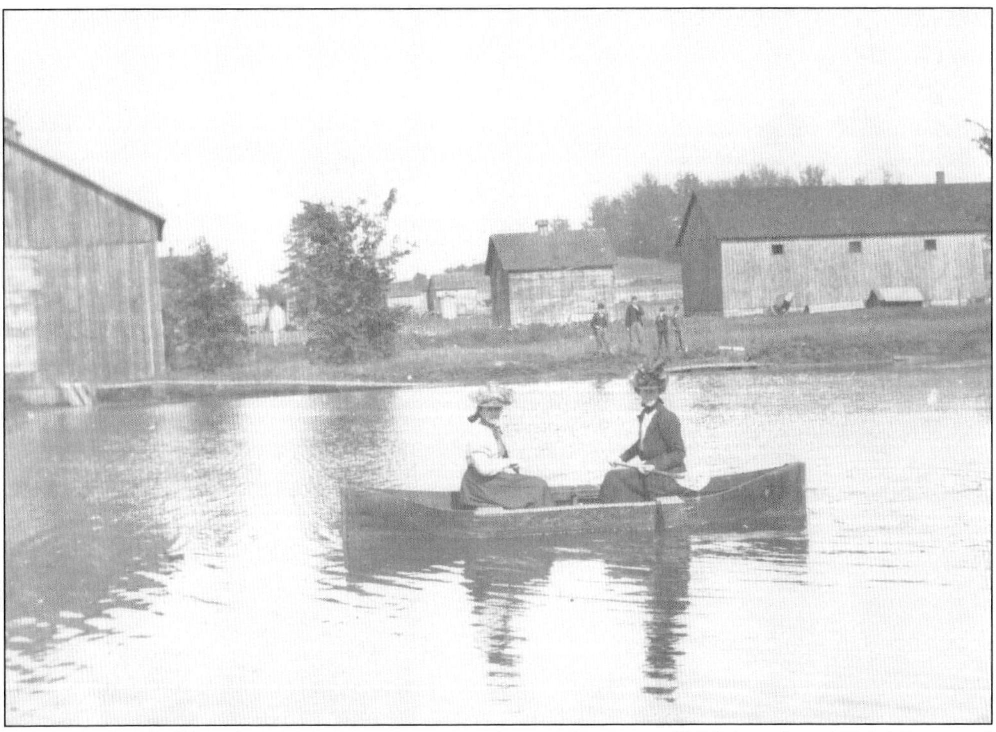

Nell Drushel (left) and Dora McIntyre enjoy a boat ride on Griffith's Pond in 1900. The pond was home to Robinson's Cold Storage and the Griffith's Icehouse.

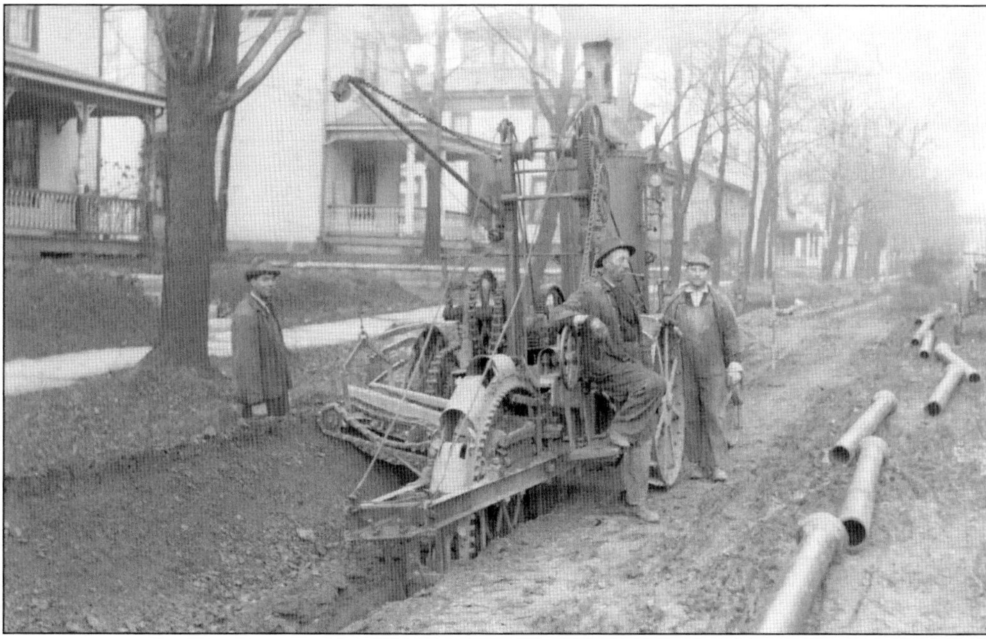

David Markey (center) and two unidentified men work with a ditching machine used to place water lines on Oak Street.

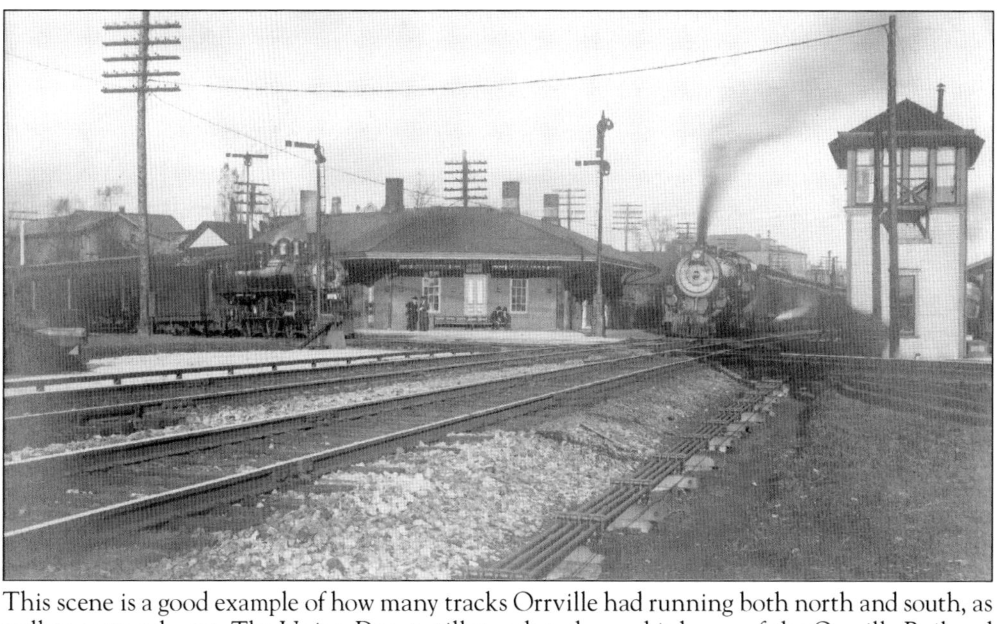

This scene is a good example of how many tracks Orrville had running both north and south, as well as east and west. The Union Depot still stands today and is home of the Orrville Railroad Heritage Museum. The Railroad Heritage Society offers numerous train rides around the area throughout the year and has an extensive collection of railroad memorabilia and Orrville history on display.

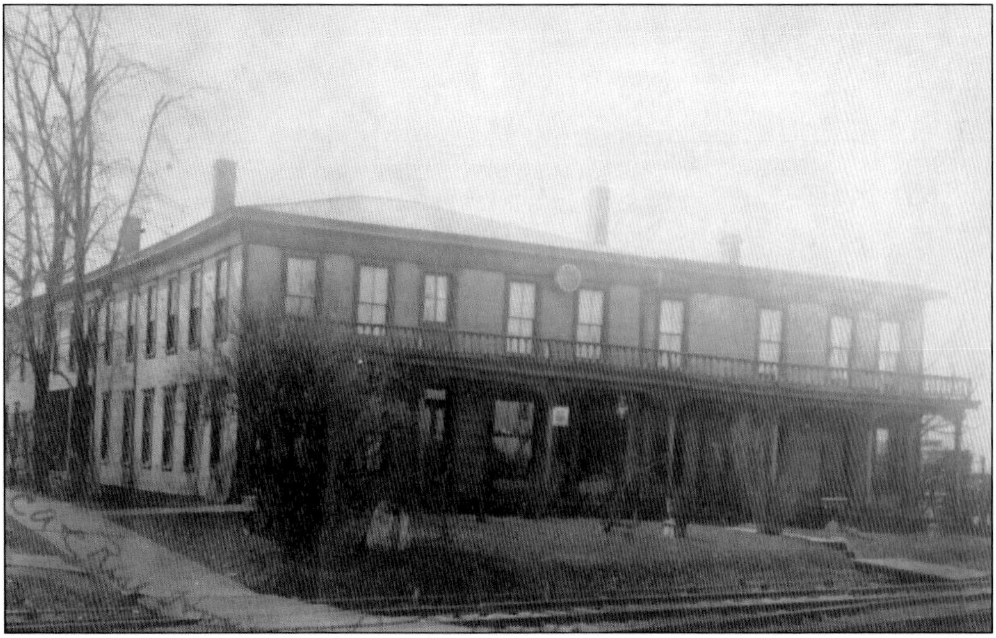

The National House sat along the railroad tracks just east of the depot. It was built in 1873 by Peter Eberly and stood until 1914, when it was pieced apart into houses and moved. Two of those individual homes still stand today on Garfield Avenue.

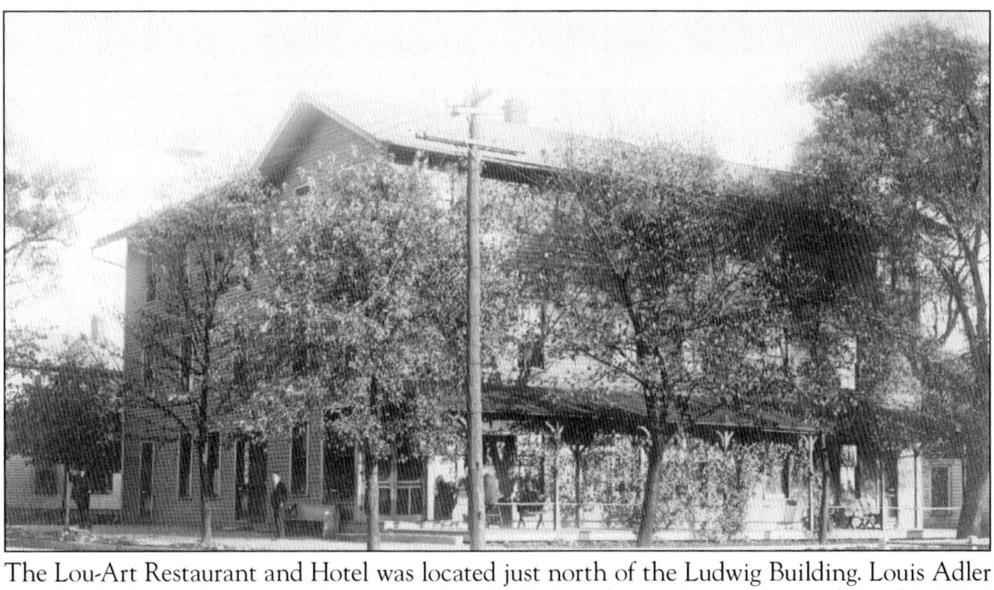

The Lou-Art Restaurant and Hotel was located just north of the Ludwig Building. Louis Adler and Art Faul were the owners. Adler later bought the Manhattan Restaurant and Hotel in 1929. (Courtesy of Wayne Liechty.)

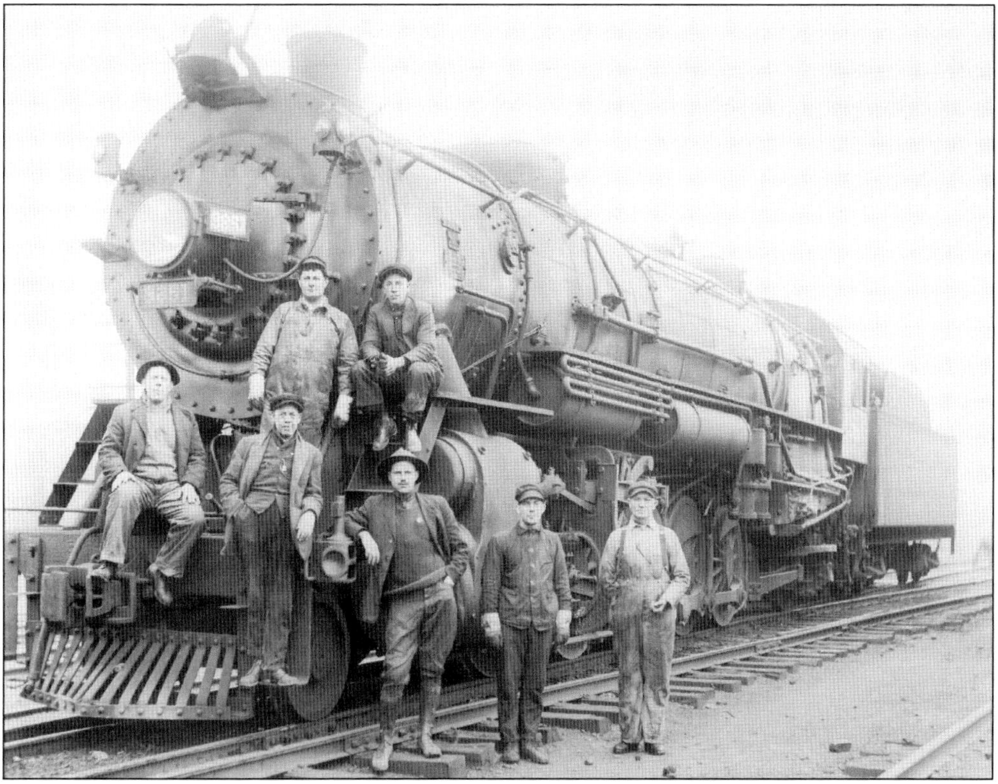

Pictured above, a group of unidentified rail yard workers takes a break near the Union Depot. Below is another group of rail workers along the Pennsylvania line. At far left is Albert Gouter, and second from the right is Enos Wagner. Pictured are two different engines at the Union Depot. (Above, courtesy of Wayne Liechty; below, Alison Wagner.)

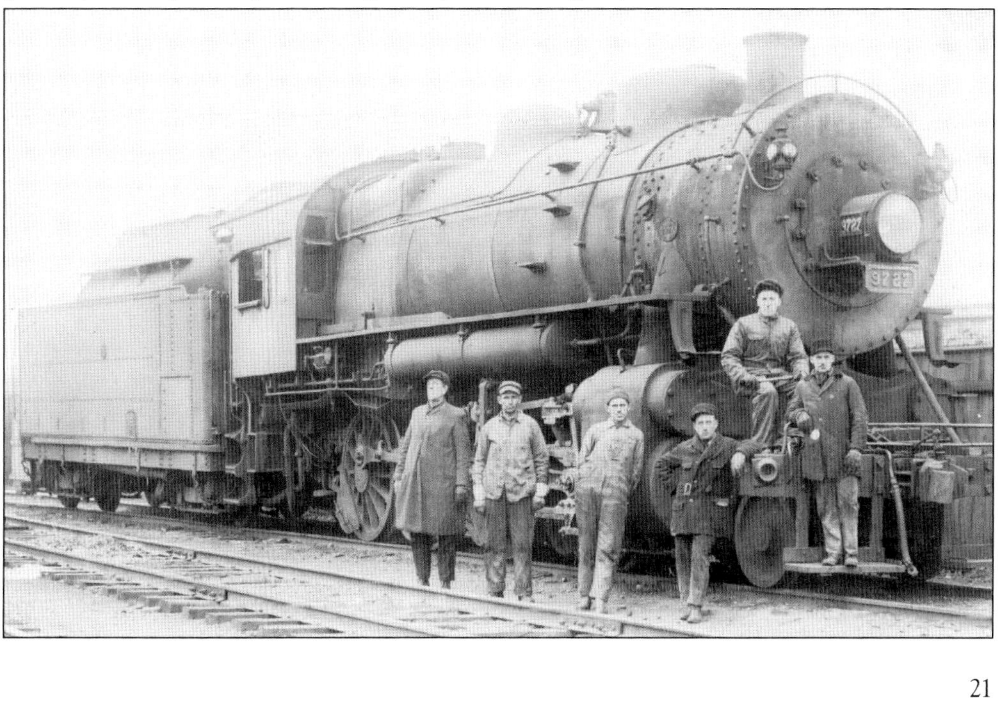

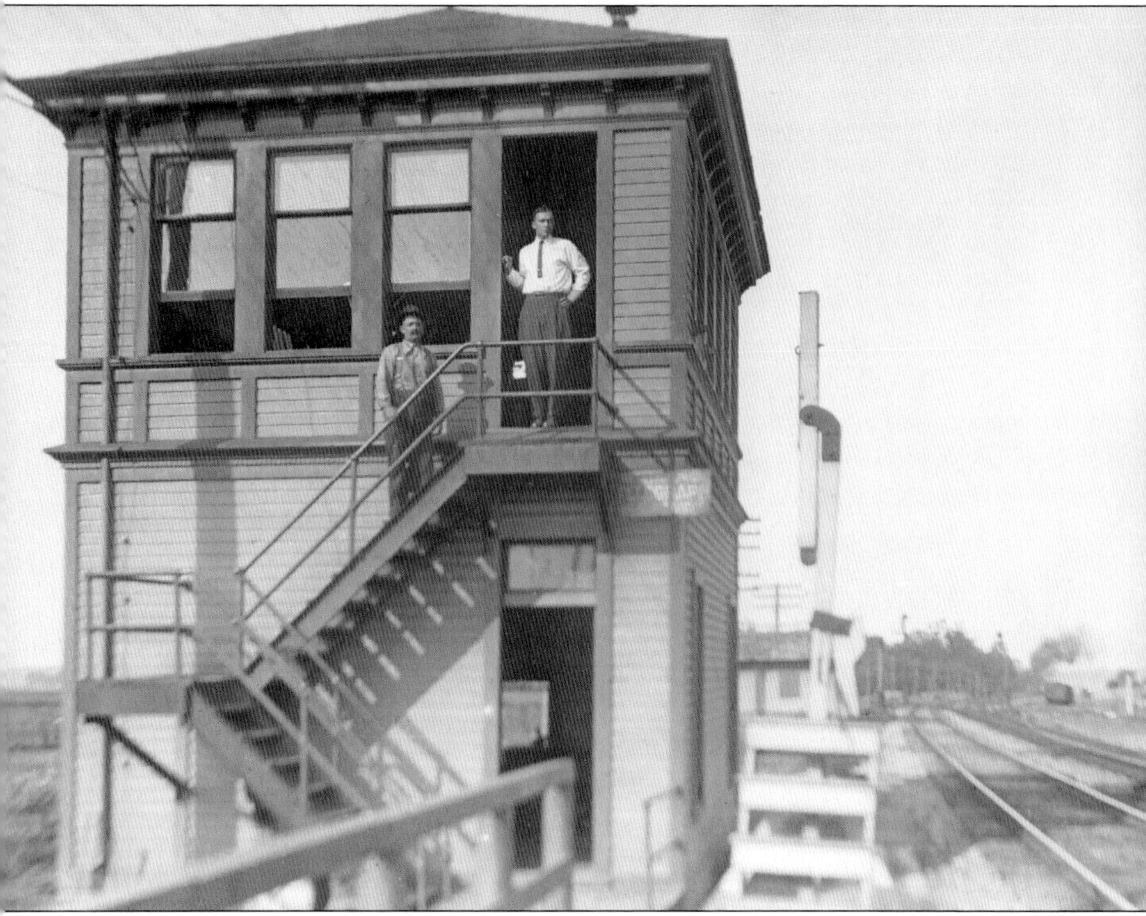

This is the railroad tower located along the Pennsylvania Railroad line by the depot. The tower was originally located on the south side of the tracks but was moved to the north side and is now owned by the Orrville Railroad Heritage Society. Repairs are in the works to help refurbish the tower and open it to the public as part of its museum and displays. (Courtesy of Wayne Liechty.)

Two

DOWNTOWN

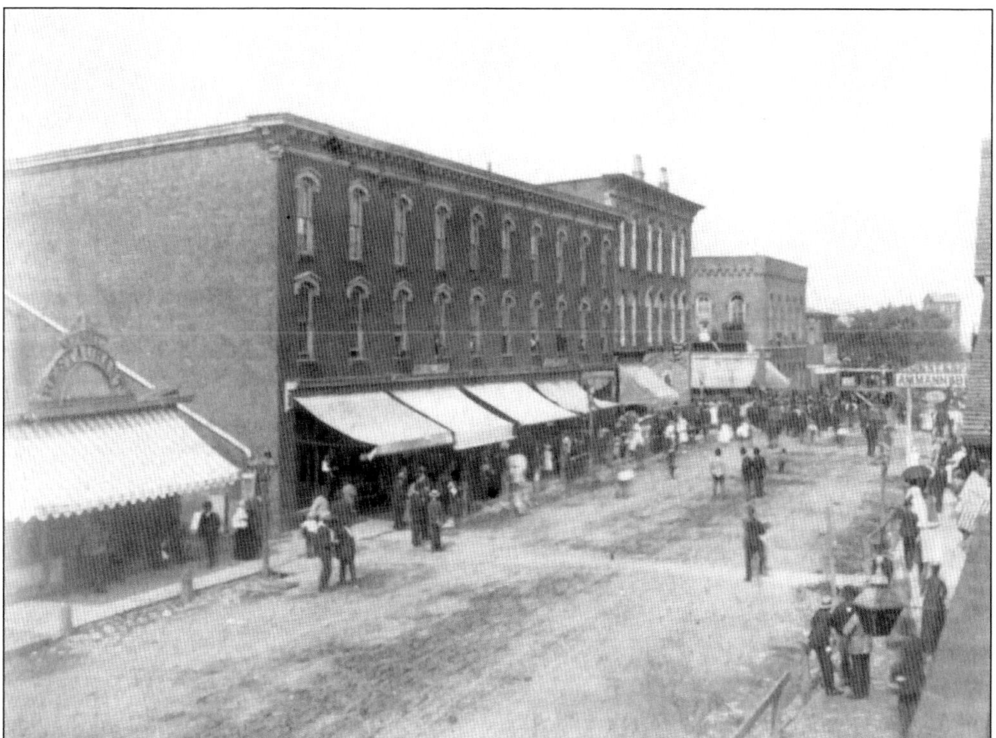

This view of Market Street in 1885 faces east. The large brick building in the center of the photograph was known as the Brenneman Building, one of the only three-story structures in the downtown area.

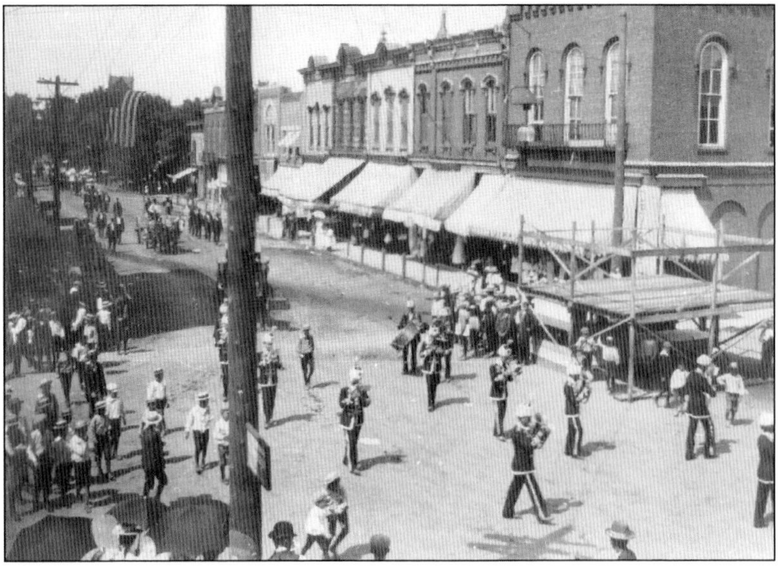

Much like today, a Fourth of July parade was held yearly. This particular photograph is from the parade in 1897. It looks as though the parade route went east on Market Street. East Market Street was a residential neighborhood at the time. Today, it is an extension of the downtown business district.

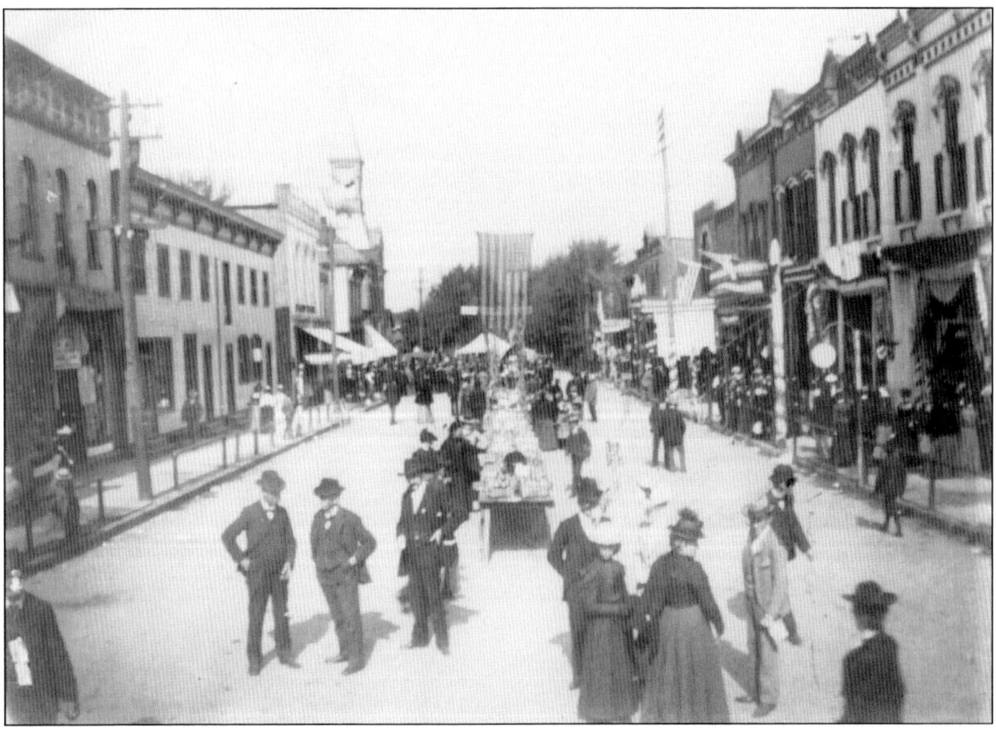

This 1905 street fair brought many residents to the downtown business area. In the background to the left, city hall is easily identifiable. With dirt streets and hitching posts for horses, the main street of downtown is recognizable but much more modern today.

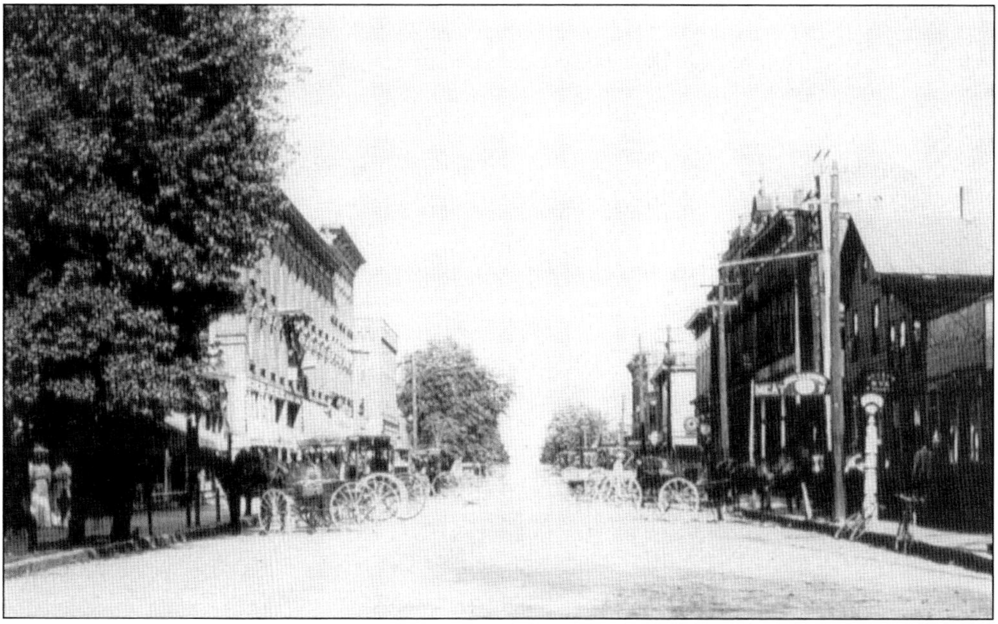

This is West Market Street, looking east, in 1910. In an interview, a Mr. Wolbach states, "Orrville may pride itself, with justice too, upon its general appearance." He called the town neat and tidy and also stated that Orrville had an appearance that was "quite metropolitan" for its time.

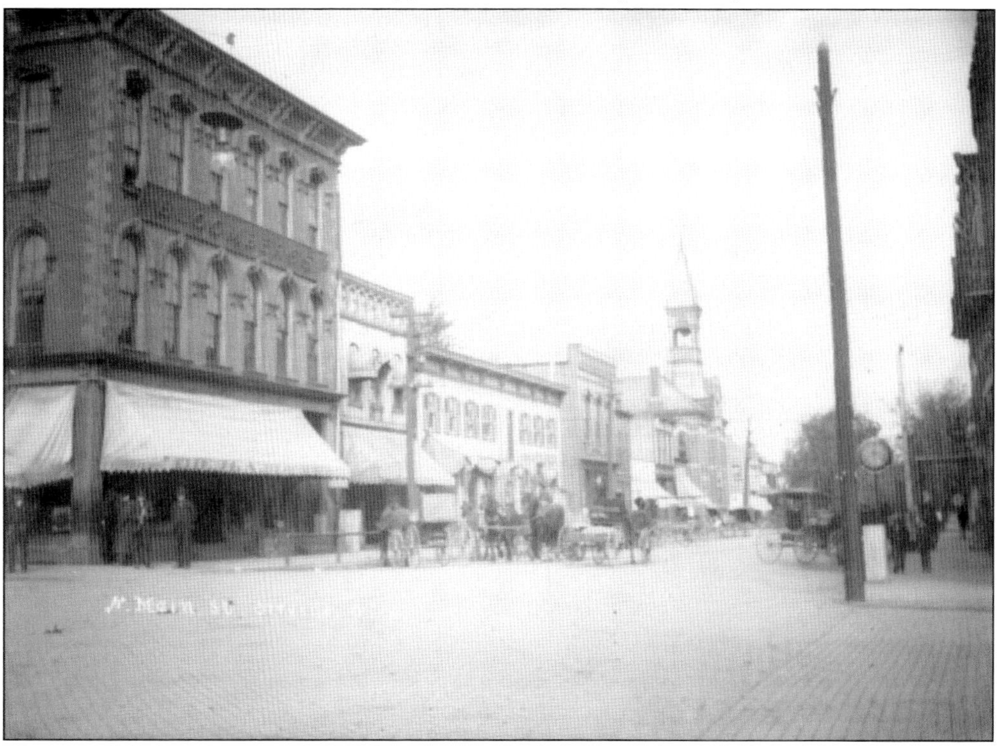

This original glass negative shows Bloomberg's on the corner of Main and Market Streets. In an 1897 advertisement in the *Independent*, a local paper that was published from 1897 to 1898, the business boasts being "the only one priced clothiers" in Orrville.

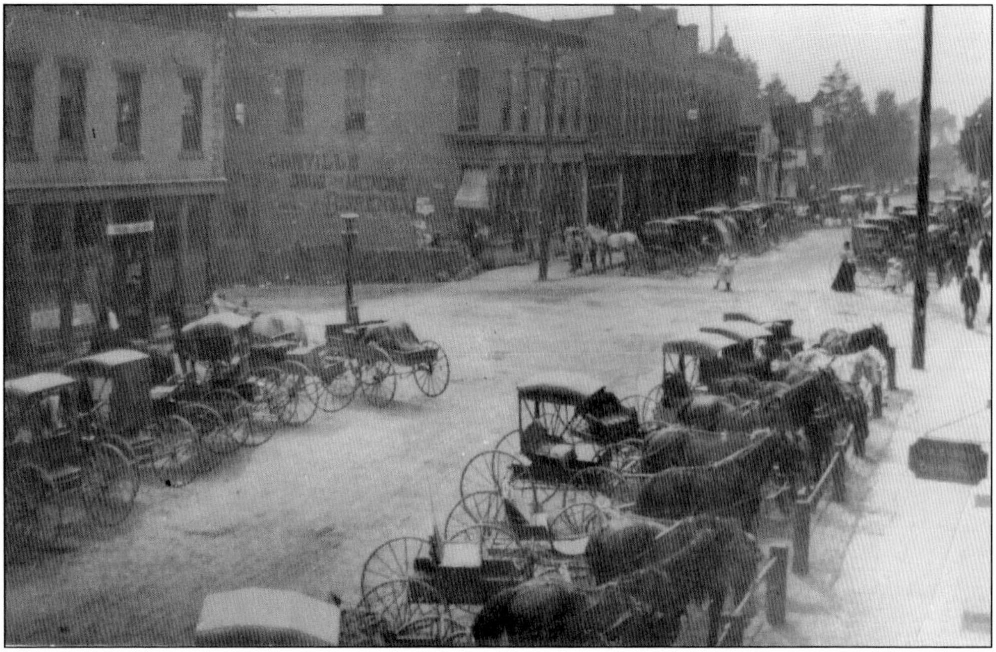

This photograph looks west on Market Street across Main Street. The building painted with "the Orrville Drug and Medicine Dispensary" housed numerous drugstores for over 110 years. The most recent, Seifried's Pharmacy, occupied the space until 2010. The building is now home to the Orrville branch of the Wayne County Community Federal Credit Union.

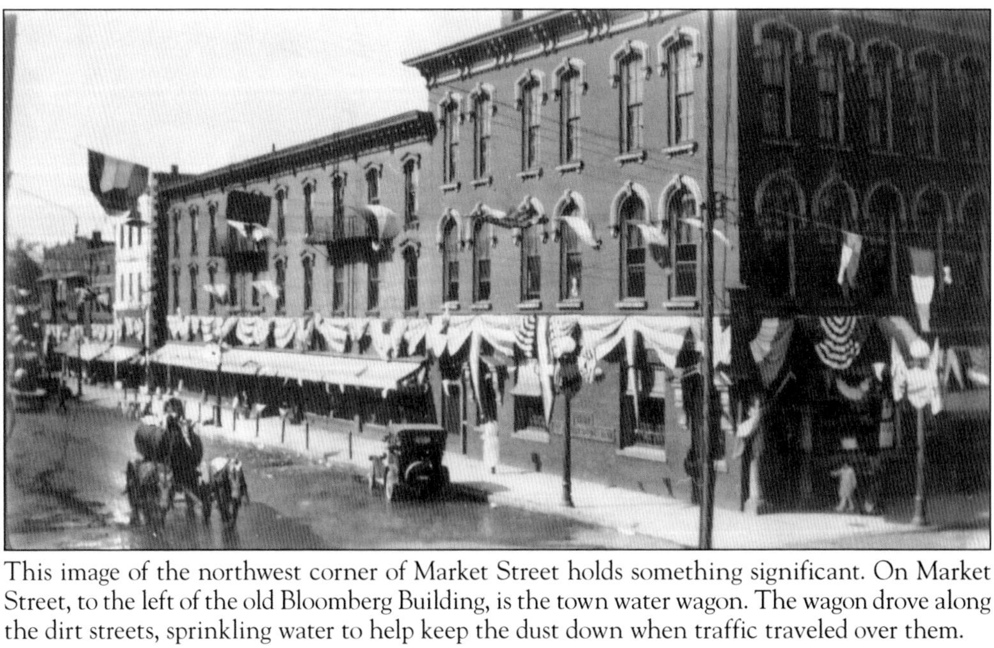

This image of the northwest corner of Market Street holds something significant. On Market Street, to the left of the old Bloomberg Building, is the town water wagon. The wagon drove along the dirt streets, sprinkling water to help keep the dust down when traffic traveled over them.

The Orrville Post Office was relocated in 1910 to what was known as the Golden Corners, which was the southeast corner of North Main and Water Streets. Pictured here from left to right are Gid McIntire, postmaster Dan Forrer, Irene Drushell, and Elmer Tschantz.

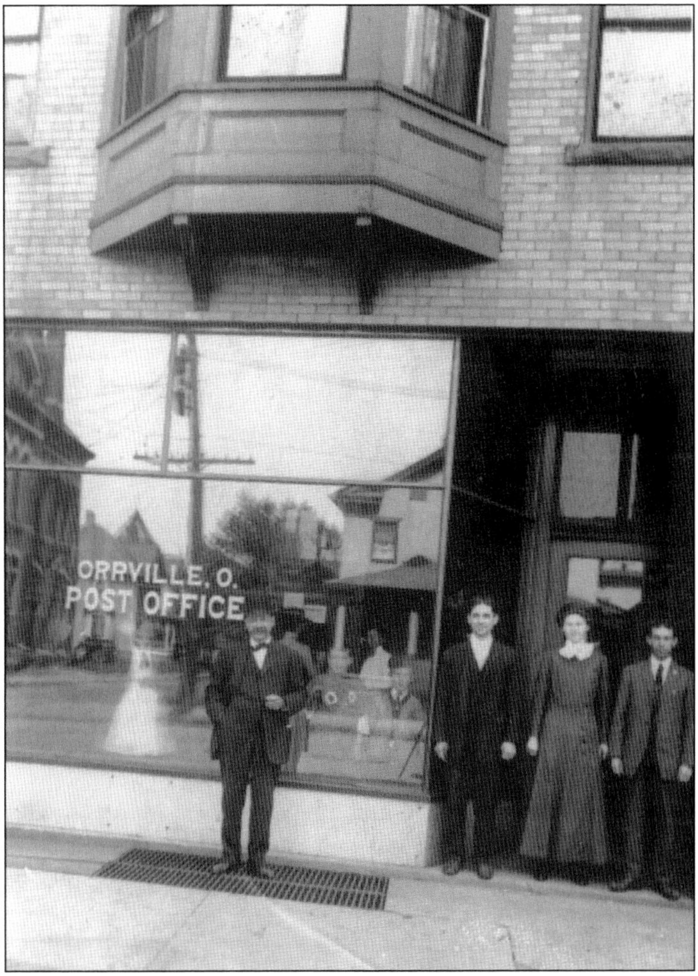

This photograph faces west on Market Street from the square. In an interview, a man identified as Mr. Wolbach said, "The village is laid out with the points of the compass; the streets crossing each other at right angles," with Main and Market Streets as "the principal business thoroughfares."

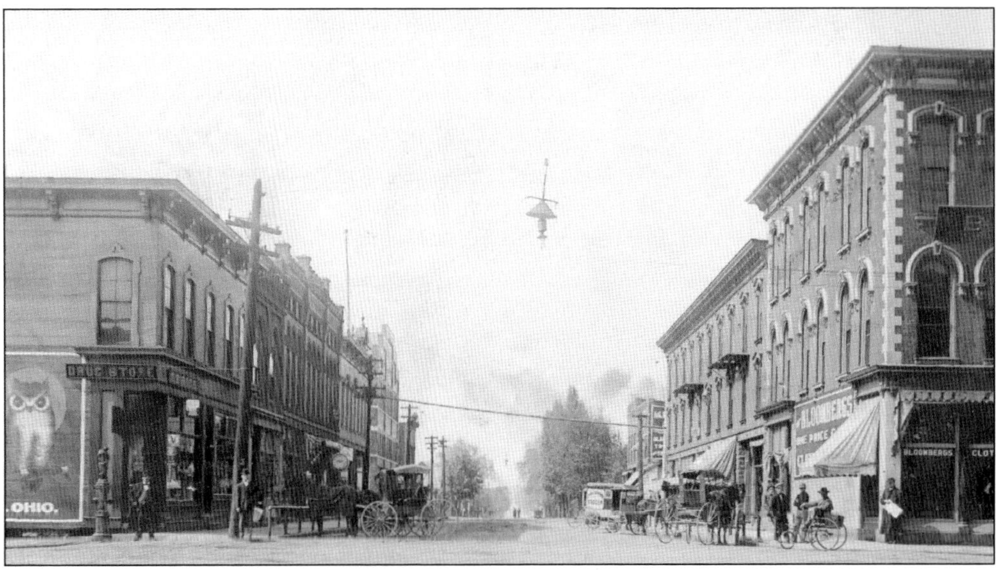

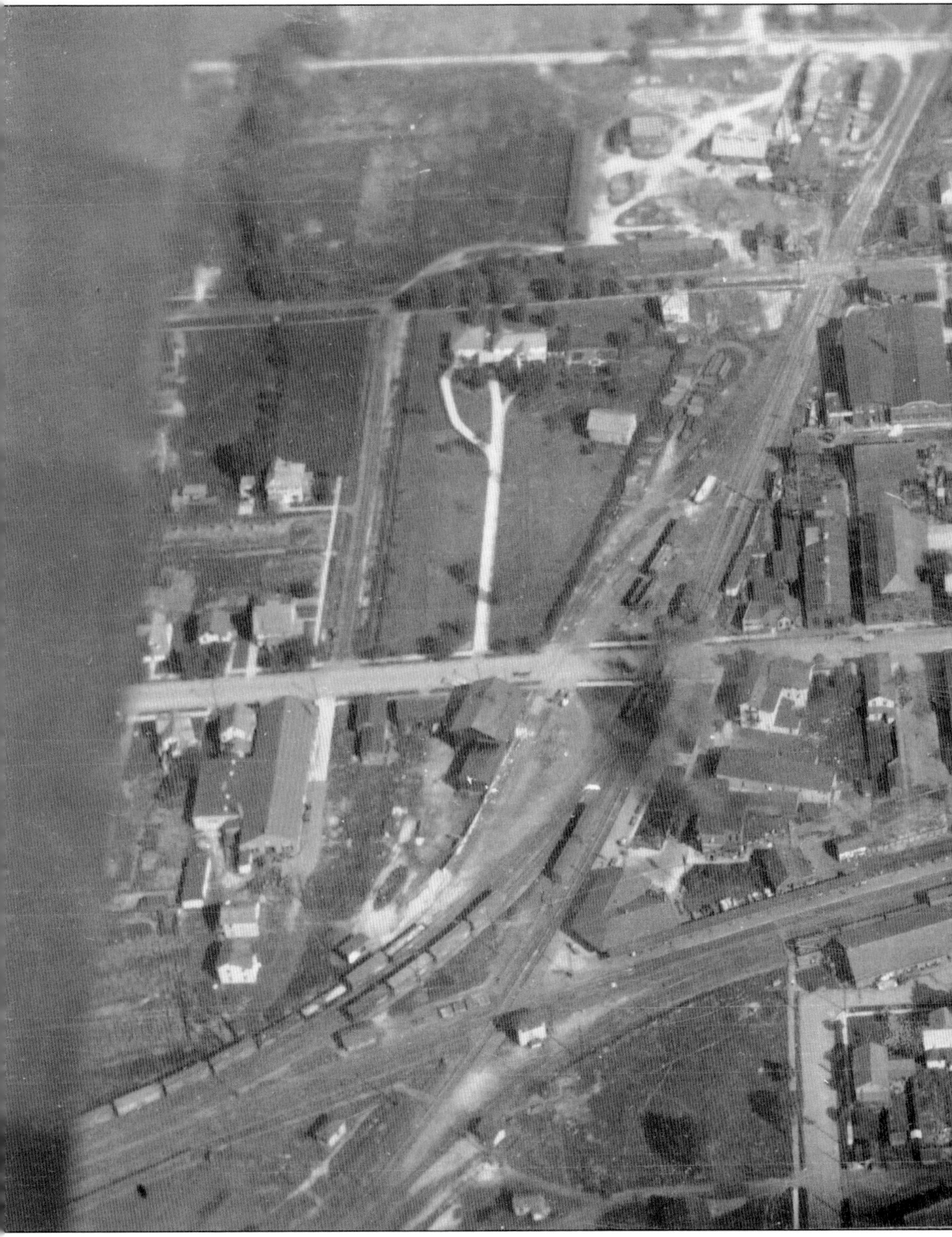

This aerial photograph of downtown Orrville was taken in 1910. Looking closely, numerous landmarks can be identified. In the upper-left corner, the Smith Orr homestead is visible with a

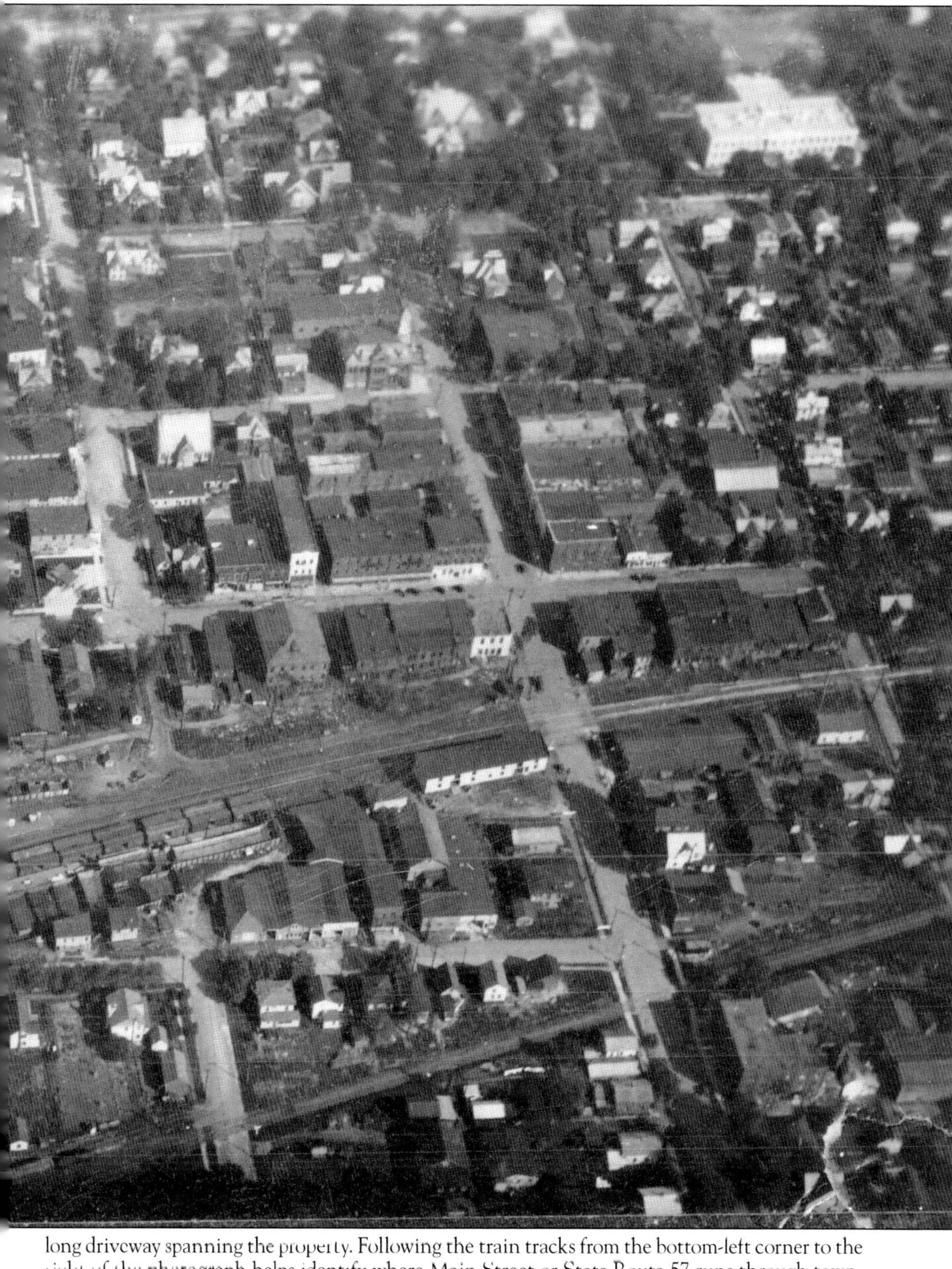

long driveway spanning the property. Following the train tracks from the bottom-left corner to the right of the photograph helps identify where Main Street or State Route 57 runs through town.

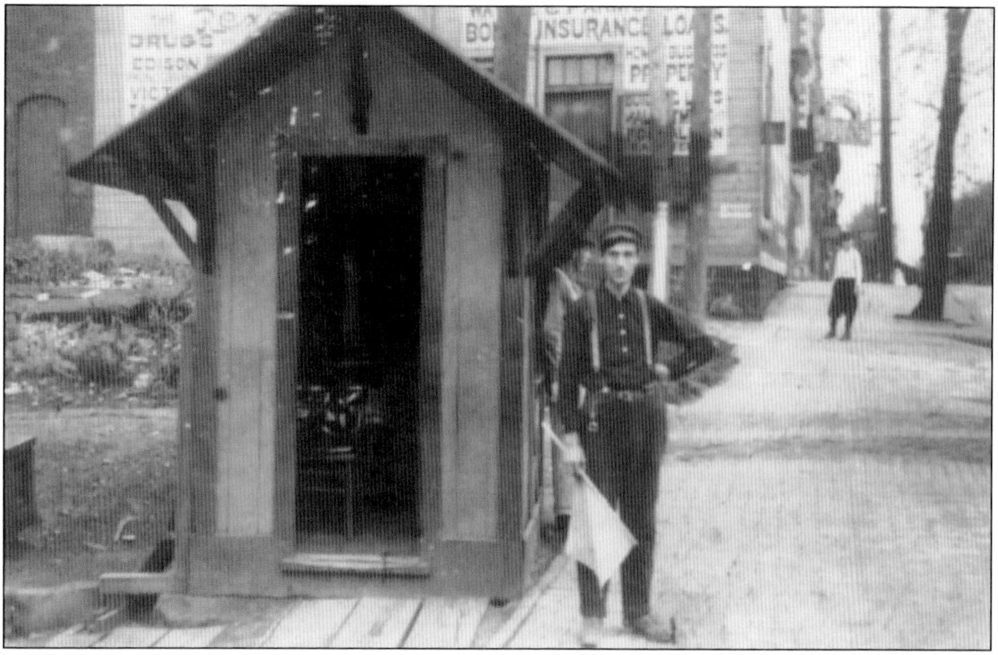

James Cline is shown here in 1911 as the flagger on the main Pennsylvania Railroad line that ran east and west through Orrville. Behind him is the rear of the drugstore on the southwest corner of Market and Main Streets. This rail line is still active today; modern railroad crossing gates, bells, and lights replaced the flagger and manual operator in 1963.

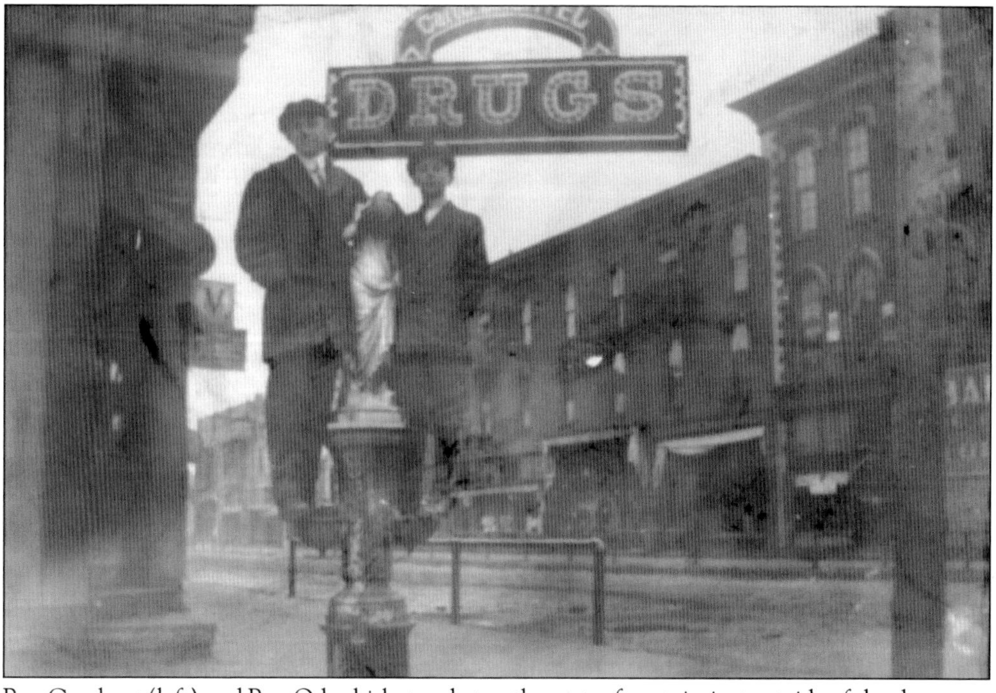

Roy Gearhart (left) and Roy Odenkirk stand atop the water fountain just outside of the drugstore on the southwest corner of Market and Main Streets in 1912.

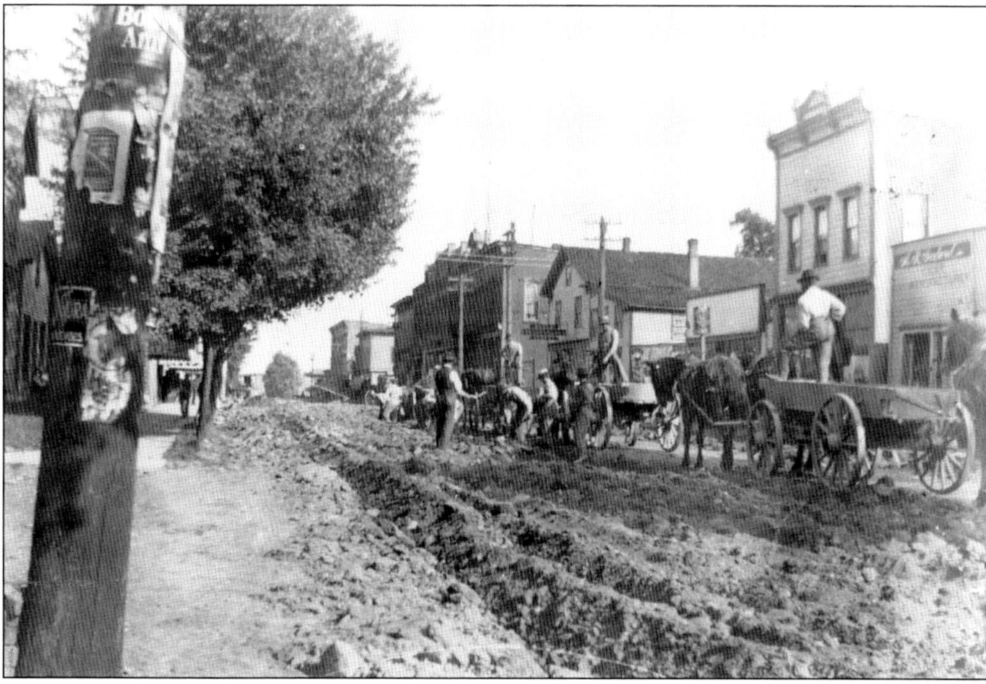

This image was captured on the day Market Street was paved in 1898. It was the first street in Orrville to be paved. A section of the original brick is still exposed on West Market Street in front of the historic Smith Orr homestead.

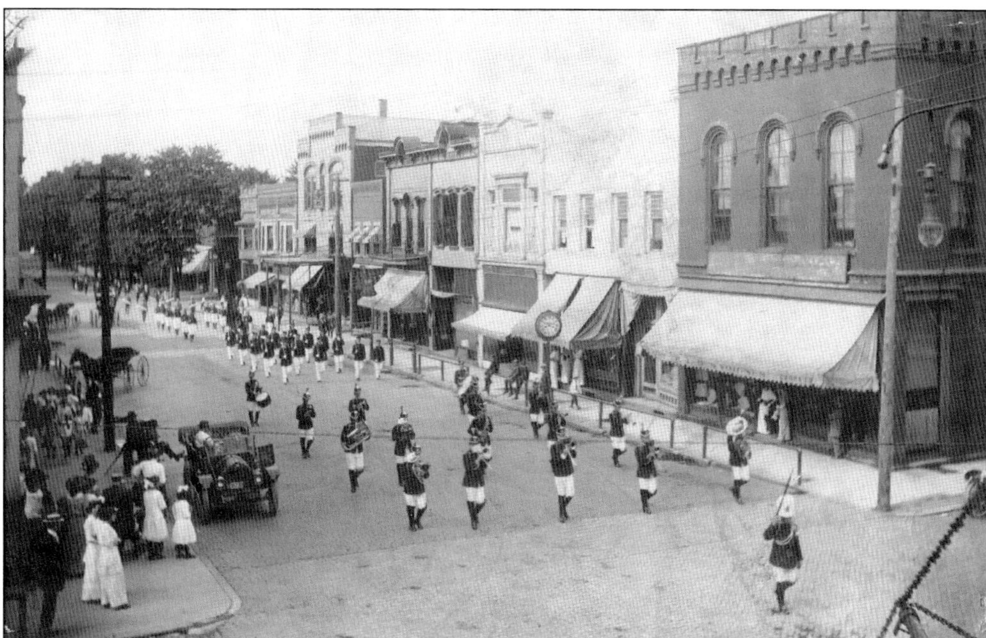

This photograph was taken during the 1914 Modern Woodman Memorial Day Parade held downtown. This view shows the east side of North Main Street, as well as the new brick roads that were being laid throughout town.

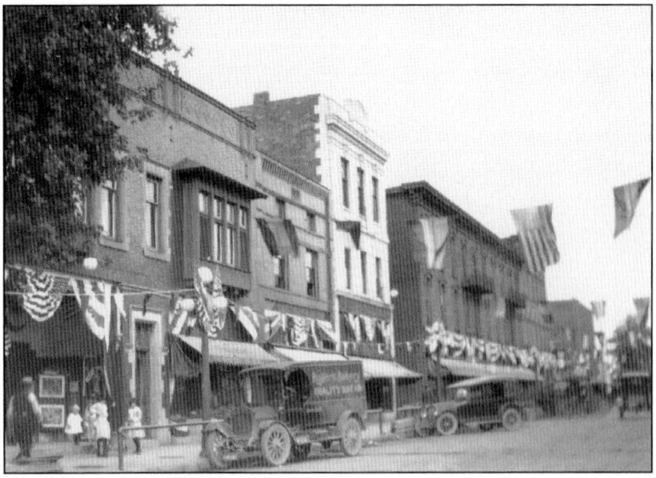

Seen here on the far left are some children at the entrance of the Grand Theater, managed by Gus Lambrigger. Additions were made to the building in 1926, bringing the seating capacity to 600. Located on the north side of West Market Street, just east of Vine Street, the building still stands today. Those familiar with downtown would recognize it as Michael's Bakery and the law offices of Kropf, Wagner, Hohenberger & Lutz.

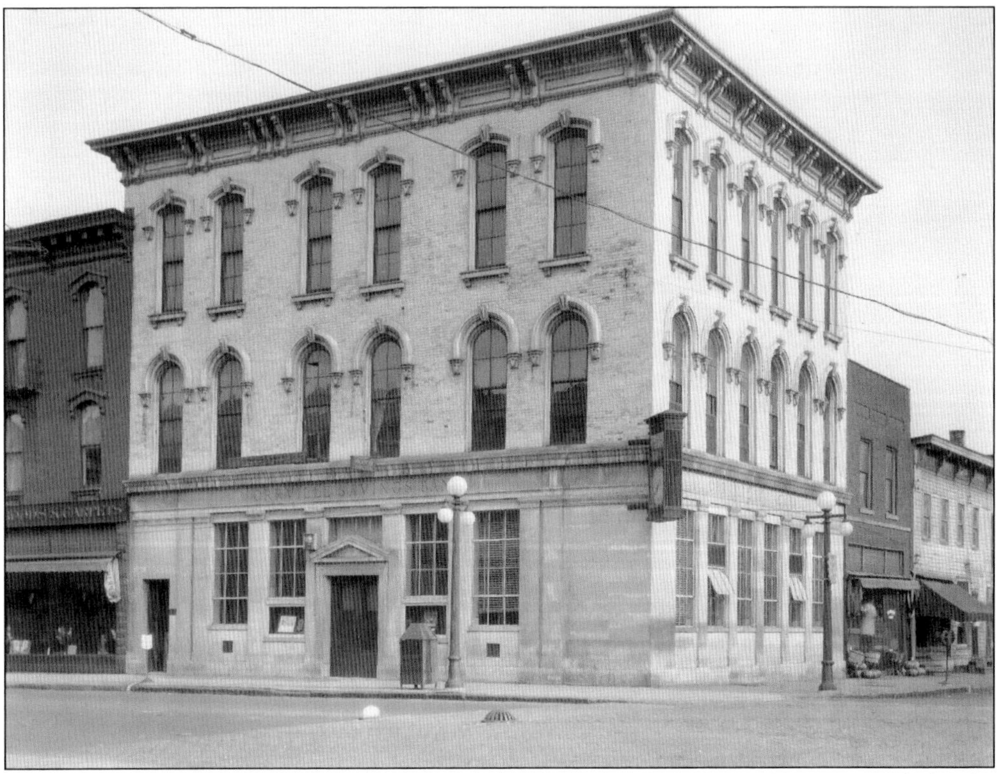

The Orrville Savings Bank, pictured here, housed the first Will-Burt stoker ever made by the company. The building still stands today as a two-story structure, and the sandstone engraving bearing the bank's name is still visible; it is currently the home of PNC bank. The Will-Burt Company is one of the largest businesses in Orrville, building emergency lighting masts. These masts are used locally by the city's fire department, as well as worldwide, providing US troops overseas with their advanced lighting technology.

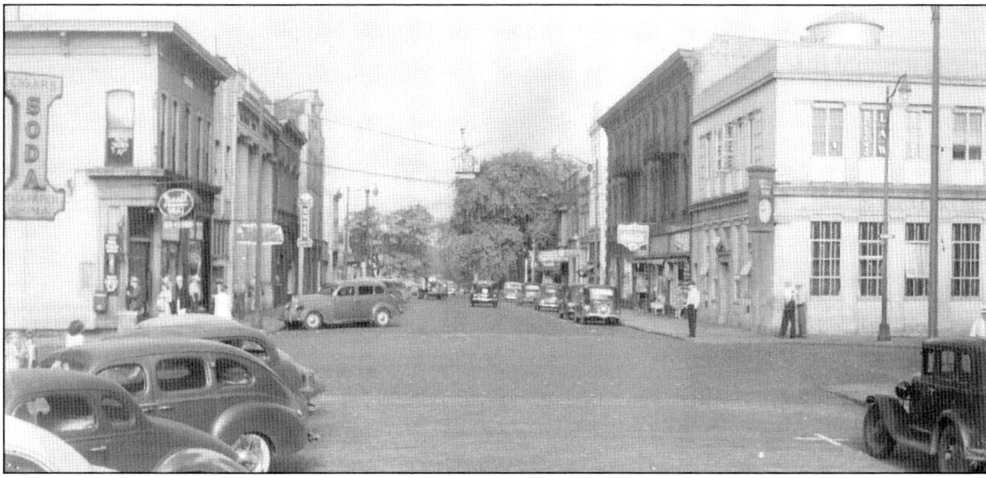

Looking west on Market Street, this c. 1950 photograph depicts downtown with a slightly more modern feel. Many changes had taken place by this point in time. The water tower was constructed and peaks over the buildings. The Orrville Savings Bank Building was no longer three stories, but two. Streets were brick and automobiles replaced horse-drawn wagons. Orrville officially became a city in 1950 with a population of 5,153 residents.

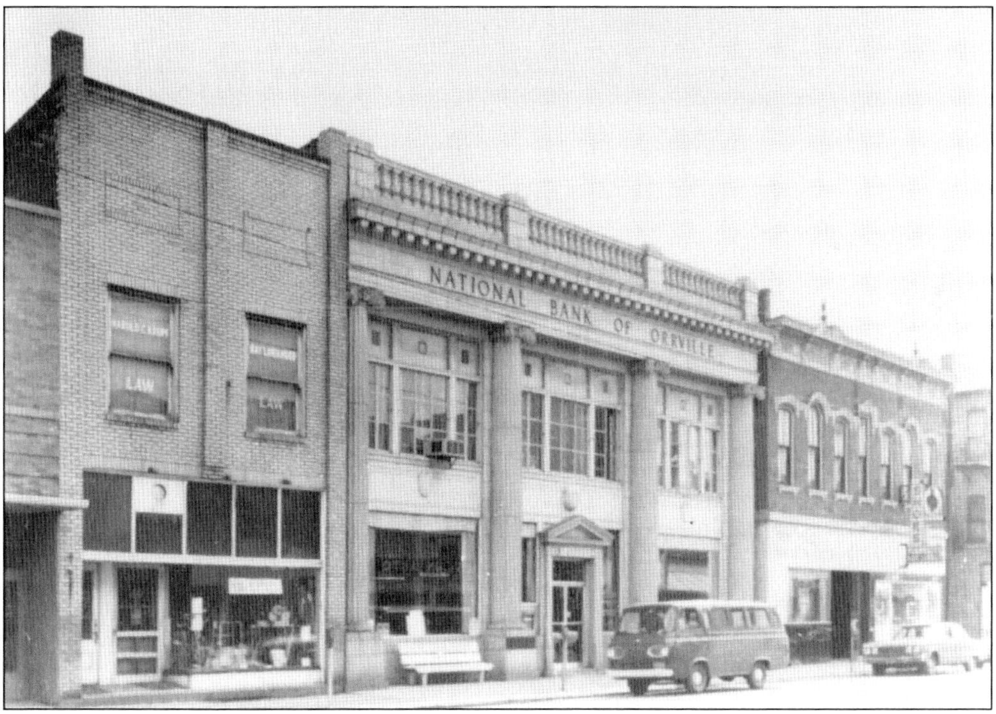

This photograph of the First National Bank was taken in 1966. Although businesses on either side of the bank have varied through the years, the bank is still there. With construction and some resurfacing being done over time, the sandstone pillars are still a part of the architecture that can be seen on West Market Street today.

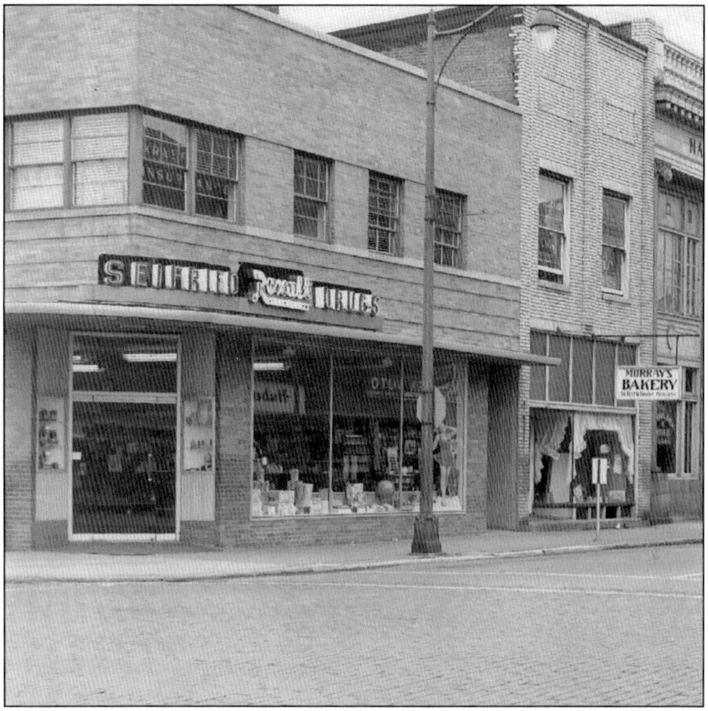

Seifried's Pharmacy, a long-standing business in Orrville alongside Murray's Bakery, is shown here on West Market Street. Paul Seifried, a second-generation pharmacist, owned the drugstore beginning in 1970. With a full pharmacy and soda fountain, Seifried's was a hub for much activity up until the day it closed its doors on September 20, 2010. Murray's Bakery was located originally on Market Street and then moved to the northeast corner of Main and Market Streets. Murray's served "made fresh daily" baked goods in all varieties.

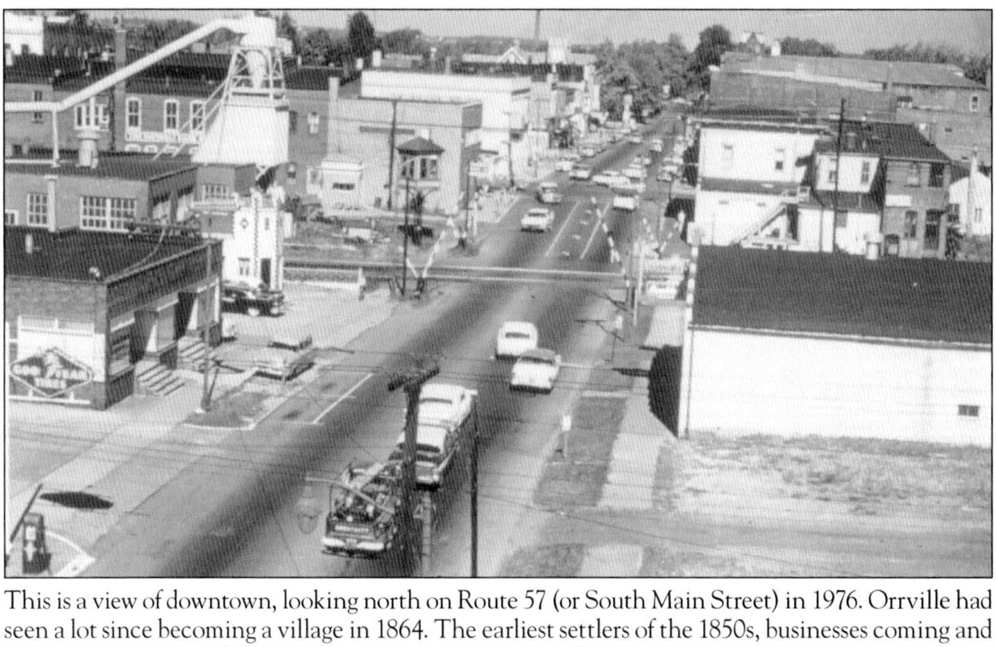

This is a view of downtown, looking north on Route 57 (or South Main Street) in 1976. Orrville had seen a lot since becoming a village in 1864. The earliest settlers of the 1850s, businesses coming and going, the great fire of 1872, the downturn of the railroad in the 1920s, the Great Depression, and the centennial celebration in 1964 were just a few events that highlight Orrville's existence.

Three

ORRVILLITES

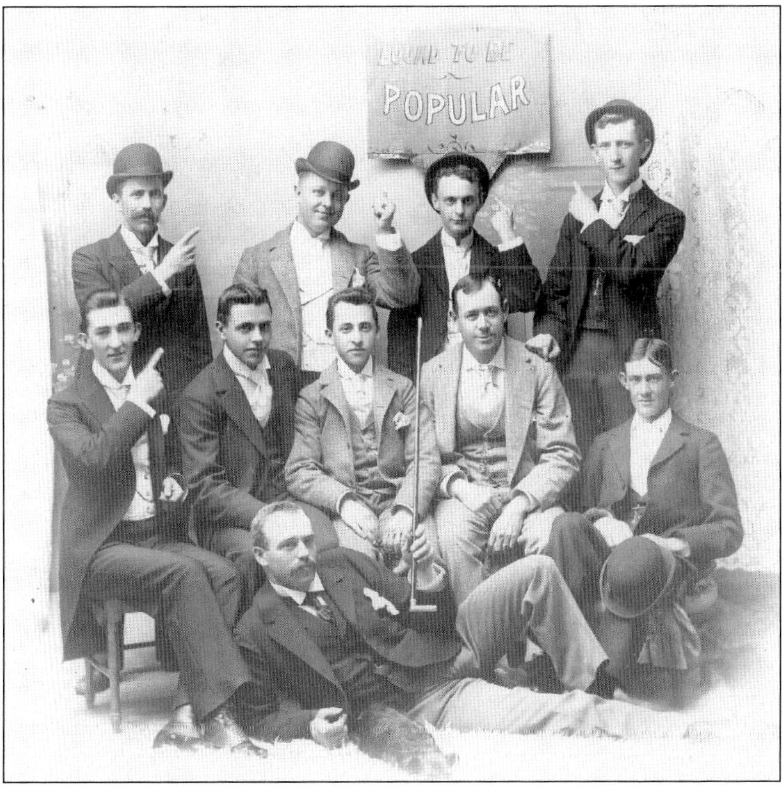

Taken in 1887, these fellows were "Bound to be Popular," as the sign declares. From left to right are (laying down) Rube Steiner; (first row) Warren Wirth, Charles Wright, Louie Bloomberg, E.P. Willaman, and Billy Taggart; (second row) George Young, Harry Taylor, Proctor Seas, and Ed Wirth.

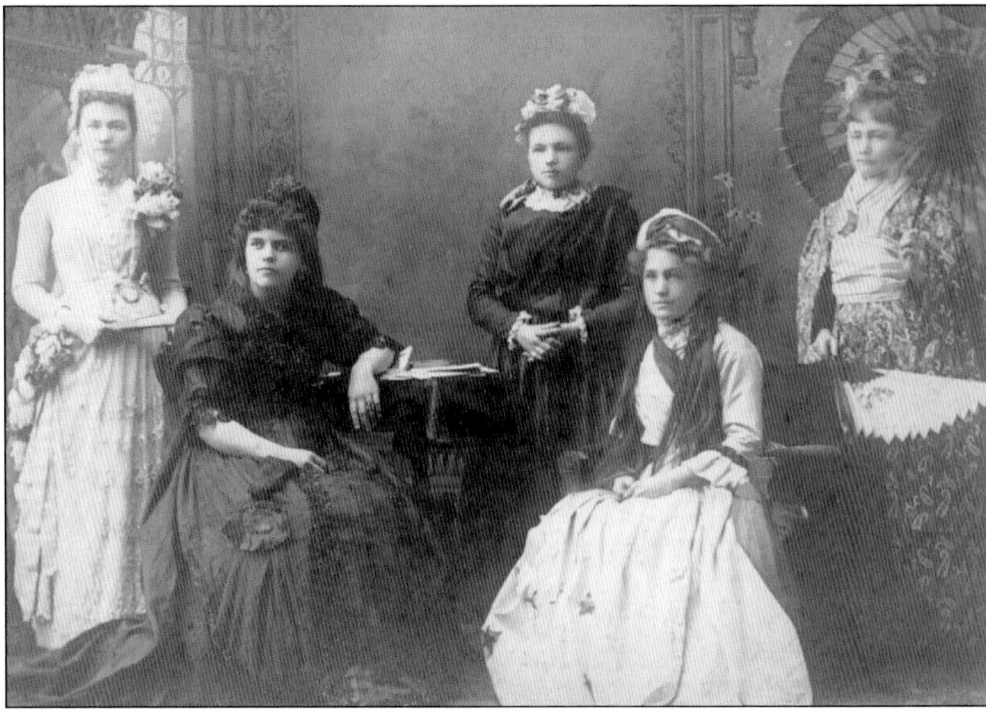

These members of the "Mystic League" were attending a party at town hall in 1888. Pictured from left to right are Mary Taggart, Jennie Leickheim, Mary Grabill, Nettie Gailey, and Jennie Taggart.

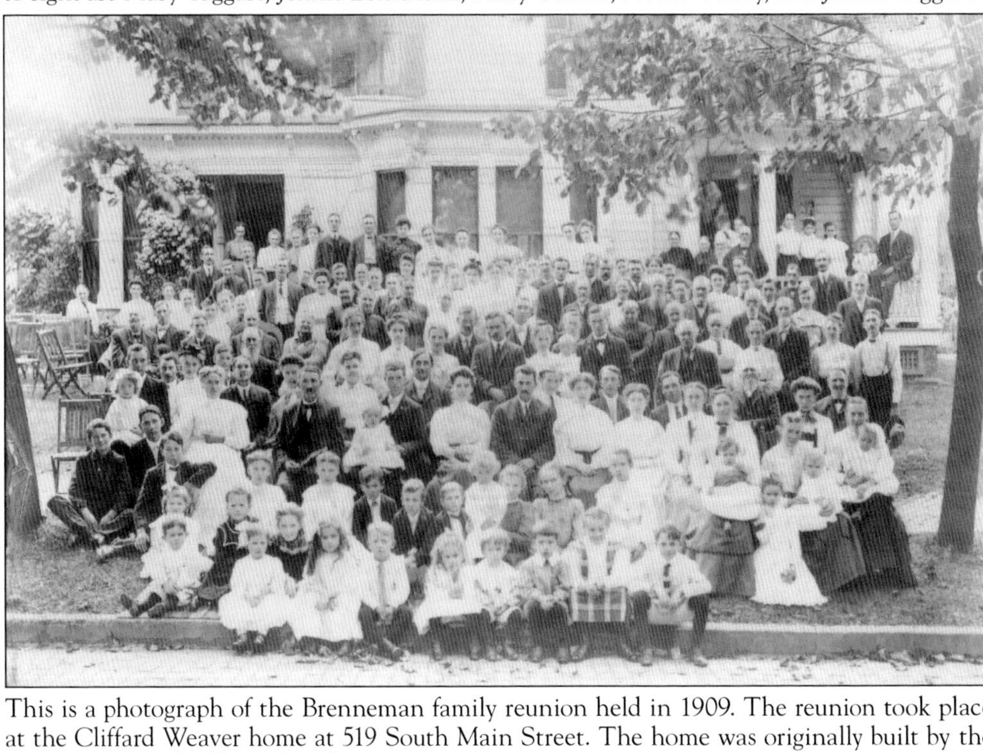

This is a photograph of the Brenneman family reunion held in 1909. The reunion took place at the Clifford Weaver home at 519 South Main Street. The home was originally built by the Brennemans and still stands today.

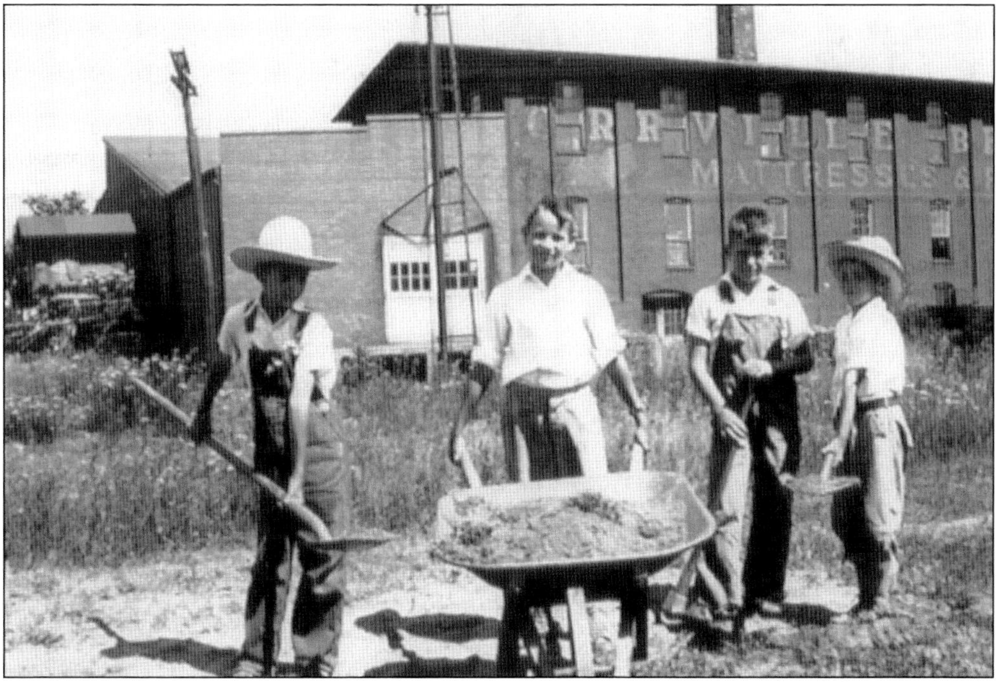

This photograph of the two Congdon boys Carl (center) and Rowland (far right) with some unidentified friends was taken in the side yard of the Congdon property, today known as the Smith Orr homestead. Seen behind the boys is the Orrville Bedding Company; this building remains part of Smith Dairy, located on south side Church Street just west of Vine Street.

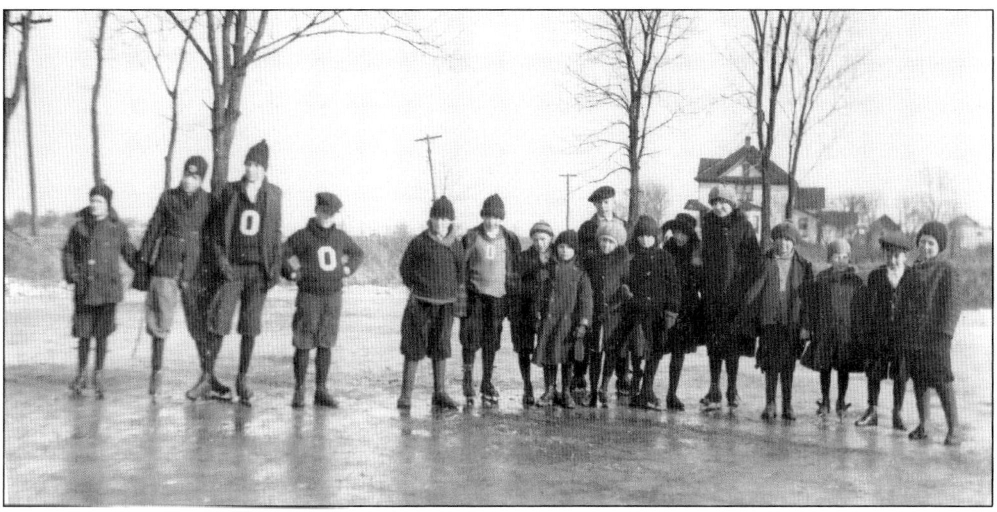

This group of kids is seen ice-skating on Griffith Pond, or "Millpond," in the winter of 1921. The pond supplied water to the Orrville Milling Company for the flour mill.

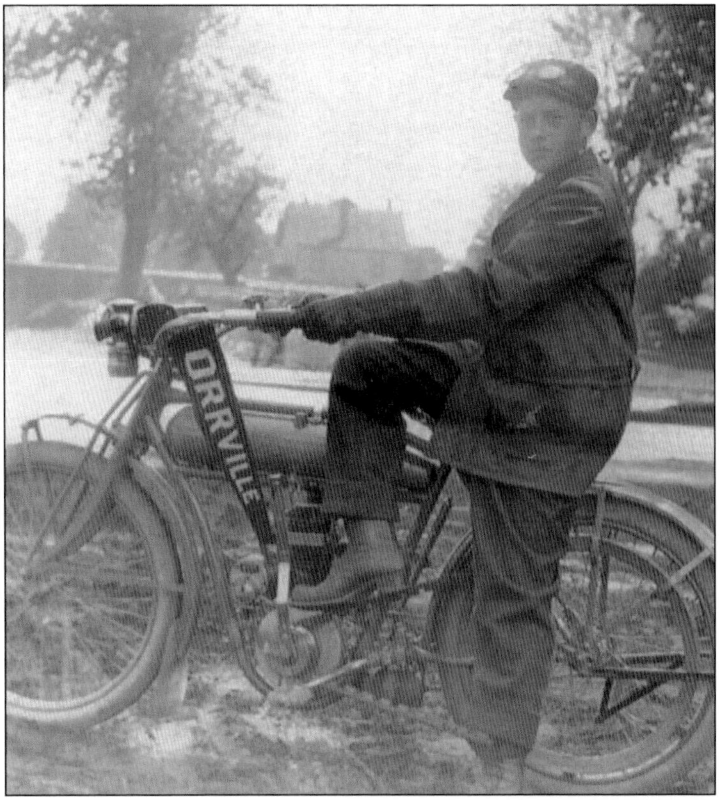

This unidentified boy rides in town on his motorbike, which displays an Orrville pendent.

This is an early picture of the labor force at the Sanderson Cyclone Drilling Company. The only two men identified are Shorty Metzger (front row, arms folded) and Henry Marty (back row to the right of the left post).

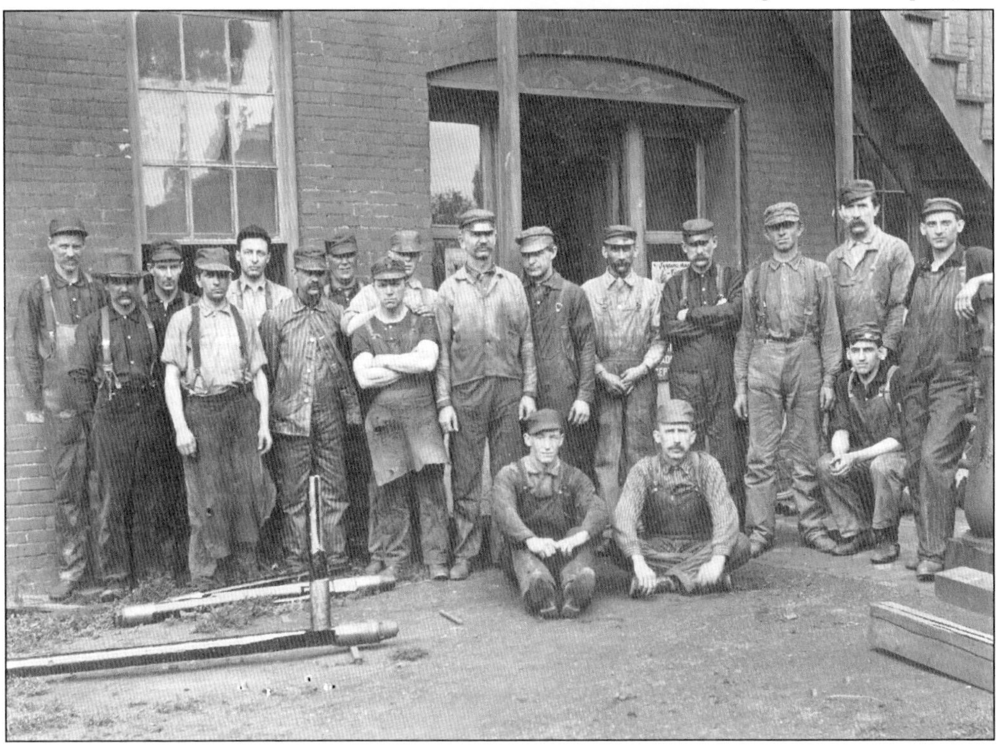

This unidentified couple holds up the "Orrville Corporation Limit" sign on the edge of town. Signs entering town before 1936 were inscribed with the city name of Orrville and "the Friendly City."

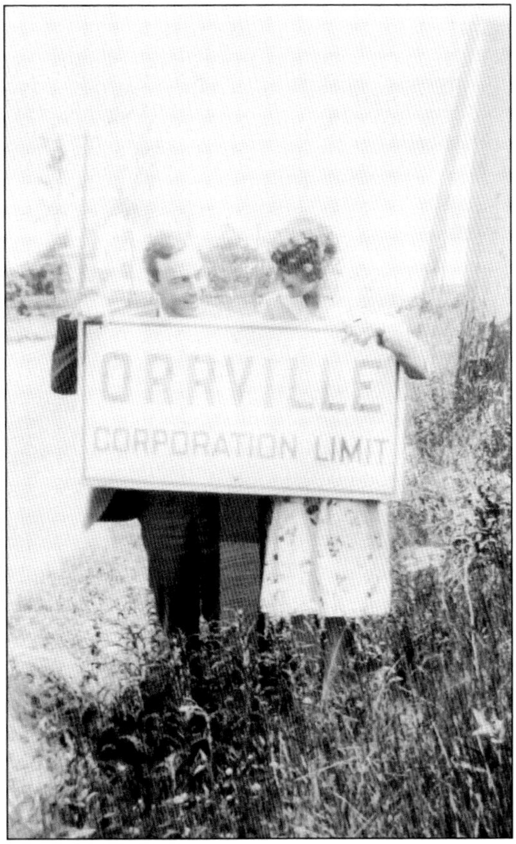

Simply written on the back of this photograph is the "comb shop gang." These are some of the workers from the Orrville Comb & Novelty Company.

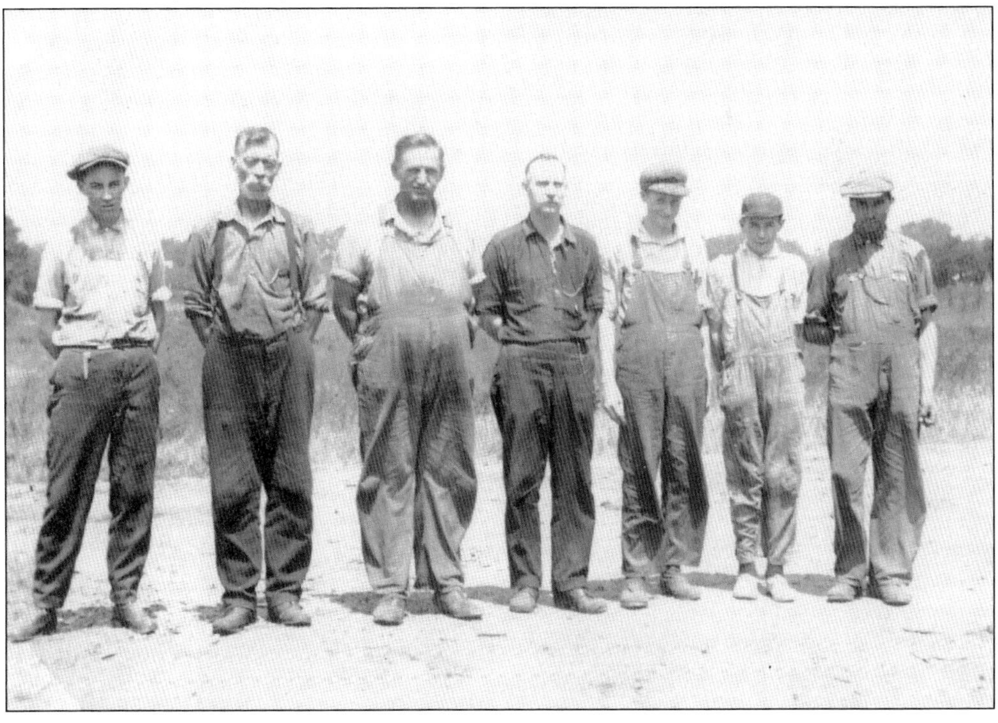

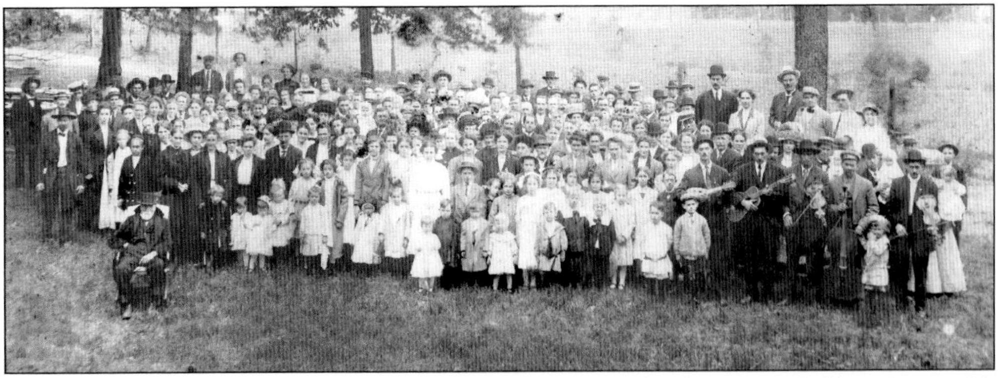

This is an extended-family photograph from the Brenneman family reunion held on August 30, 1911. The Brenneman family has a long-standing history in Orrville, being directly related to Orrville founder Smith Orr. Smith Orr's only granddaughter, Maria, married Samuel Brenneman and went on to keep the Smith Orr homestead in the family, living there with her husband and their two daughters, Charlotte and Maud.

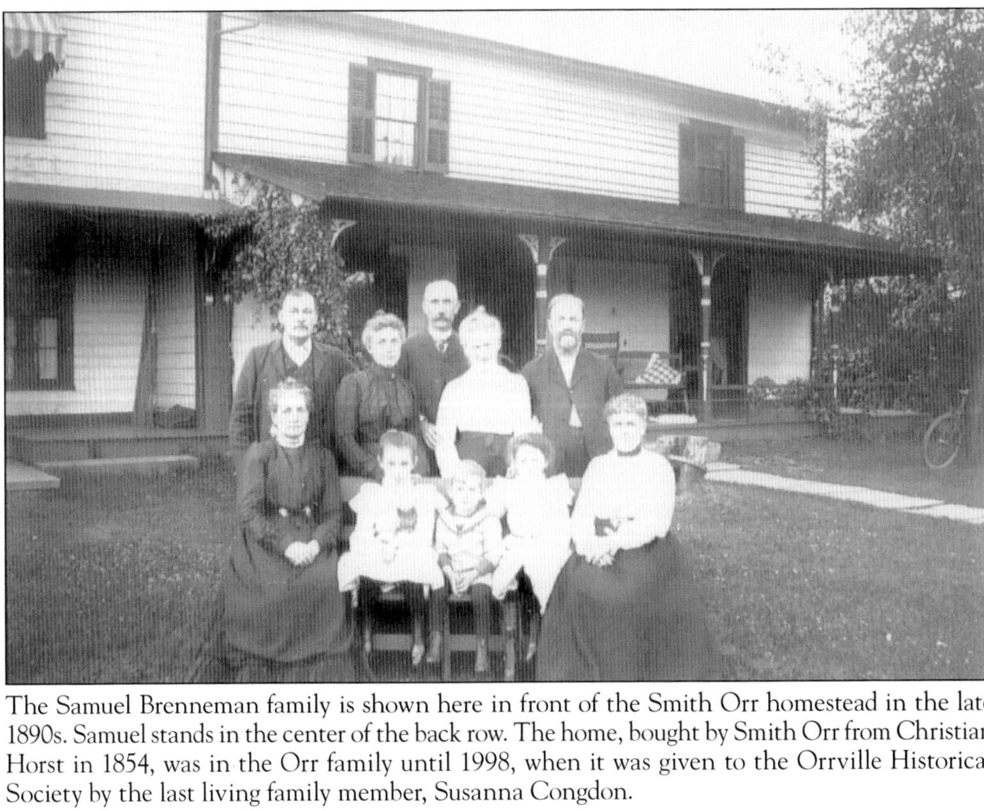

The Samuel Brenneman family is shown here in front of the Smith Orr homestead in the late 1890s. Samuel stands in the center of the back row. The home, bought by Smith Orr from Christian Horst in 1854, was in the Orr family until 1998, when it was given to the Orrville Historical Society by the last living family member, Susanna Congdon.

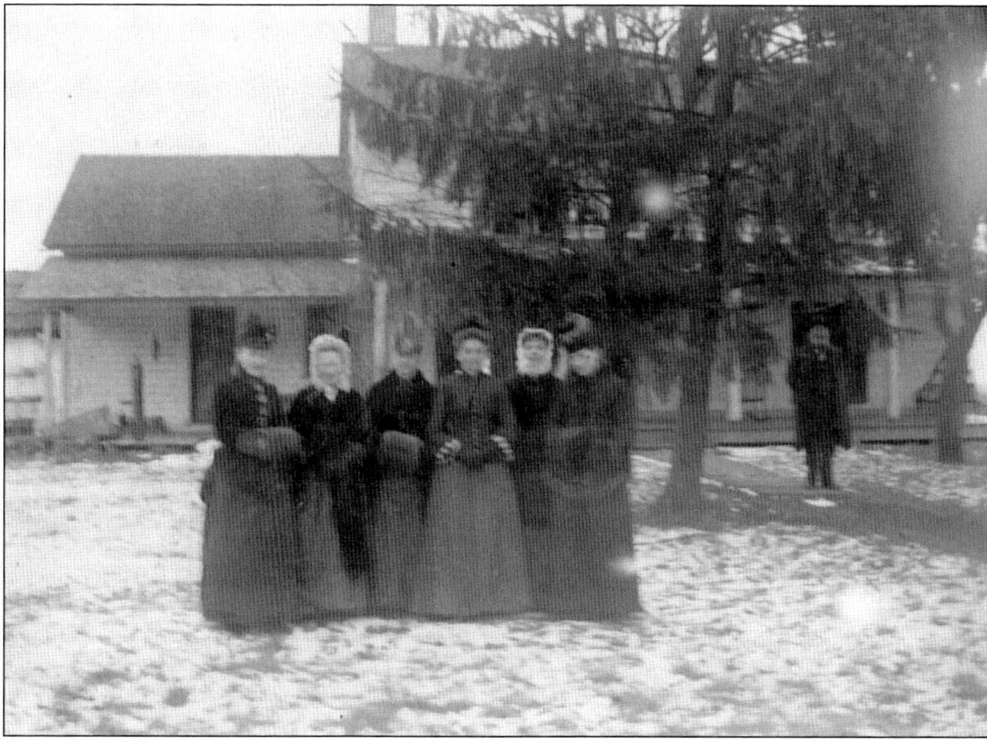

A party was being hosted here for out-of-town guests at the Smith Orr homestead. Even though it was a chilly day, the women of the group gathered outside for a photograph after the luncheon. It is said they requested that Smith Orr's only son, William, be in the picture, but he declined. Being a larger man, he did not want to overpower the women in the image. The photograph was snapped, and when it was developed, William ended up in the background, walking down the sidewalk toward the photographer.

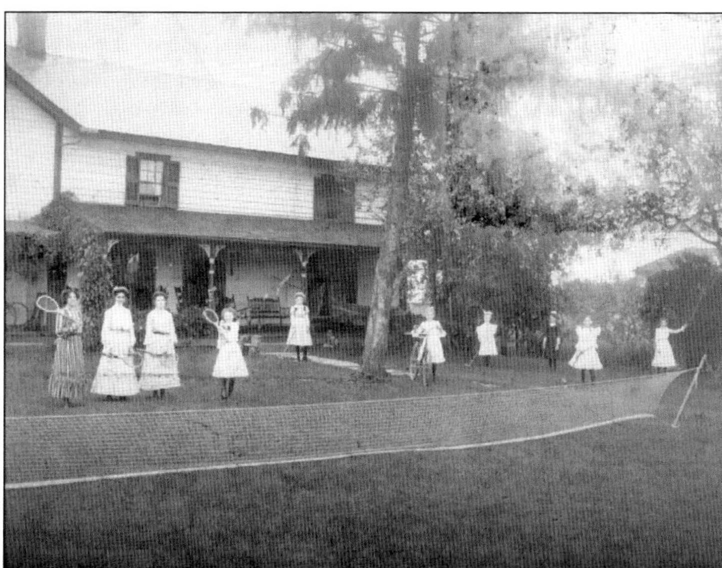

This picture was taken at a birthday party at the Smith Orr homestead. The house can be seen in the background before its 1916 exterior remodel. Charlotte (forth from left) and Maud Brenneman (sixth from left) lived in the home at the time. The girls were the great-granddaughters of Orrville founder Judge Smith Orr.

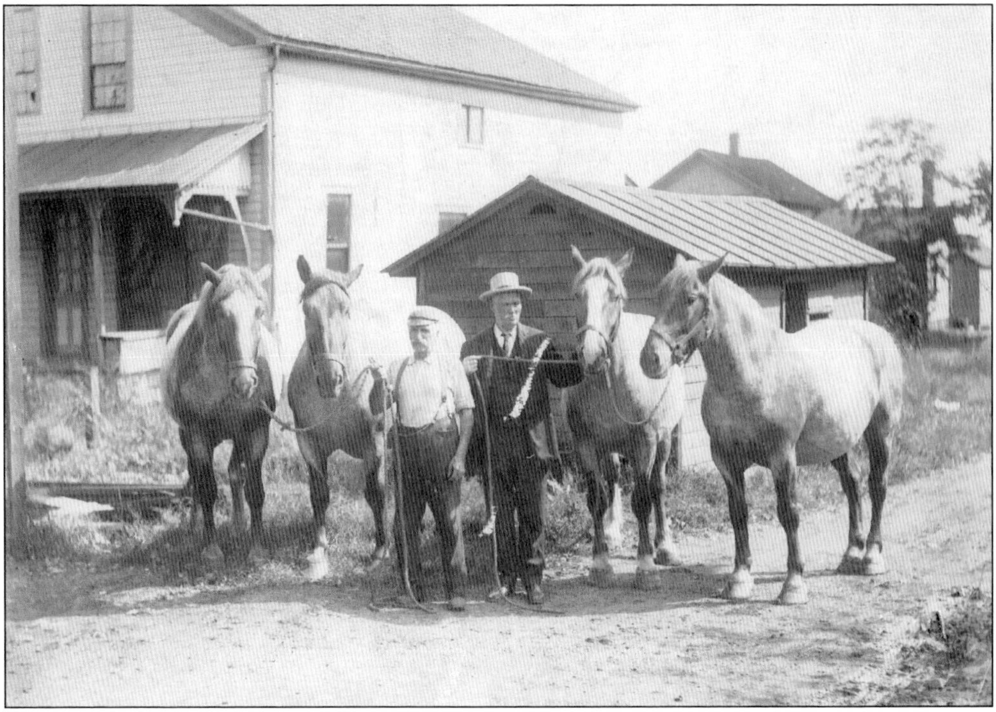

John Gerhart (left) and Ed Brown are seen here in 1900 with a few of their horses. Horse trading was a big deal at this time in US history, and Orrville had one of the largest horse traders east of the Mississippi with the Winker Horse Trading Company.

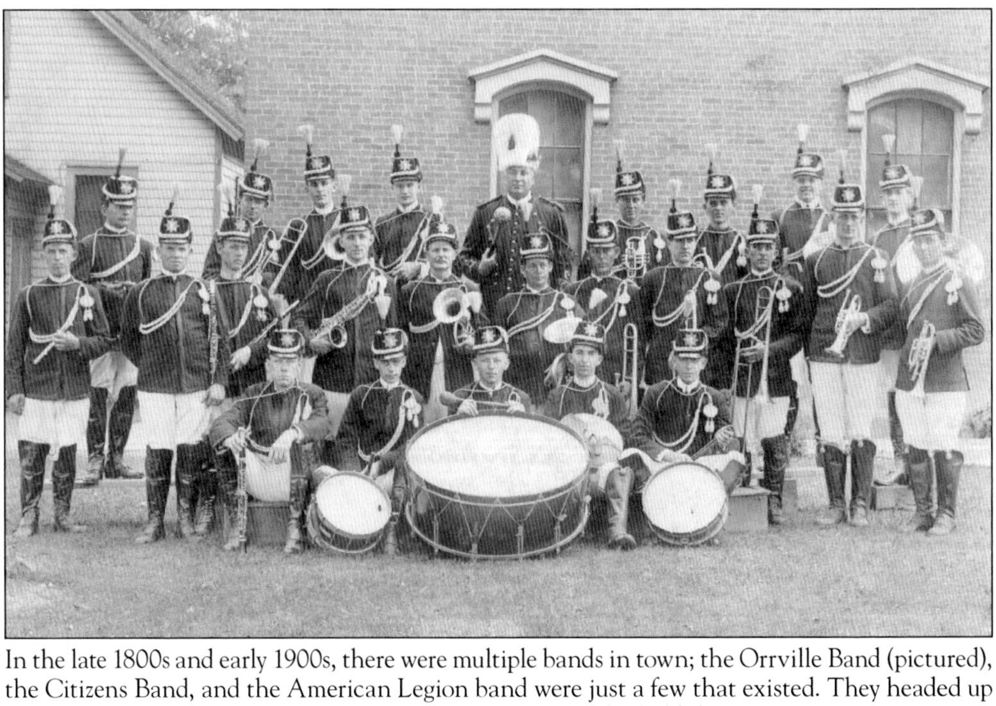

In the late 1800s and early 1900s, there were multiple bands in town; the Orrville Band (pictured), the Citizens Band, and the American Legion band were just a few that existed. They headed up many celebrations and numerous parades that were annually held downtown.

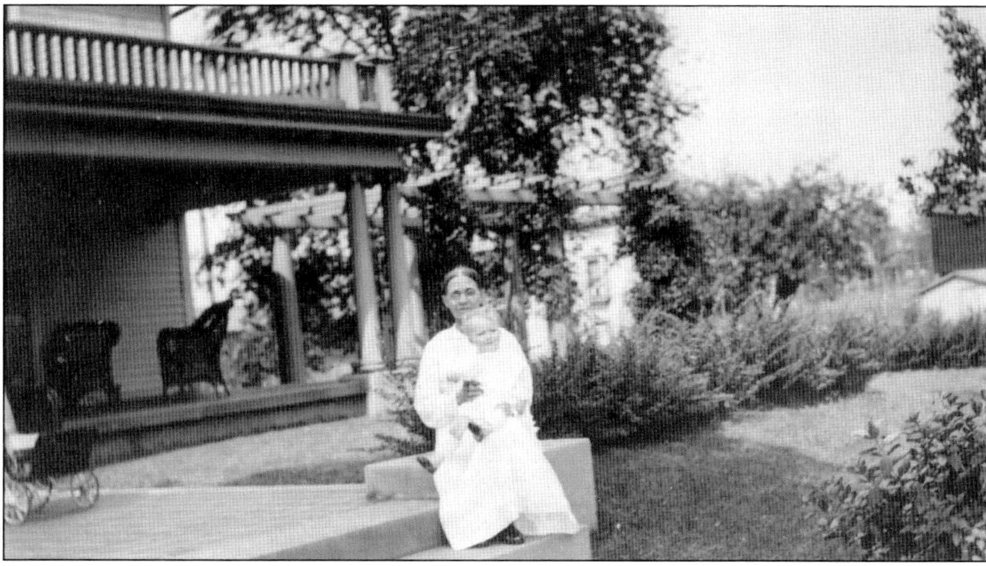

Congdon housekeeper Ricki Bartel is pictured above with either Carl Jr. or Rowland Congdon on the front steps of the Congdon home. Below, Bartel is seen standing on the driveway along the peony bushes that still bloom annually at the Smith Orr homestead.

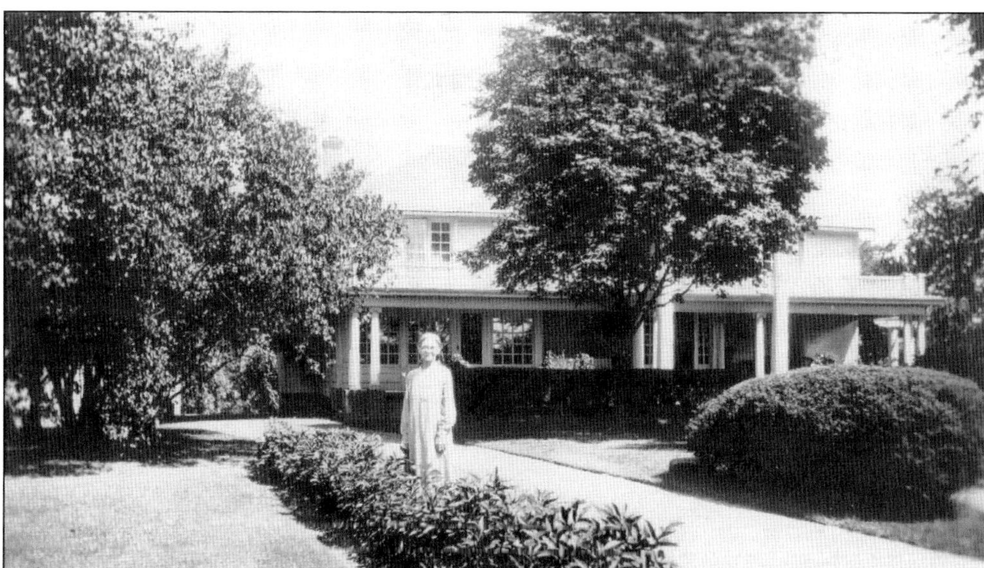

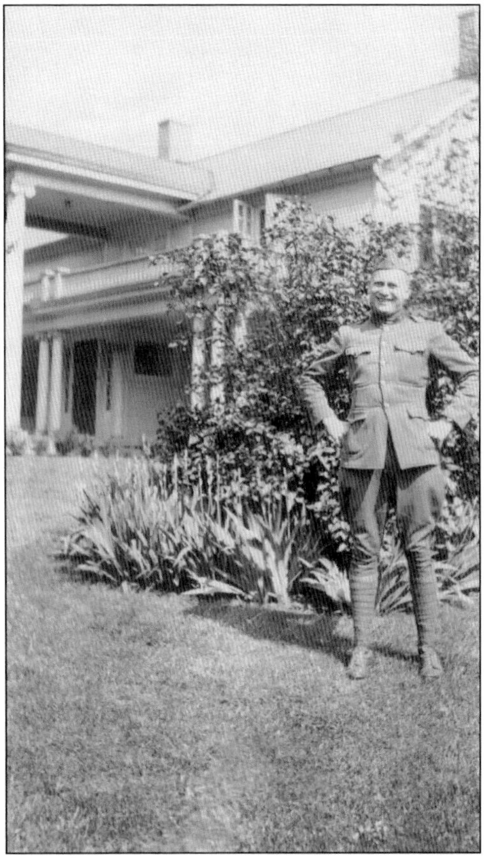

Carl Congdon Sr., the husband of Maud Brenneman, poses in the gardens of the Smith Orr homestead in his World War I uniform. The complete uniform is now a part of the Orrville Historical Museum's collection.

This is Warren Wirth in his automobile around 1905. The little girl to the left of the vehicle is unidentified.

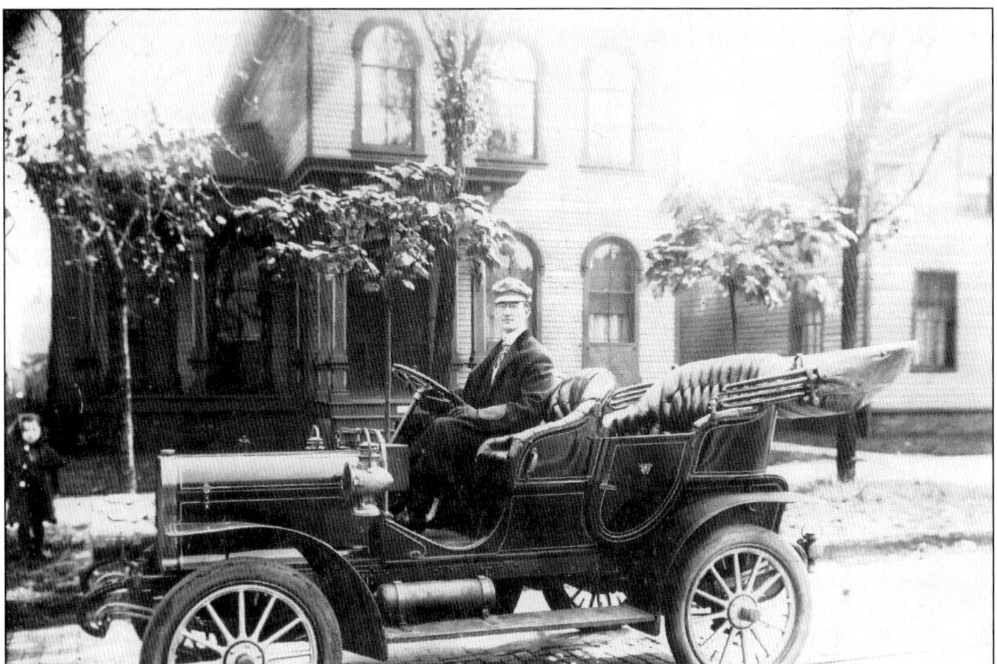

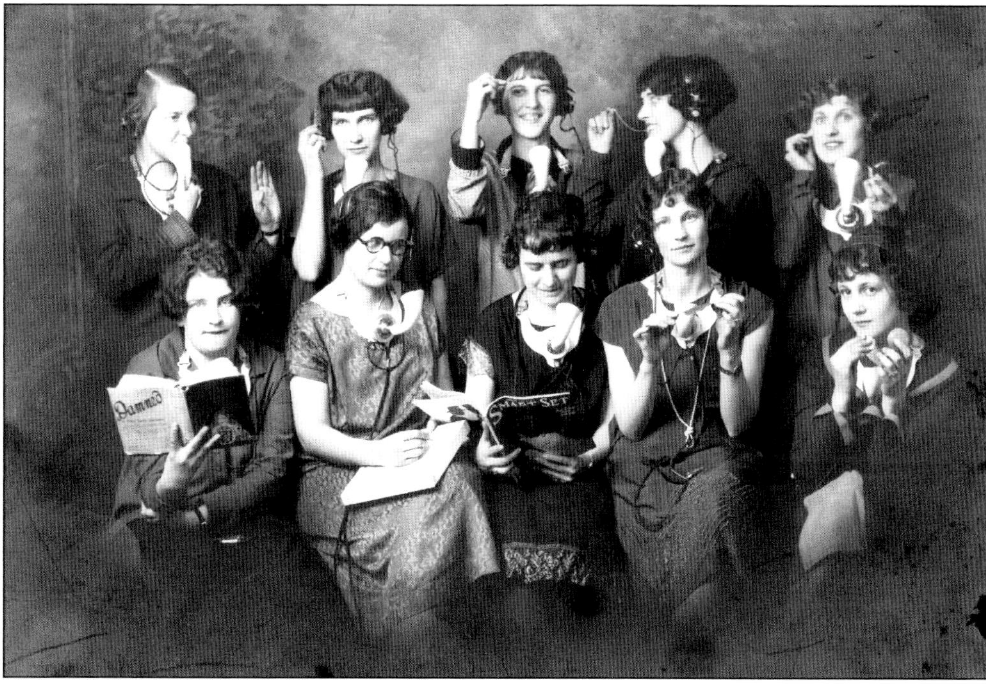

Poking fun at themselves, these telephone operators pose for a photograph. Identified are Evelyn Simon Wagner (third from left in the first row) and Edith Cook (second from left in the second row).

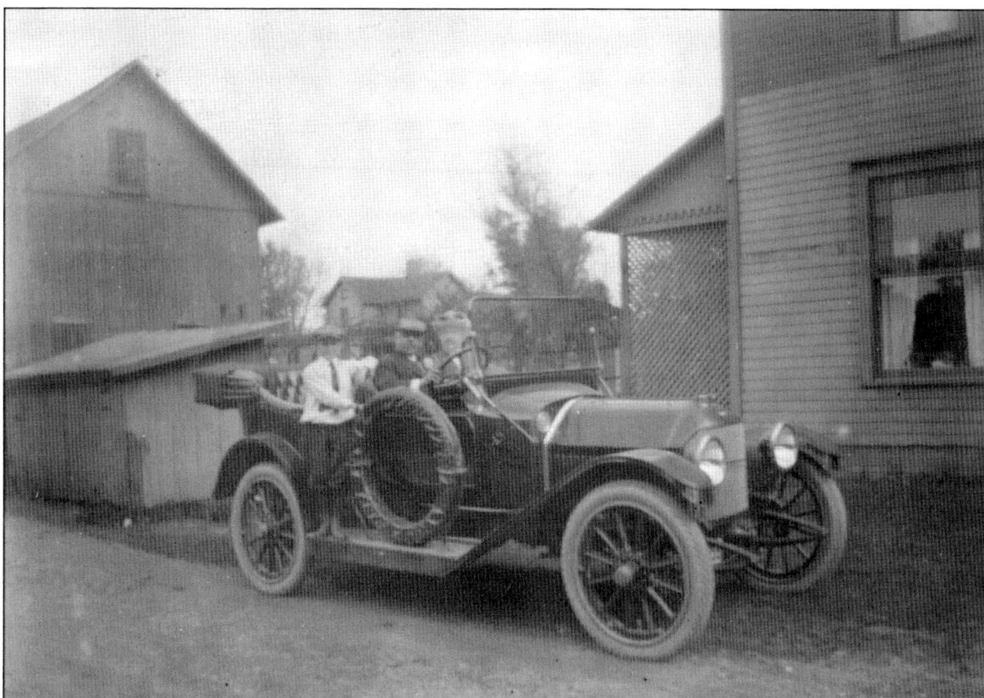

Sam and Lizie Eshelman drive their automobile in 1907. Roy Odenkirk is seen standing on the sideboard.

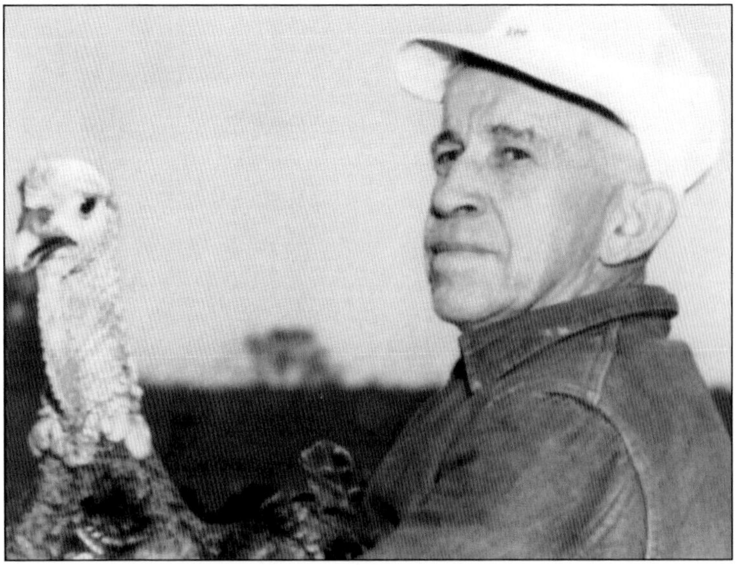

Ammon Hostetler is pictured here with one of his turkeys. Hostetler, along with his eight sons, Wayne, Norman, John, Alvin, Irvin, Ammon Jr., Homer, and Orie, raised dairy cows, turkeys, hogs, and horses. The boys ran a garbage route throughout Orrville to help feed and maintain the hogs on the farm. (Courtesy of the Irvin Hostetler family.)

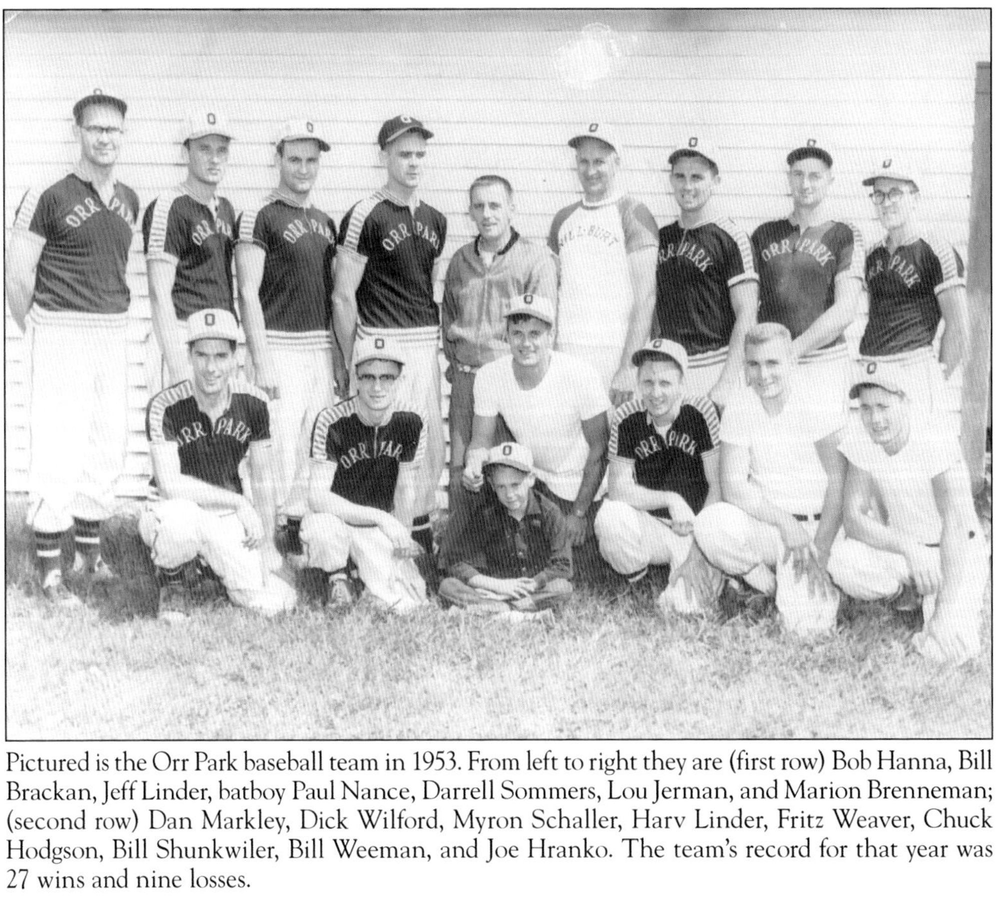

Pictured is the Orr Park baseball team in 1953. From left to right they are (first row) Bob Hanna, Bill Brackan, Jeff Linder, batboy Paul Nance, Darrell Sommers, Lou Jerman, and Marion Brenneman; (second row) Dan Markley, Dick Wilford, Myron Schaller, Harv Linder, Fritz Weaver, Chuck Hodgson, Bill Shunkwiler, Bill Weeman, and Joe Hranko. The team's record for that year was 27 wins and nine losses.

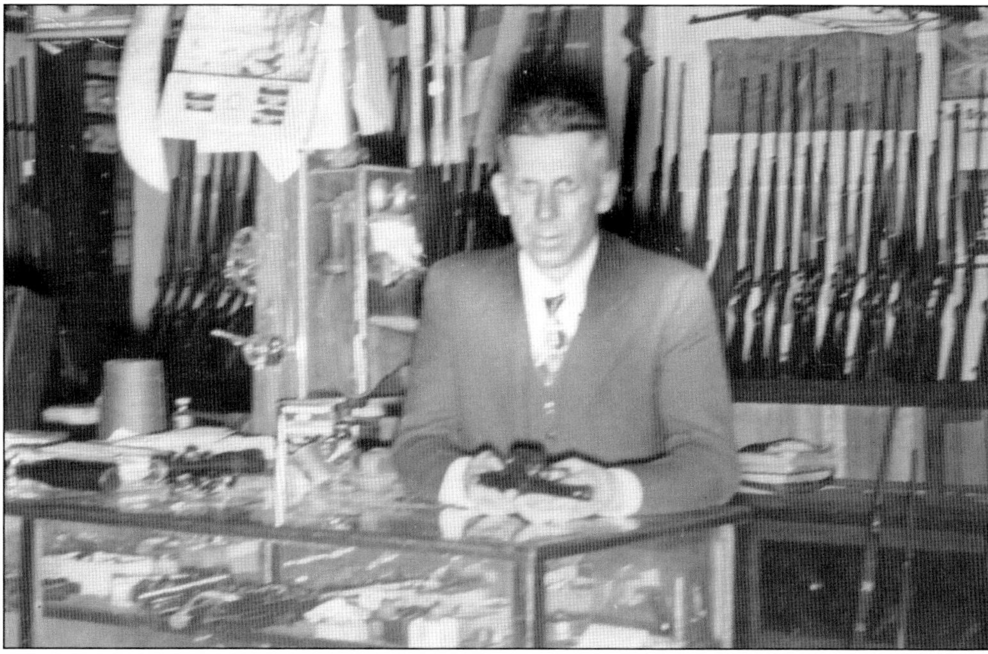

Seen above is Vernon Hershey with his guns. Vernon owned and operated a gun shop on Tannerville Road from 1943 until he passed away in 1956. Pictured below with his son Malcolm, Vernon shows off his extensive gun collection. Malcolm was later the owner of the MMM Trailer Park. On January 5, 1976, while serving an eviction notice, Malcolm was shot to death by an offending tenant.

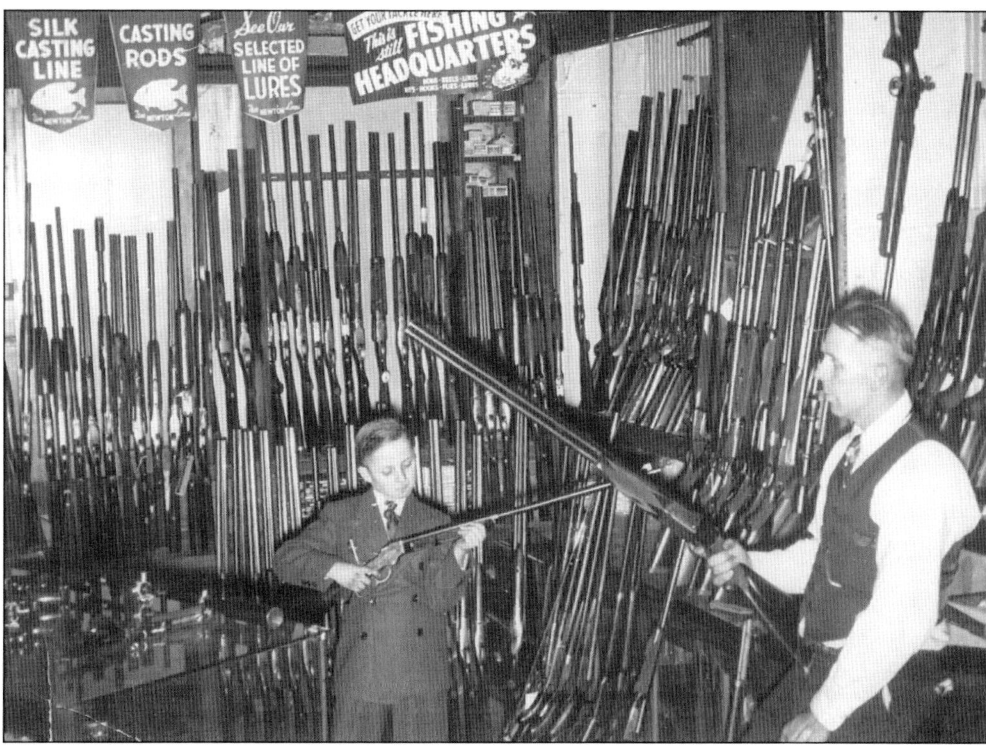

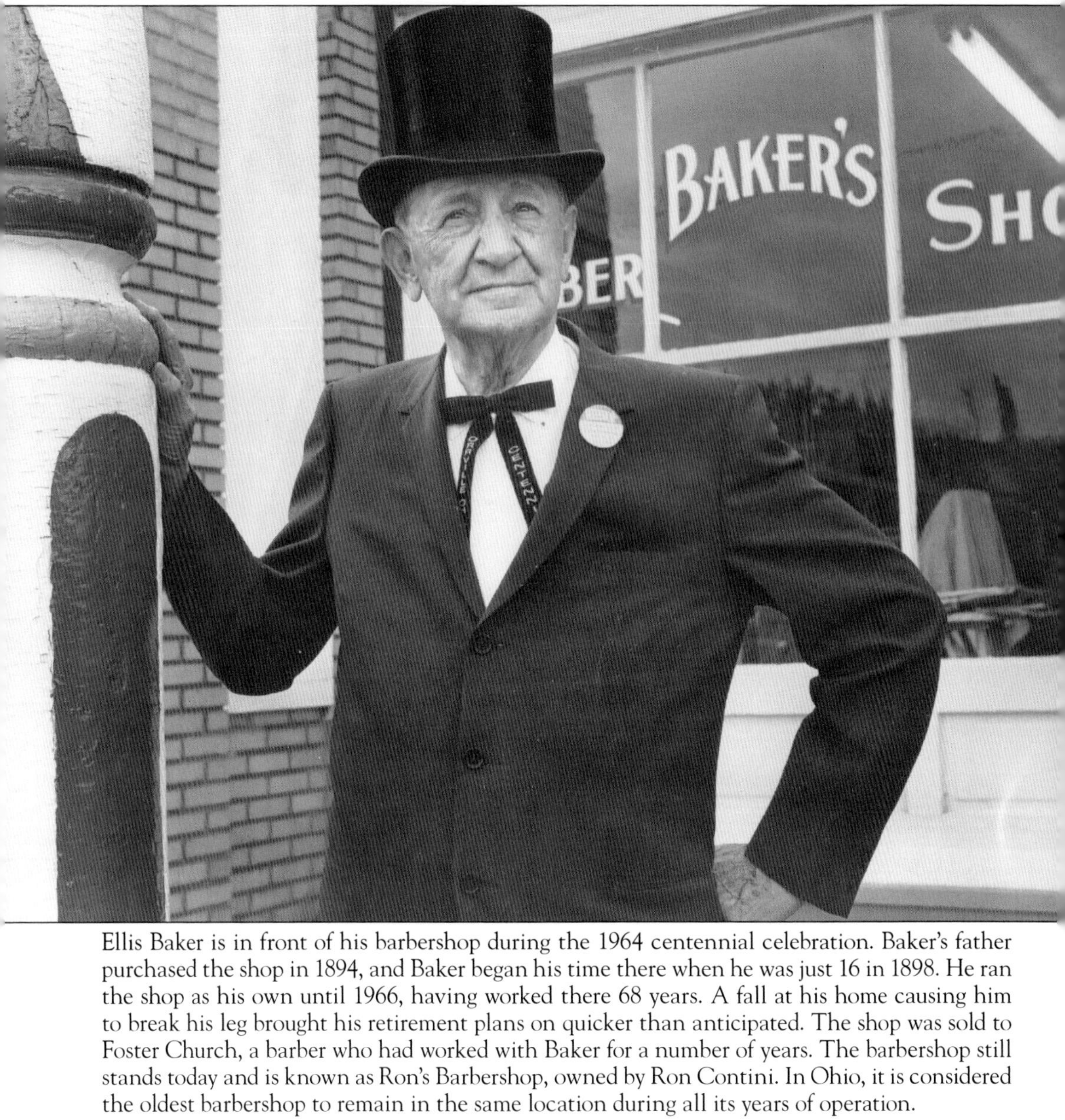

Ellis Baker is in front of his barbershop during the 1964 centennial celebration. Baker's father purchased the shop in 1894, and Baker began his time there when he was just 16 in 1898. He ran the shop as his own until 1966, having worked there 68 years. A fall at his home causing him to break his leg brought his retirement plans on quicker than anticipated. The shop was sold to Foster Church, a barber who had worked with Baker for a number of years. The barbershop still stands today and is known as Ron's Barbershop, owned by Ron Contini. In Ohio, it is considered the oldest barbershop to remain in the same location during all its years of operation.

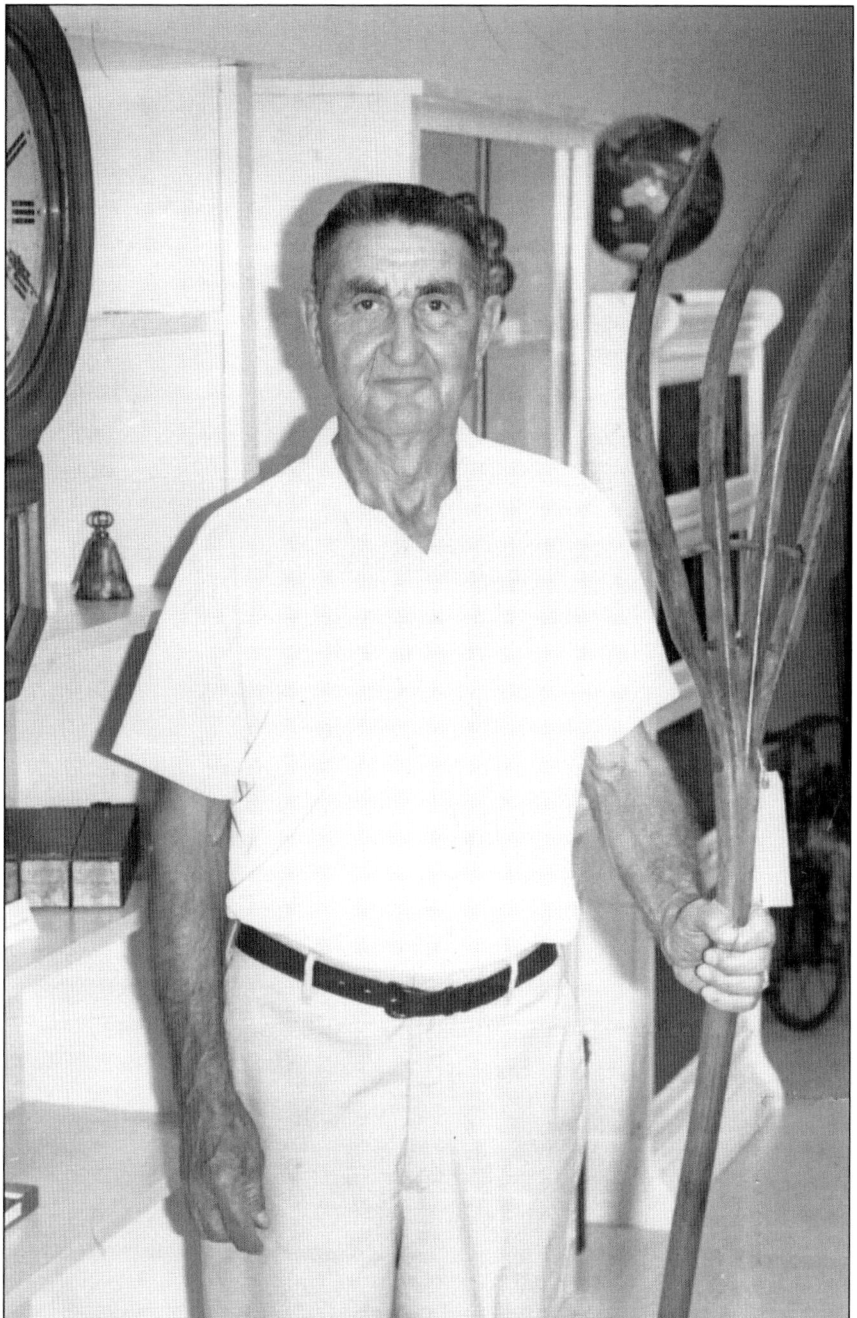

L.O. Weiss, whose full name was Lister Oliver, is seen here at the Orrville Historical Museum. Weiss was an integral part of the historical society during his retirement, stating historical and genealogical research as a hobby. He was a teacher and coach at Orrville High School from 1920 to 1925. He continued his career in education in Akron from 1925 until he retired in 1964. He wrote articles for the local newspapers describing what life was like for the pioneers of Orrville and complied numerous volumes of research and articles relating to Orrville history. All of his published research can be found at the Orrville Historical Museum.

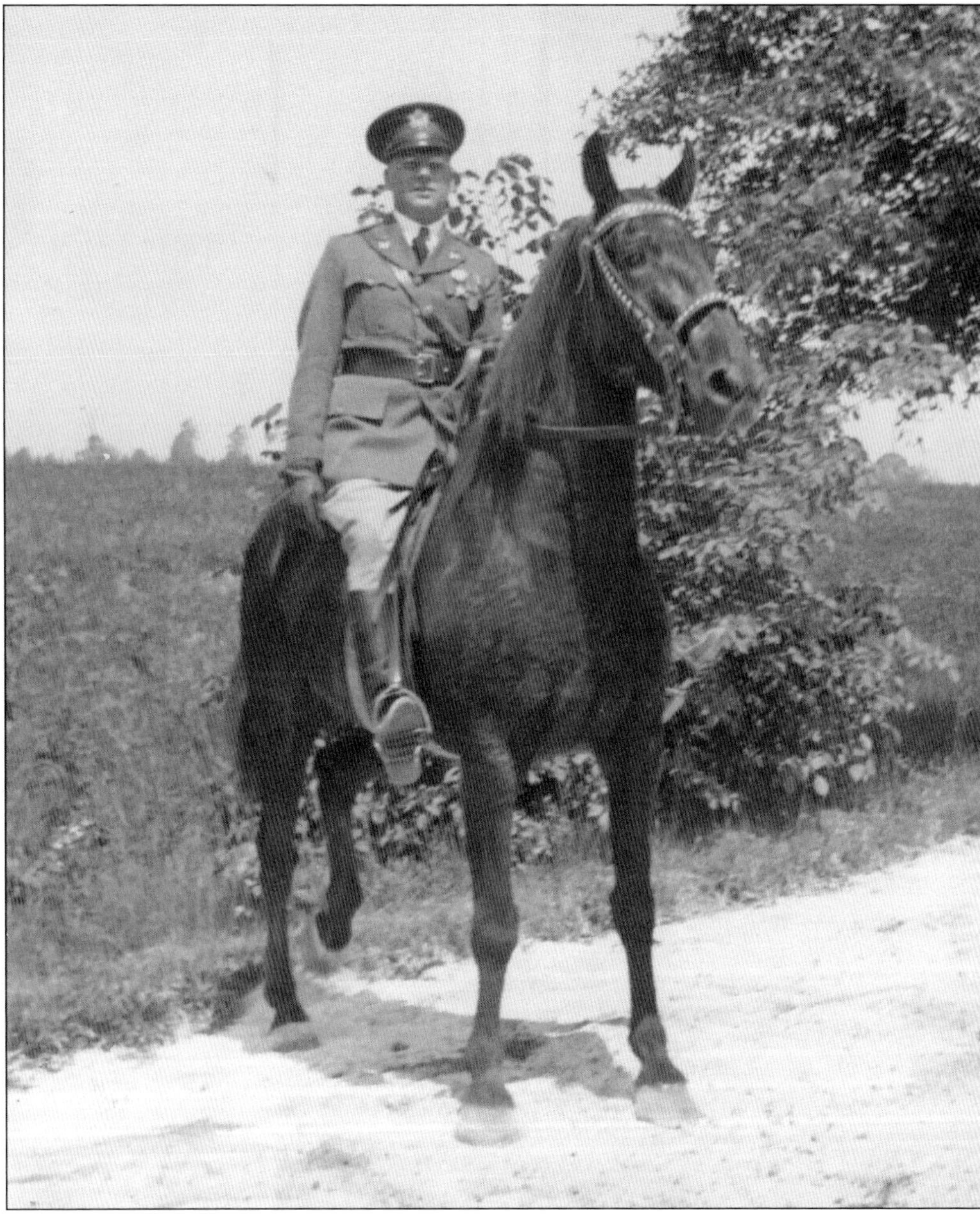

Raymond Murphy is shown here atop a horse, ready to lead the Memorial Day parade. Every year, Murphy went to one of the local horse traders in town to select the horse he would lead both the Memorial Day and Independence Day parades with. Born July 1, 1889, Murphy served for 27 months in World War I and was stationed in the Philippines and Honolulu. After the war, he returned to Orrville and worked as a conductor on the Cleveland, Akron & Columbus (CA&C) Railroad for 24 years before a tragic accident on the lines took his life in 1944. Murphy was serving as a brakeman on the Canton-to-Columbus freight train near Brink Haven when he was crawling from the engine over the coal car to his post and struck his head on an overhead bridge. He was killed almost instantly. He was survived by his wife, Bertha Louise (Tschantz), son Richard, and daughters Margaret and Della Mae. Murphy was buried at Crownhill Cemetery, and the American Legion assisted with the service. (Courtesy of Jim Musser.)

Four

Booming Business

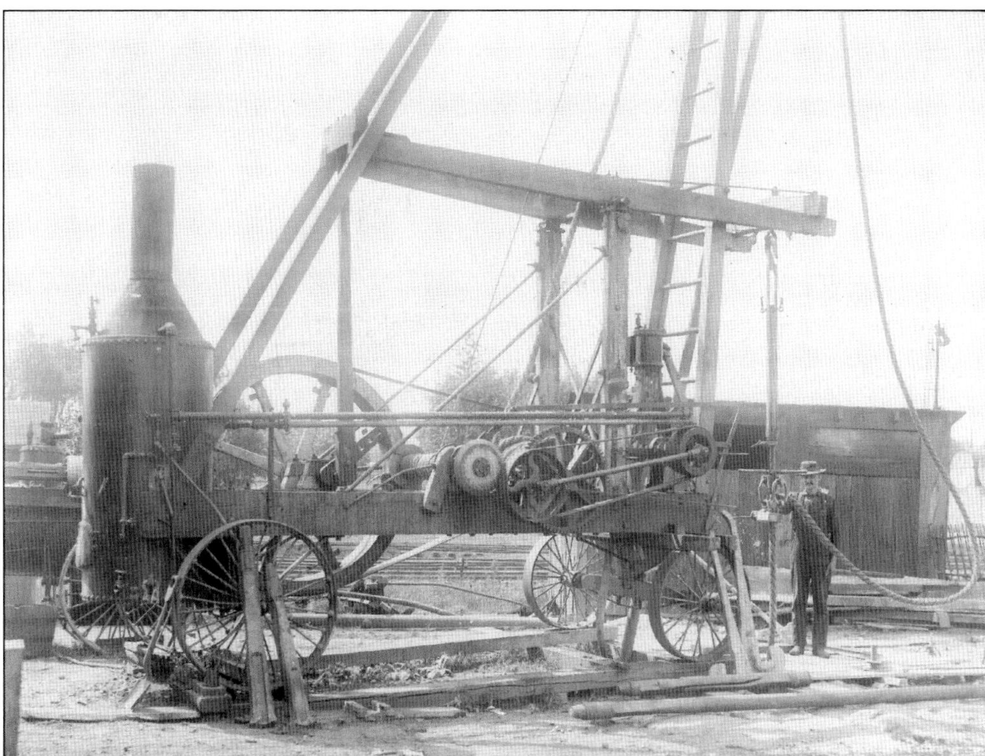

This is a photograph of the first Cyclone drilling machine produced by the Sanderson Cyclone Company. It was steam powered with an all-wood frame and steel wagon wheels.

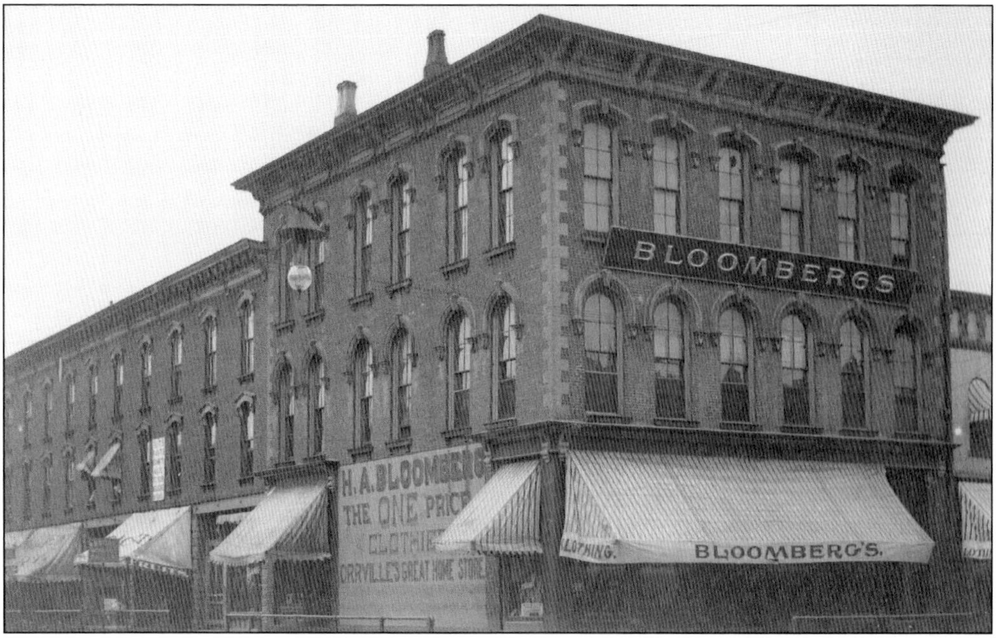

H.A. Bloomberg & Company sat on the northwest corner of the square at the center of downtown. The building towered over others in the downtown area, boasting three full floors. Today, the building is just two stories. (Courtesy of Wayne Liechty.)

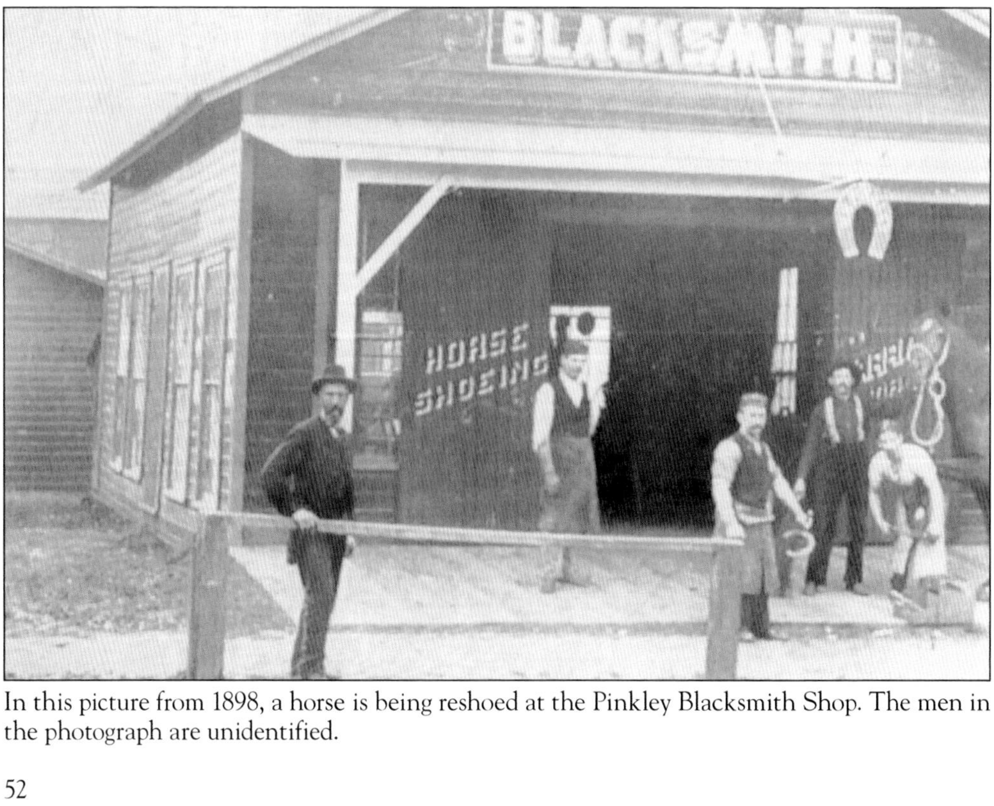

In this picture from 1898, a horse is being reshoed at the Pinkley Blacksmith Shop. The men in the photograph are unidentified.

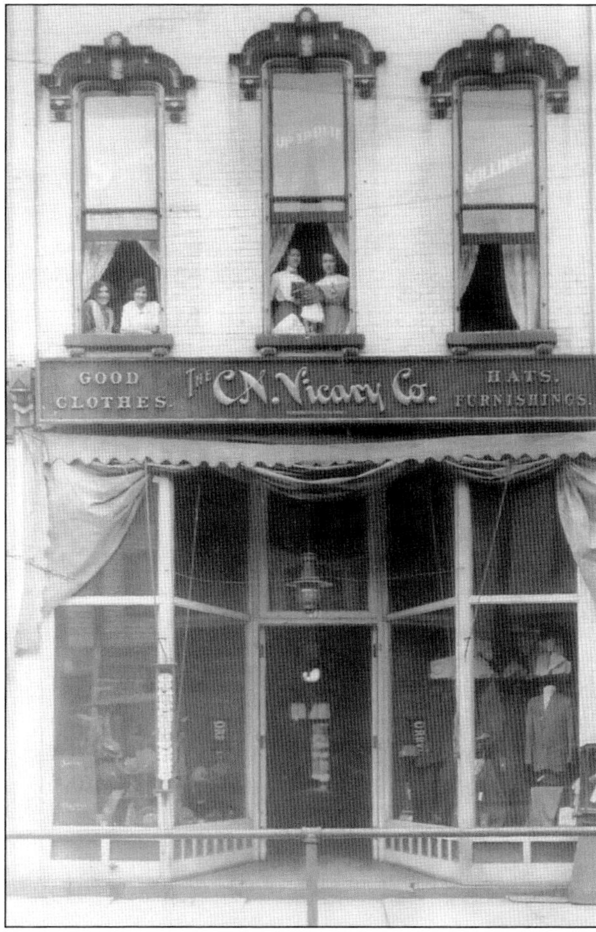

Unidentified women at the C.N. Vicary Company look out the second-story windows in the photograph to the right. This business block was constructed in 1912 and situated on West Market Street, currently home of the Brown's furniture sleep shop. The photograph below is from a company party held for Vicary employees. The sign at the celebration states, "C.N. Vicary Co. BLOW-OUT No. 1 Feb. 29."

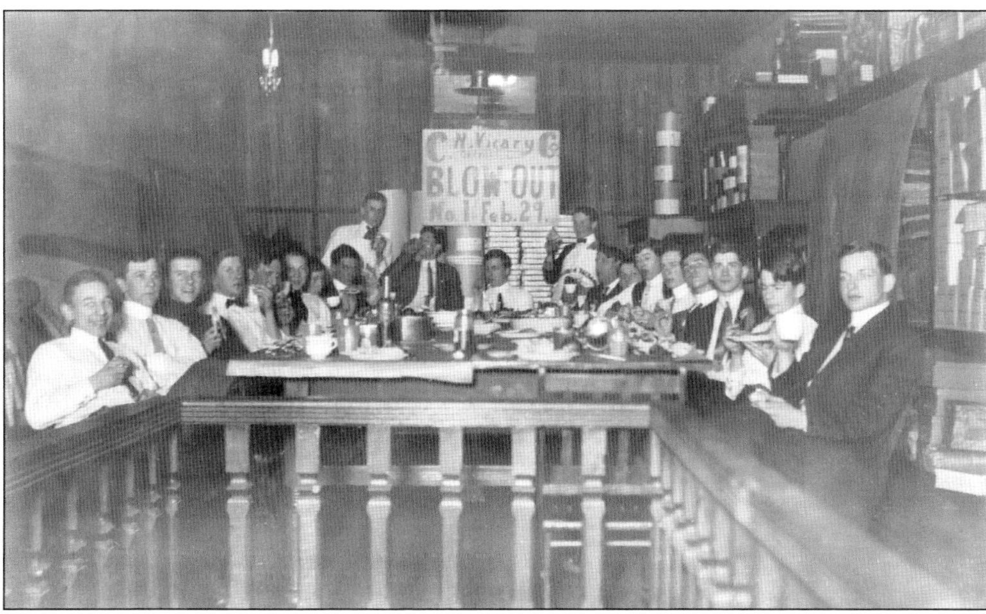

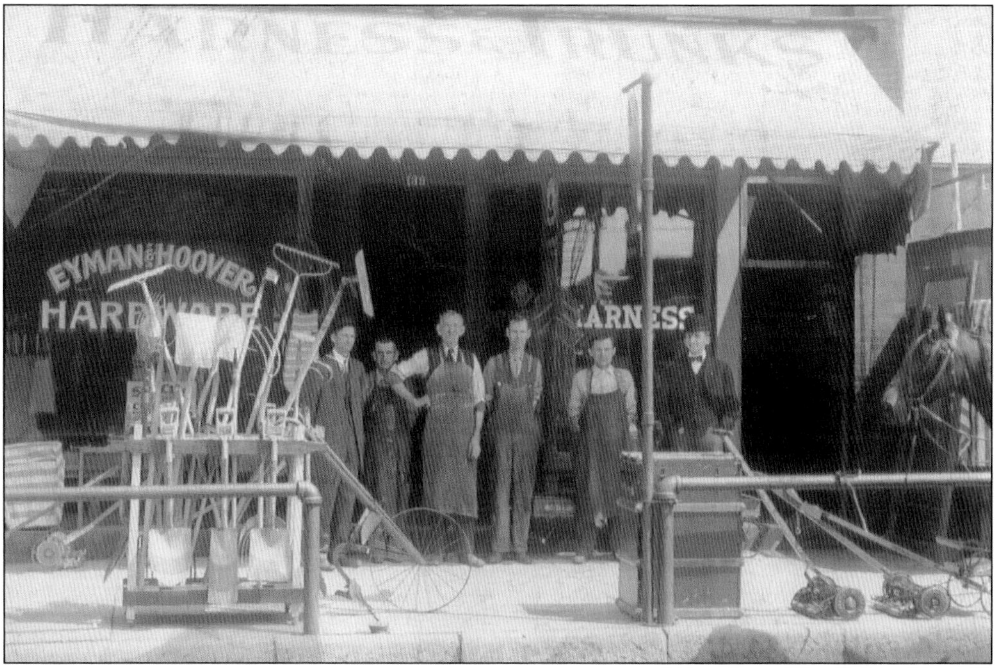

Eyman & Hoover Hardware was a harness and hardware shop located downtown. Hardware stores were always a staple in downtown Orrville, whether it was long-running Sears Hardware on East Market Street when Orrville first emerged or Johnson's Hardware, located on North Main Street until its closing in 2010.

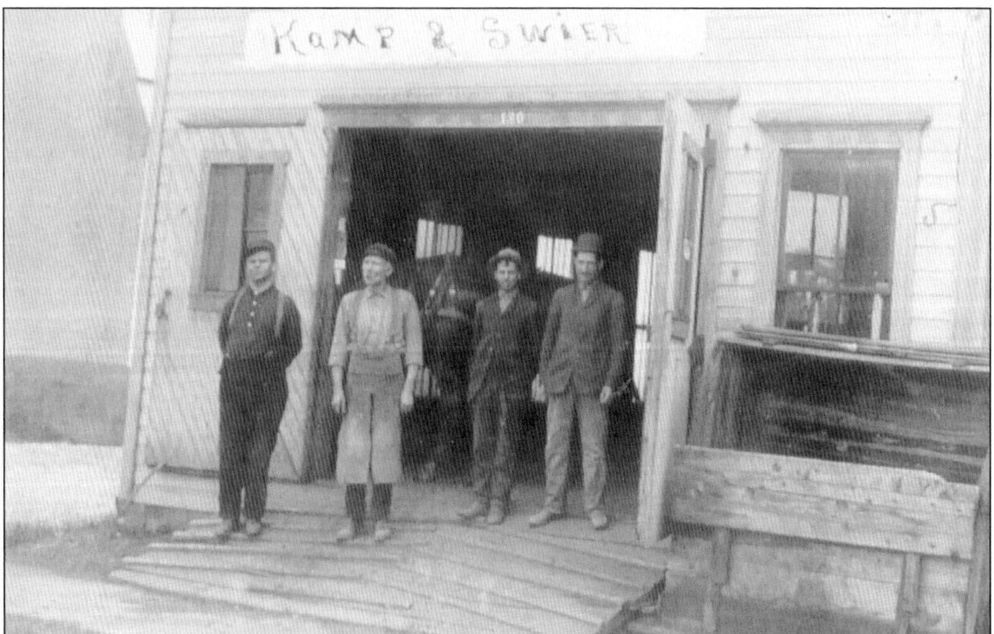

Four unidentified men stand in front of the Kamp & Swier blacksmith shop, located on North Vine Street just south of the Lutheran church. Smith Dairy was later at this location, and today, it is a parking lot for the church and lawyer's office on the corner of Market and Vine Streets.

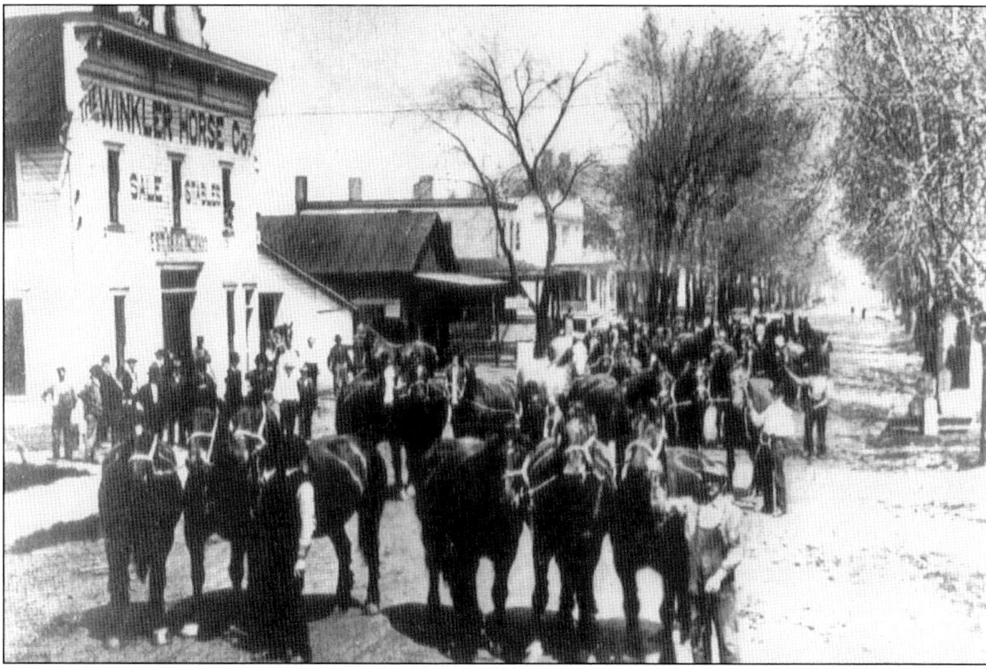

Winkler Horse Trading feed and sale stables was located in the rear of the Mansion House Hotel on the corner of West Market and Vine Streets. An 1898 ad states that they were the "Dealers of the best grade, farm and shipping horses." Operating from 1883 to 1912, it was one of the largest horse dealers west of Buffalo. In 1888, horses were shipped in from Indiana, Illinois, Iowa, and Kansas on a weekly basis. In 1897, horse sales totaled 1,260 horses with $123,500 in profit. In 1912, the business was sold to C.A. Wyer and Clyde Rudy; they expanded and ran it until 1916, when they closed horse sales and sold the rest of their stock.

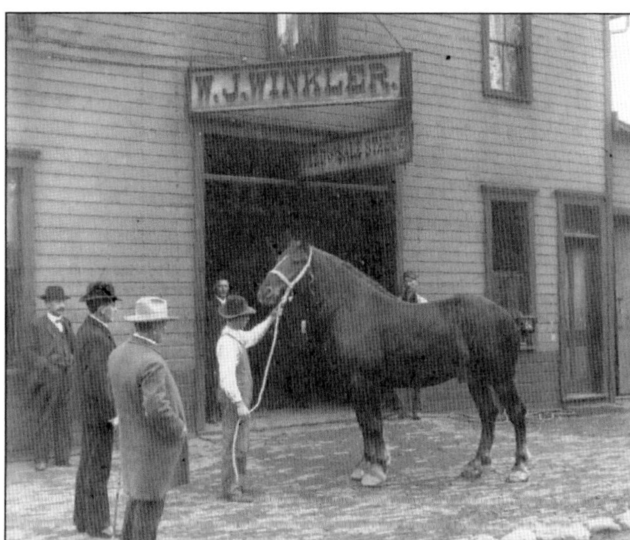

Taken in October 1903 by Karl Beckley, this picture shows a sorrel horse that weighed 1,980 pounds and was sold to a Mr. McCarshegan, a buyer in New York, for $8,500. From left to right are Elmer Bownam, who sold the horse; W.J. Winkler, sale barn owner; Mr. McCarshegan; John Winkler in the doorway; John Seigenthaler, holding the horse; and John Brandt, standing behind the horse. In 1904 alone, over 4,000 horses were shipped to Eastern markets, such as New York, Philadelphia, and Boston.

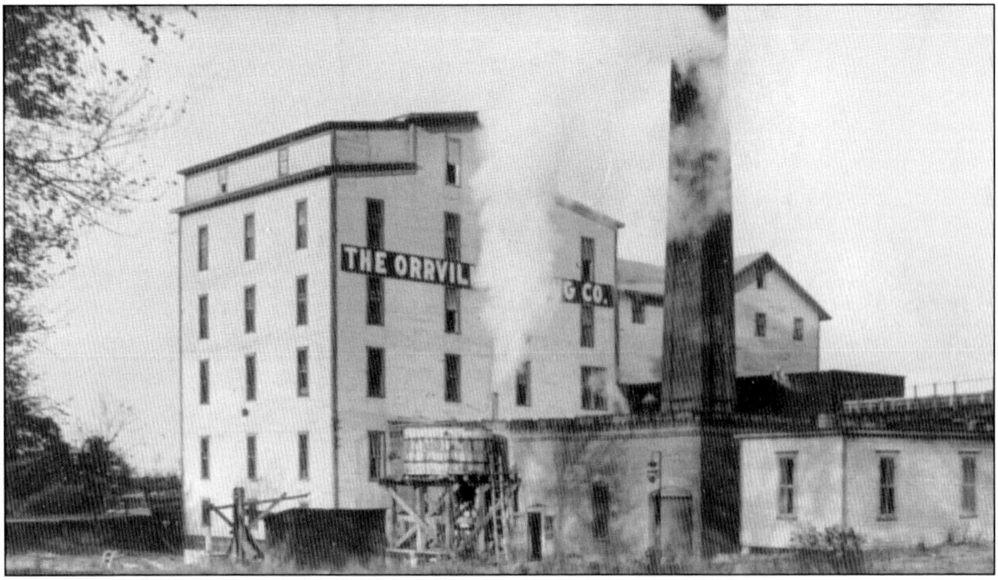

Above is an early photograph of the Orrville Milling Company. The flour mill operated 24 hours a day, seven days a week, manufacturing "Our Best" and "Table Belle" flour. The mill opened in 1874, and by 1890, three additions had been made to the mill. At that time, the mill employed 50 people and was open for sales 12 hours a day. The Orrville Milling Company is also pictured below in 1900. It had the capability to produce 800 barrels of flour a day, one of the largest productions in Ohio at the time. The mill on the left is still standing today at the end of East Market Street; unfortunately, the Orrville Milling Company went out of business in 1923.

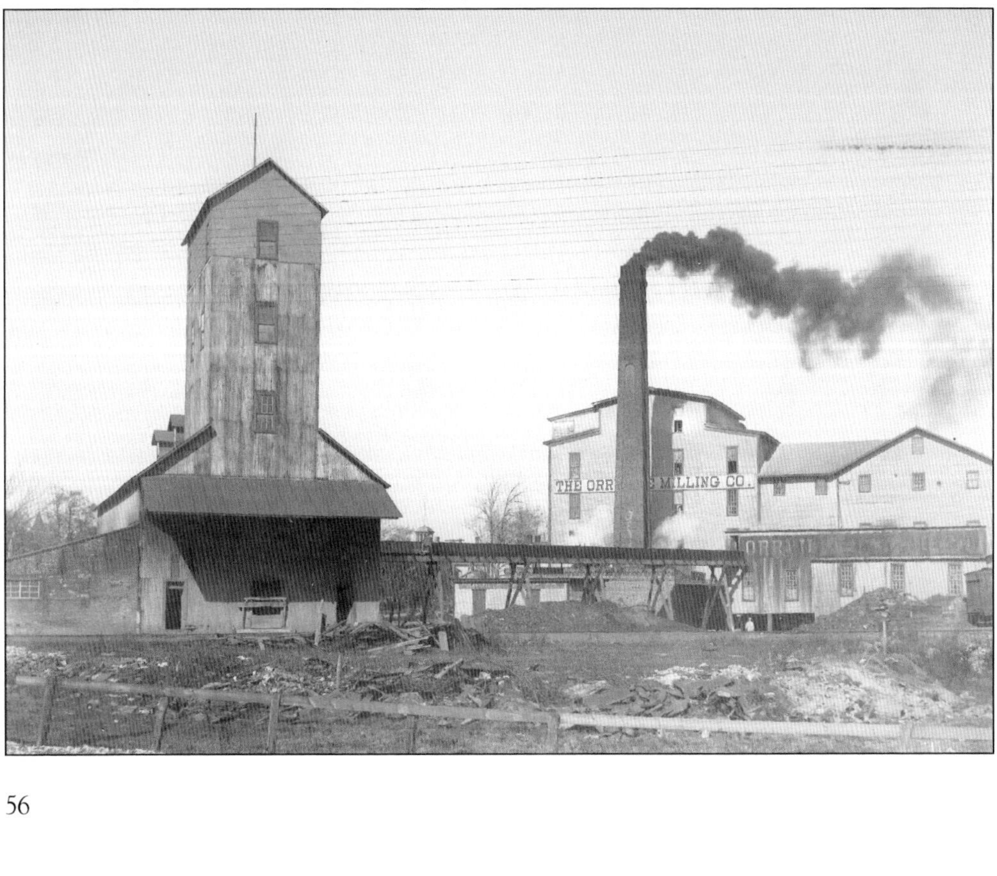

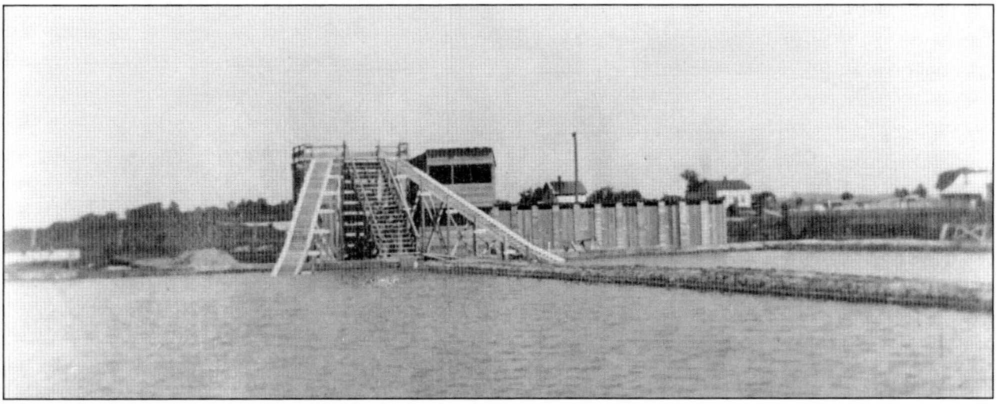

The ice ponds on North Main Street were built in 1895 as two separate swimming holes, operated by Joseph Snavely. One pond was for men, and the other for women. Due to the thick muck on the bottom, it was only a swimming area for a short time because no one wanted to swim. The swimming hole was then changed into ice ponds that furnished all the ice for the residents and Orrville businesses for many years.

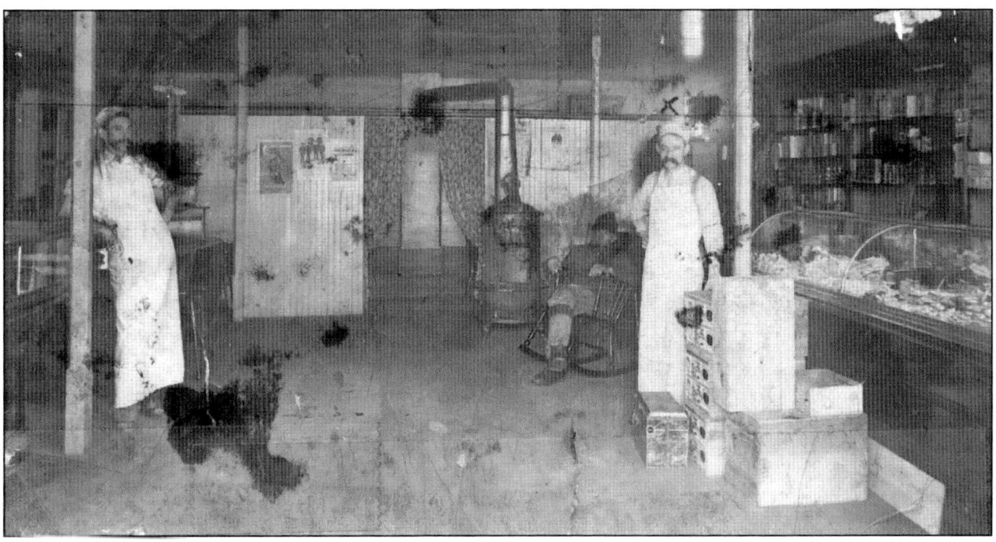

This is an interior shot of the City Bakery in 1899. The only man identified in the photograph is owner Hal Weygan on the far right.

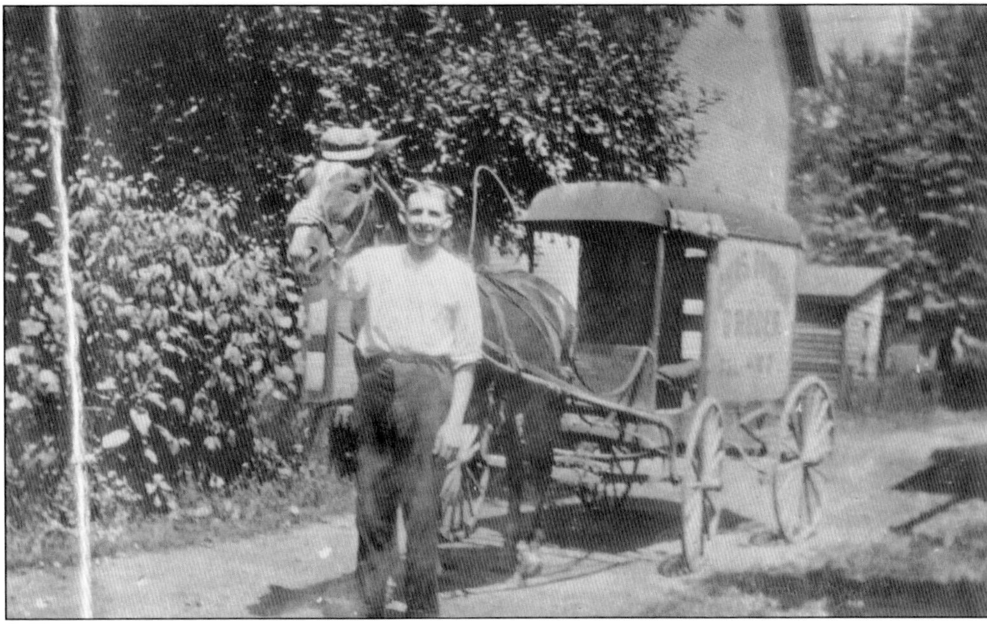

Pictured in 1912, Harold Bowman stands with a grocery wagon led by Harry the horse. His father, Charles, owned Chas Bowman's Grocery. Below is an exterior photograph of Bowman's Grocery at Christmastime, taken after the store was relocated to North Main Street from Market Street. Bowman's Grocery always featured eye-catching window displays to entice customers. Bowman won second place from the Butterick Publishing Company for the National Window Display Contest; it is said that thousands of grocers nationwide entered the contest and that second place was quite an honor.

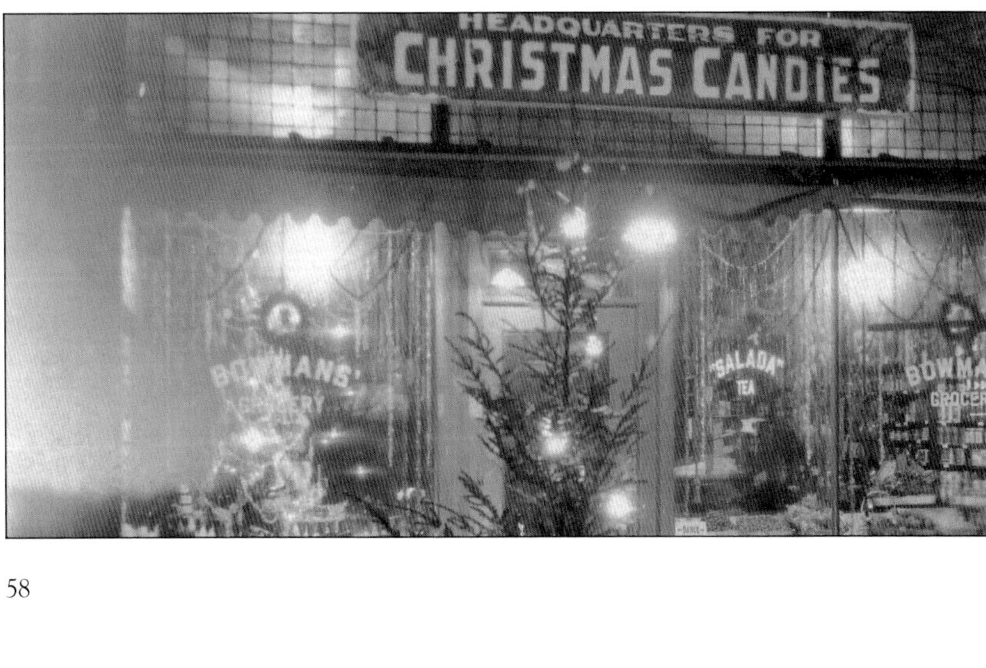

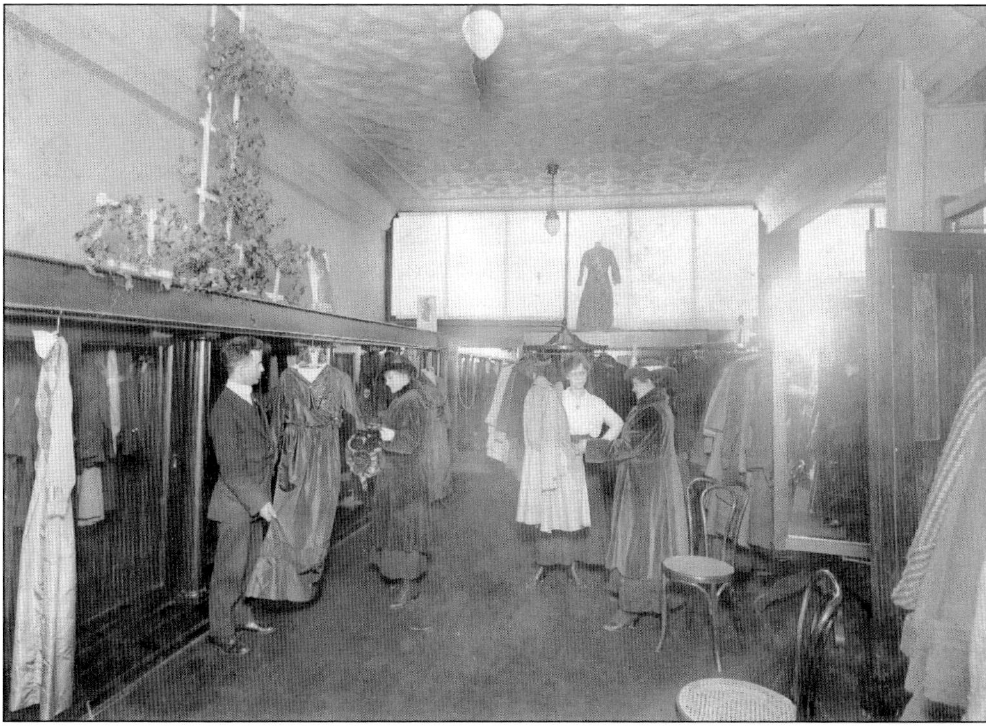

Pictured above, Henry Perilstein (left) presents ladies' garments to a customer at Jos. Perilstein Company. In 1905, Perilstein came to America through Ellis Island from Hungary. He arrived in Orrville and began working for his uncle Joseph as a janitor at his store. Once Perilstein learned to speak English, he was promoted to sales. He worked his way up through the business until his uncle passed away in 1952, when he assumed management. Today, the building is home to Brown's Furniture. Seen below is the fabric department at the Jos. Perilstein Company. The store carried women's and men's clothing, fabrics, furniture, interior decor, and floor coverings. (Courtesy of Steve Goldring.)

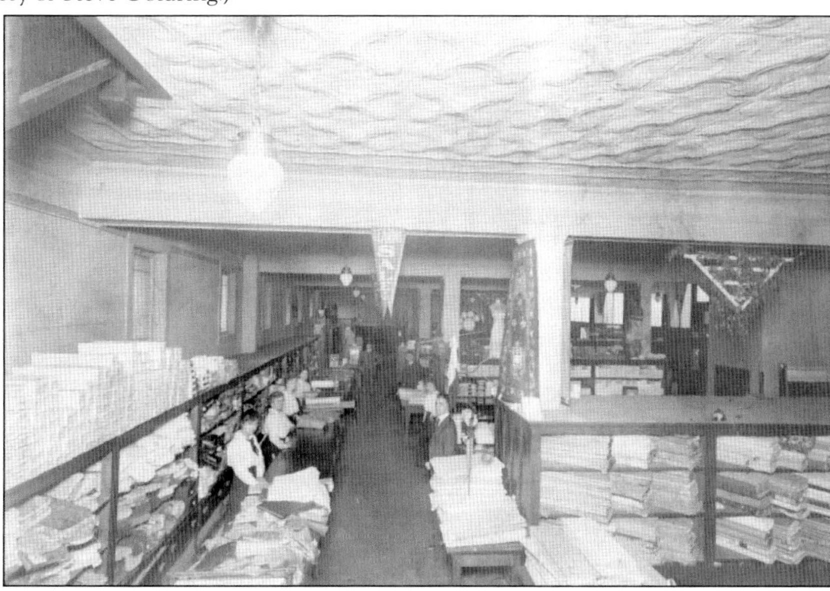

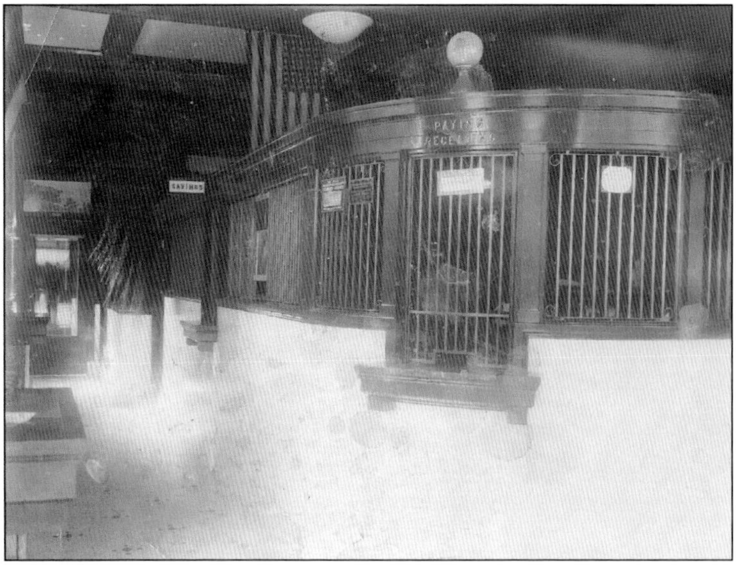

In 1868, Jacob Brenneman, D.G. Horst, and A.S. Moncreif opened the Orrville Exchange Bank, the first bank in Orrville. It failed in 1873. The Farmers Bank was opened to replace it and take over the accounts, but it also failed in 1886. This view is of the interior of the Exchange Bank.

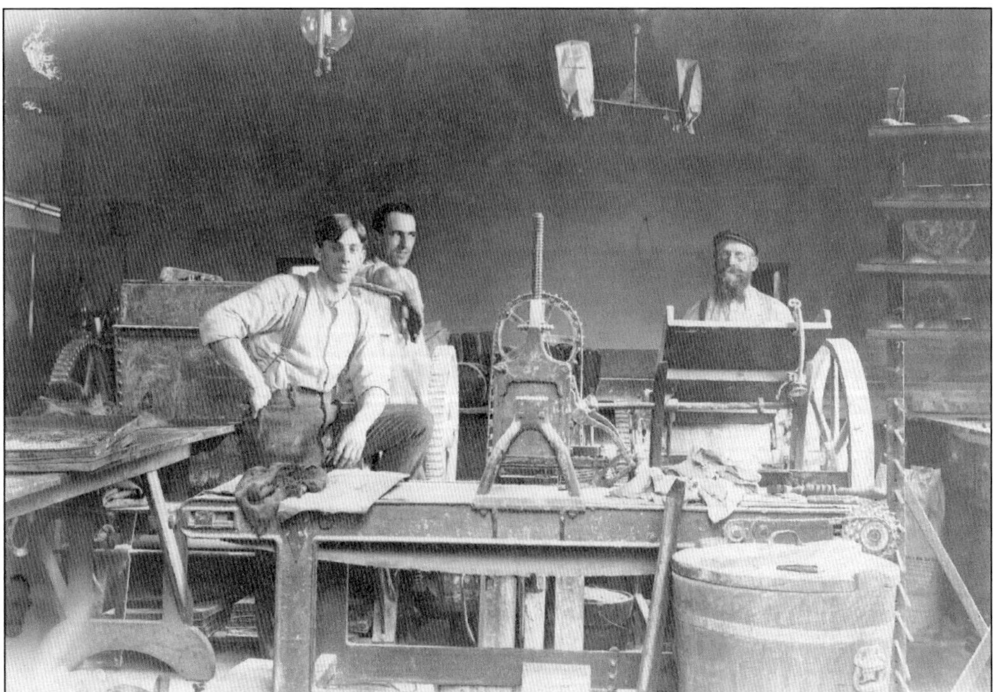

Pictured from left to right are ? Huntsburger, ? Chaffin, and Harrison "Papie" Bowman at the E.C. Bowman Bakery in 1905. According to an ad from an 1889 *Orrville Crescent*, Bowman Brothers Bakery had "Cream, Vienna, Common, Rye and Graham bread baked fresh every day."

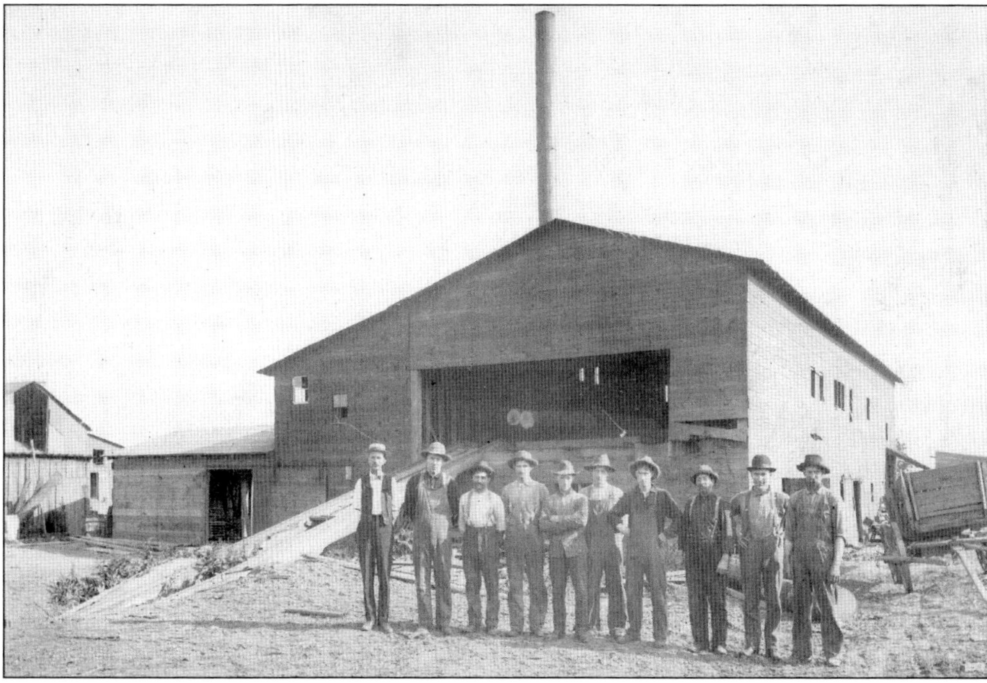

Pictured above in 1905 are, in no particular order, Kinney Lumber employees James Postalwarte, Albert Wilhelm, Jack Turner, ? Shallenberger, Charley Burkey, William Baer, Webb Huff, Frank Peterman, and two unidentified men. The lumber company sat on the exact same property as the original sawmill built by Judge Smith Orr on West Church Street and was bought by Kinney and Sons in 1902. With the railroad running right through the land, it was an ideal location. In the photograph below, Kinney Lumber wagons are seen hauling logs down Church Street. The men from left to right are Frank Zimmerman, Donald Peterman, Marvin Stocksdale, and Frank Peterman. The tree shown in the picture was one of the largest trees ever cut down in Wayne County at the time; it came from the Conrad farm in Orrville. The largest section, seen on the far left wagon, was 48 inches by 12 feet and produced 1,452 board feet of lumber. Overall, the total board length from this one tree was over 5,000 feet. (Below, courtesy Walter West Family.)

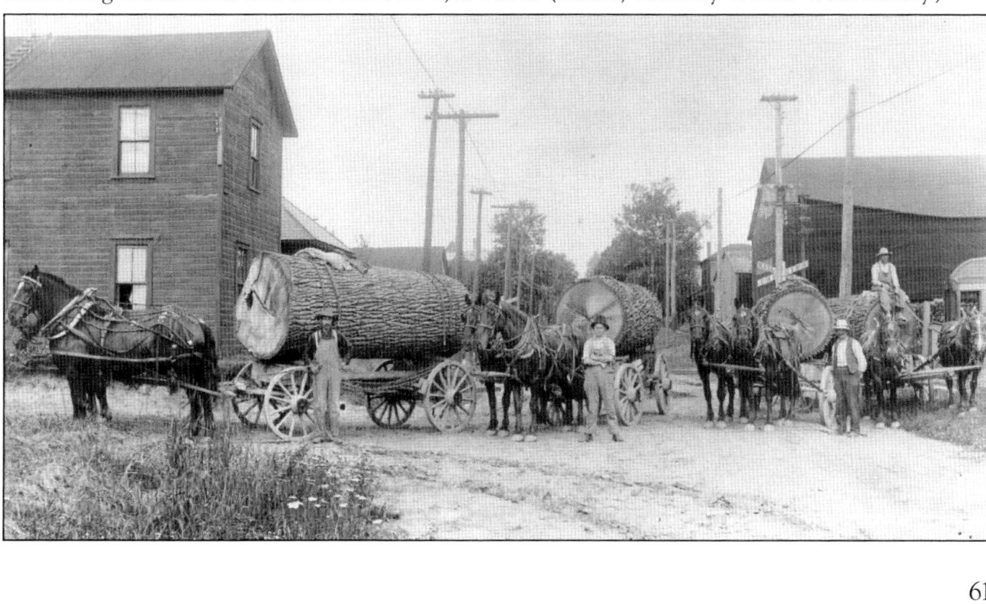

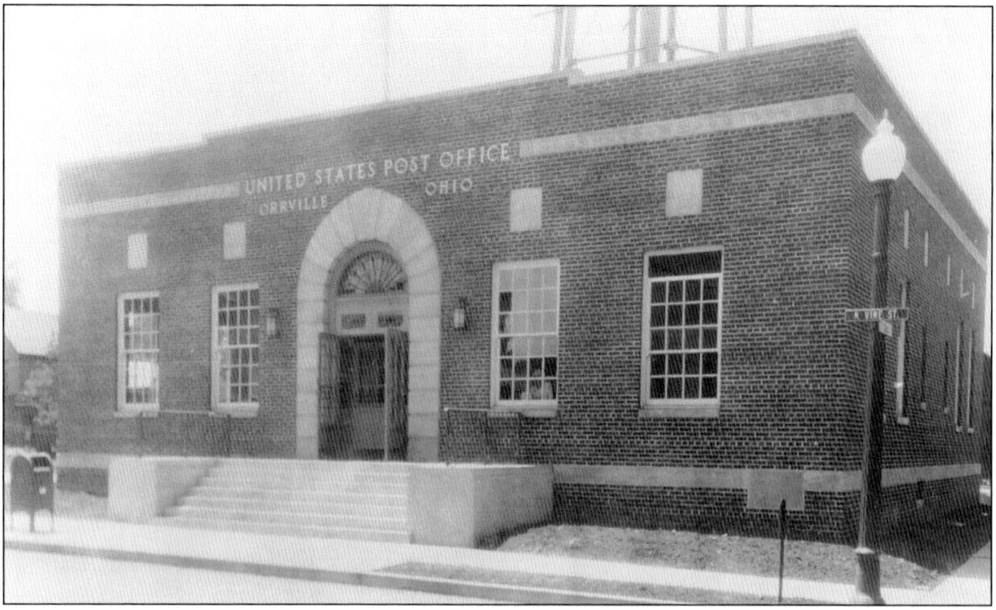

This image shows the completed new post office located on North Vine Street. The building opened in 1935 and is still the post office used by Orrville citizens today.

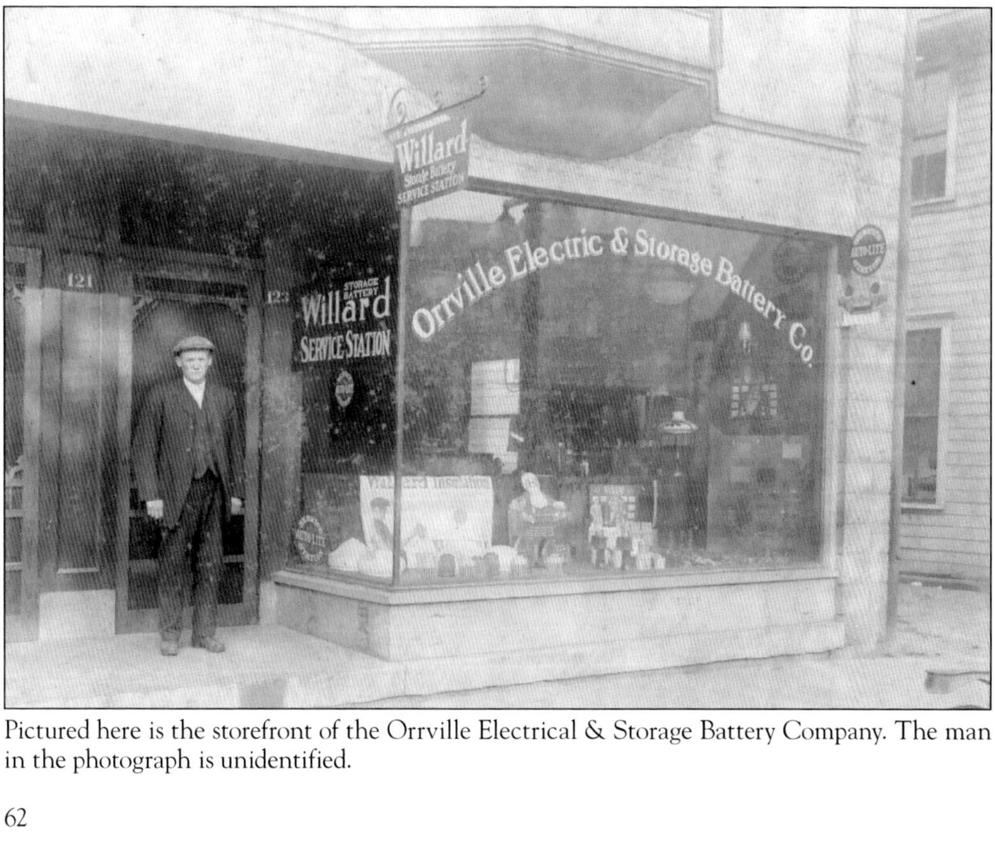

Pictured here is the storefront of the Orrville Electrical & Storage Battery Company. The man in the photograph is unidentified.

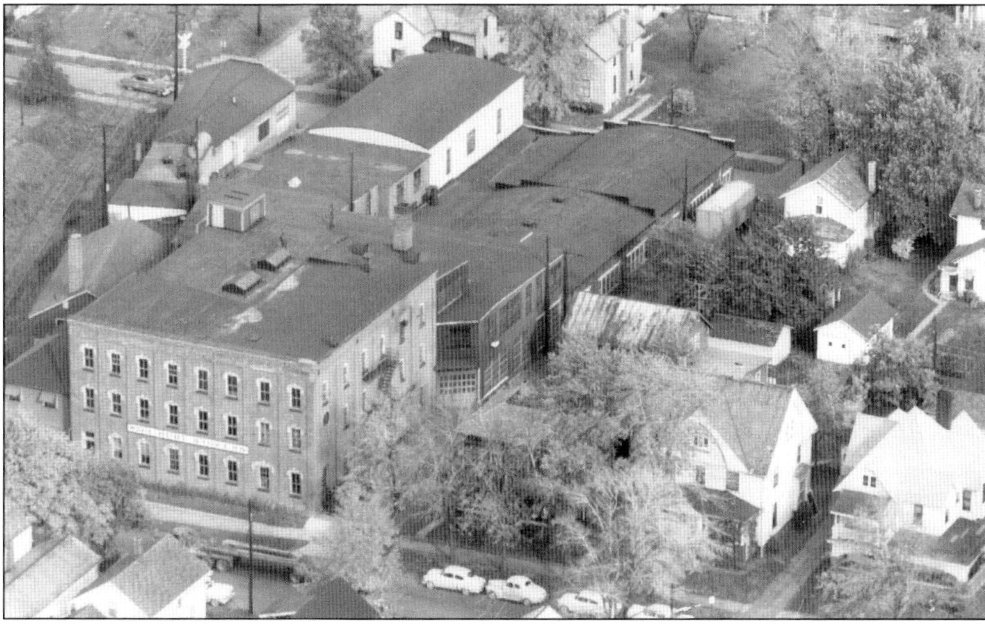

This is an aerial photograph of the Will-Burt Stoker building in 1930. The structure was originally built by the Tschantz family for the organ company and has been occupied by a number of businesses over the years. In 1878, Askin's Glass Coffin shop took over after the organ company. Later, the Chrystal Burial Casket Co. took over for Askin's, with the business failing in 1891. The building was then sold at a sheriff's sale. In 1909, the building was occupied by the Millersburg, Wooster, and Orrville (MW&O) Telephone Company. In 1914, the structure became a ladies' garment factory, which closed in 1915. In 1916, Wayne Rubber Company took over the building and manufactured tires there. Will-Burt then occupied it until it was torn down in the 1990s to make room for the Rite Aid Pharmacy that is currently there.

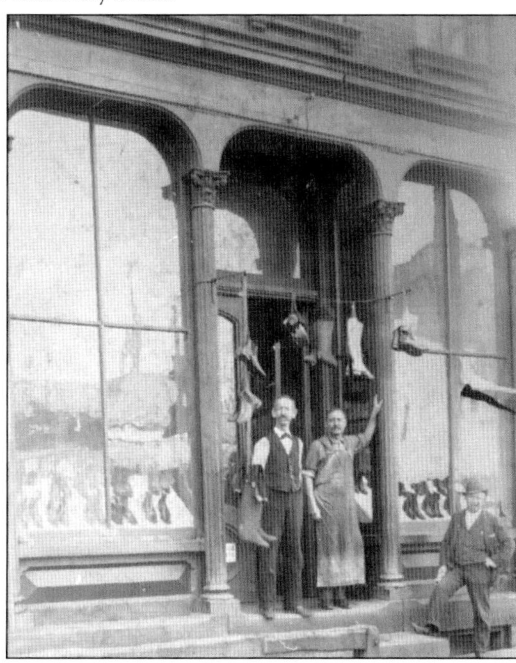

Another longtime business in the downtown area was the Wirth Shoe Store. Pictured here in the front of the store are, from left to right, owner Adam Wirth, George Fulmer, and Frank Robinson. An ad from the 1897 *Independent* states, "Here We Are! With a complete line of Fall and Winter Footwear, consisting of Ladies' and Gents' Heavy Wear, and Boys' and Girls' school shoes, at prices that make you open your pocket book. A. Wirth & Son, Shoe Merchants." Wirth passed away in 1917 after having owned his shoe business for nearly 50 years.

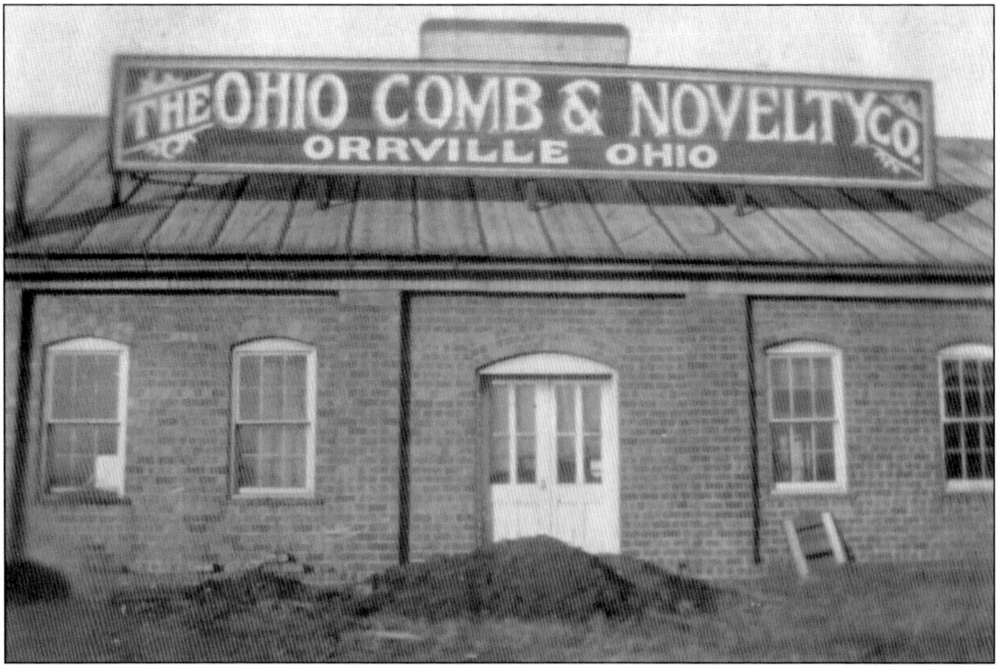

The Ohio Comb & Novelty, located on Penn Avenue, opened in 1911 and manufactured rubber combs until the 1920s before switching to aluminum; however, once ladies' styles changed and a new, short flapper hairstyle was introduced, combs were not in as high demand. So, the company expanded its product line, adding items such as hairbrushes, jewelry, beads, and letter openers just to name a few.

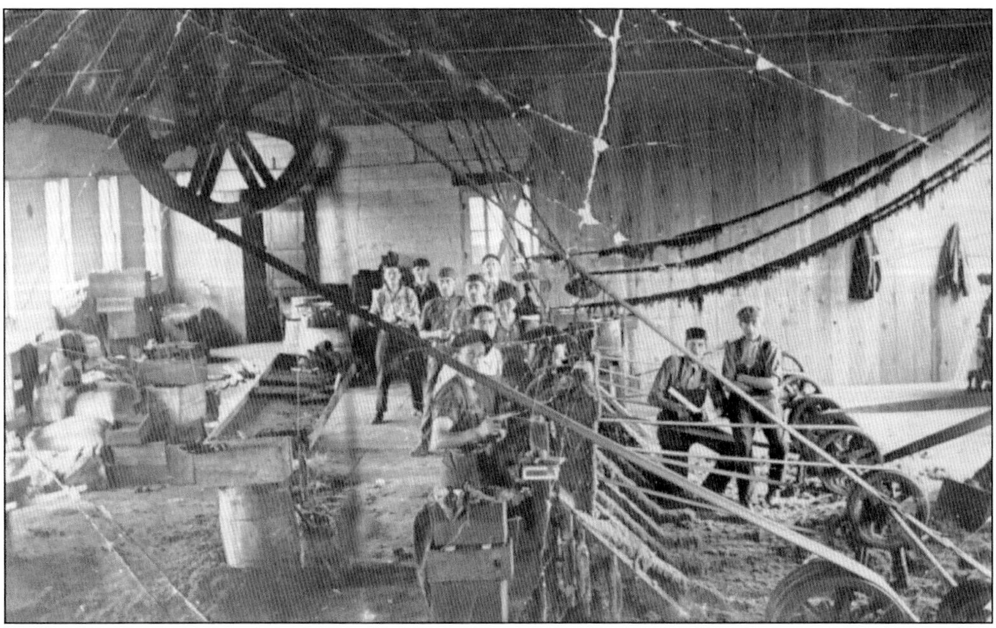

Pictured here are some of the laborers that worked at the Orrville Comb Factory. A 1920 record of the workforce states that the workers' ages varied from as young as 14 to 68 years old.

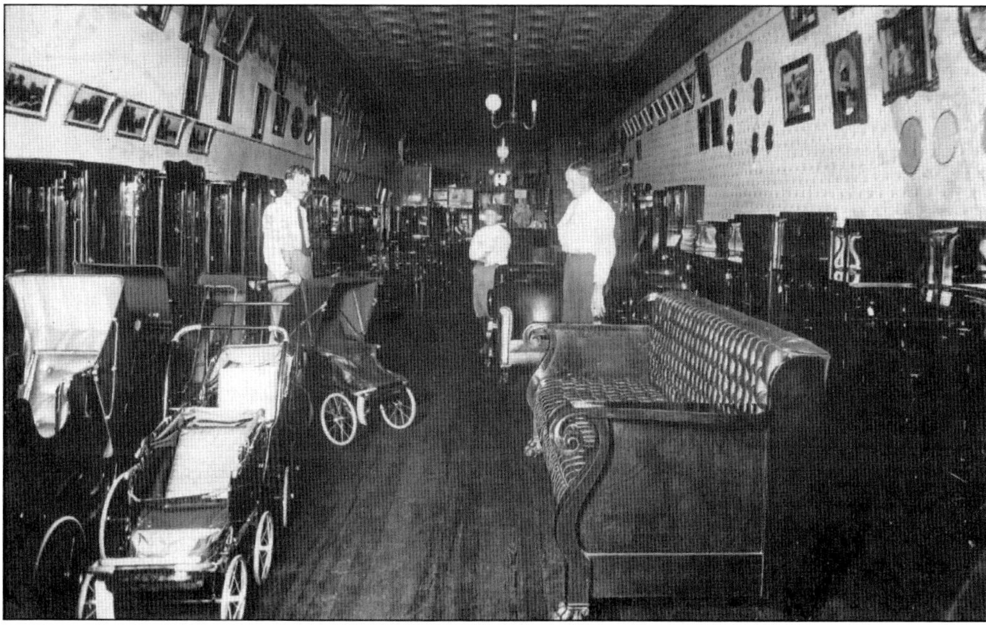

In 1907, Harvey "H.C." Auble opened a furniture and undertaking store on North Main Street. This picture was taken in 1911 with, from left to right, Auble and Perry and Vern Halteman. The first store was located in the old Masonic building on the east side of Main Street until 1912. Then, from 1912 to 1925, the business was in the Independent Order of Odd Fellows (IOOF) building, where the Municipal Building sits today. (Courtesy of Auble's Funeral Home.)

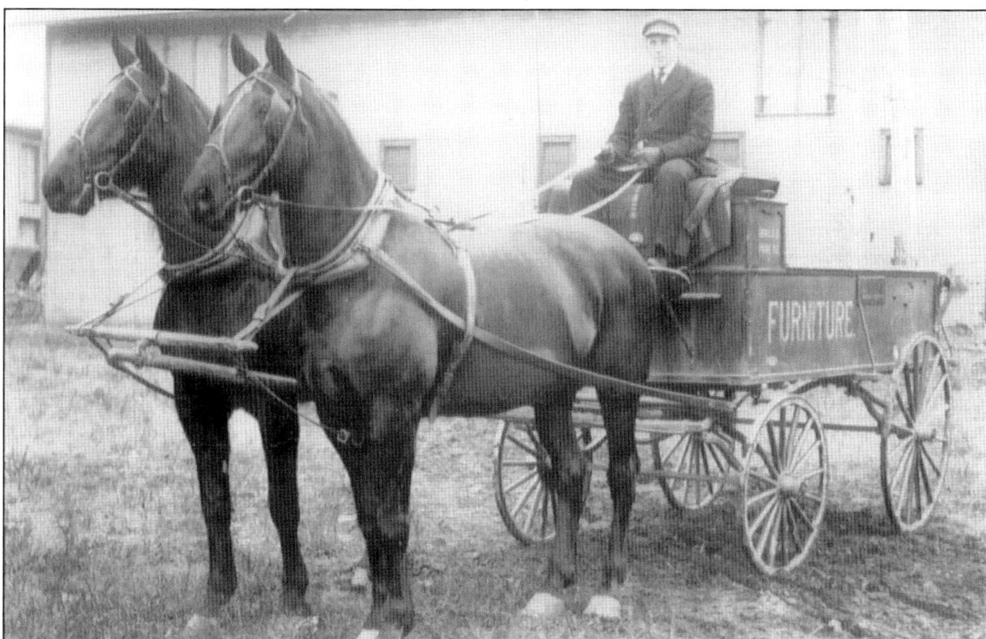

In this 1912 image, Vern Halterman drives Auble's furniture delivery wagon. At the time, furniture making included casket making, which led to most furniture stores taking up undertaking. Auble's ran the furniture part of the business until it was sold in 1933. Today, Auble's Funeral Home is located on East Oak Street. A forth-generation Auble, Mark, helps run the family business.

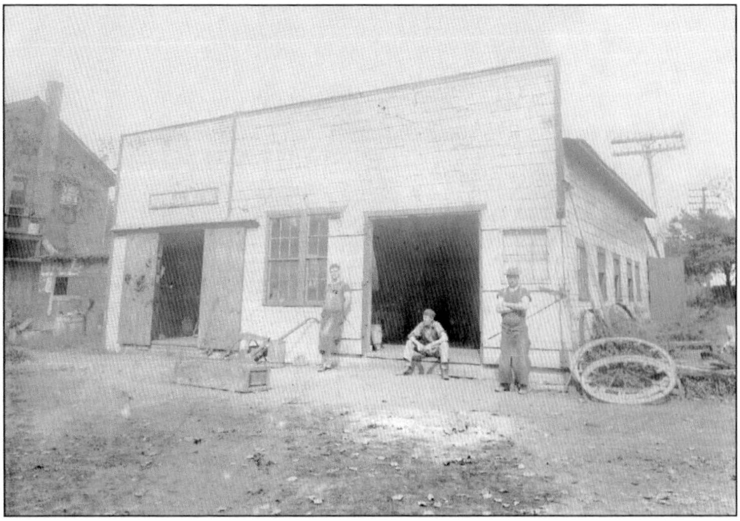

This is an early photograph of a wagon-and-buggy shop; the men pictured are unidentified. The sign above the door advertises Turnbull wagons. Much like today's numerous car dealerships, there were a number of wagon-and-buggy shops throughout early Orrville back then.

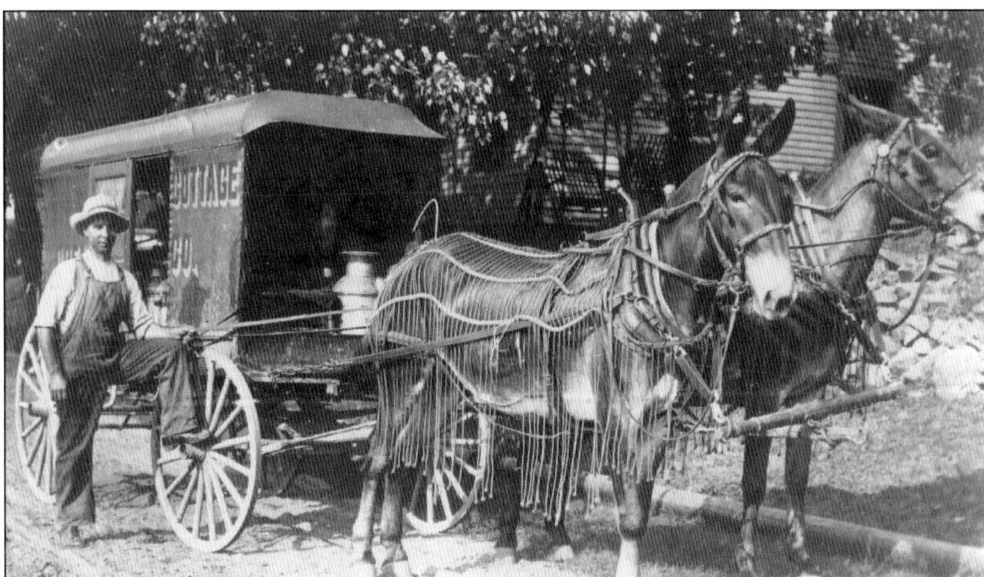

Donkeys pull the Cottage Creamery wagon in 1910. The Cleveland Cottage Creamery Company formed the creamery in 1898. At the time, the Orrville branch was the only firm that manufactured nothing but butter. Originally located on West Market Street, it moved to North Mill Street in 1910. Both locations of the creamery took advantage of being near the railroad, having all their products shipped via the railway.

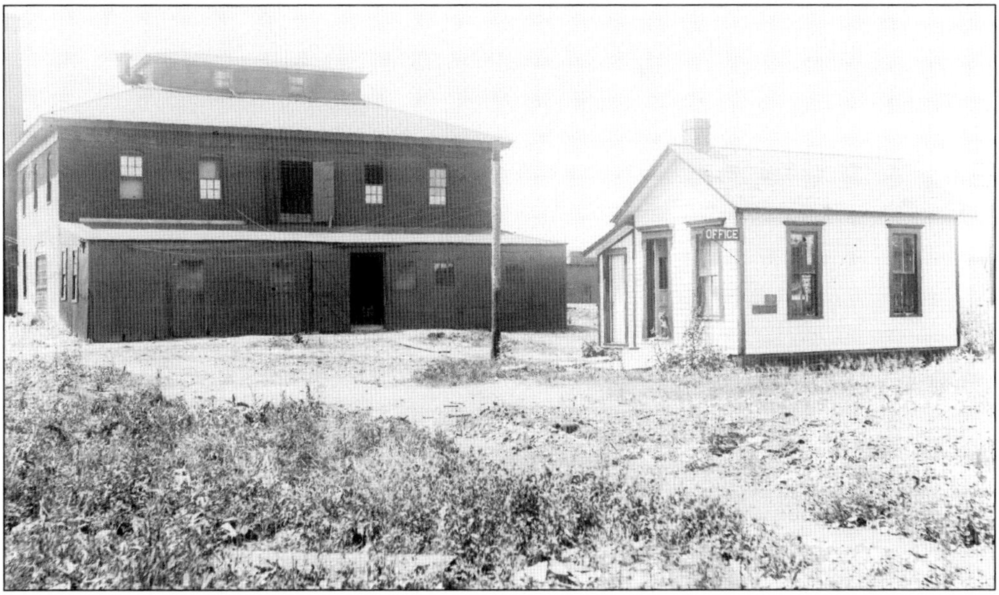

The Grave Vault Building and office were located on the West Chestnut Street extension just west on the depot. The building on the left burned to the ground in 1910, ultimately closing the business for good.

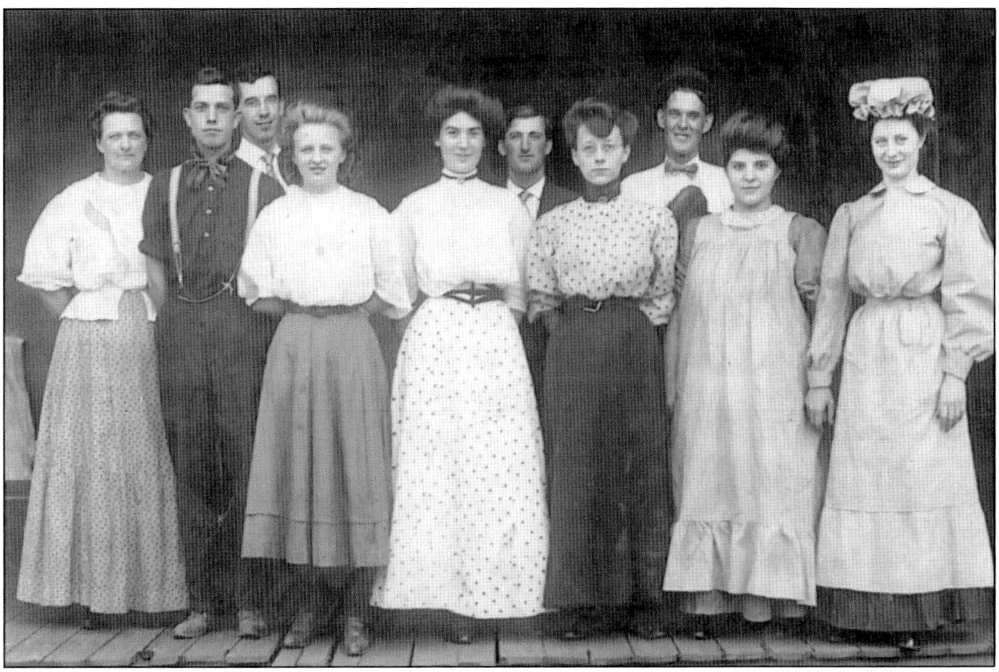

This was the Hurd House staff around 1900. The only person identified in the photograph is Grace Luelle Sell Tschantz (second from the right in the first row). The Hurd hotel, built in 1859 by Enoch Zollars for John Burkholder of Smithville, was originally named the American House. It was located on the southeast corner of Market and Depot Streets. (Courtesy of Louis Tschantz.)

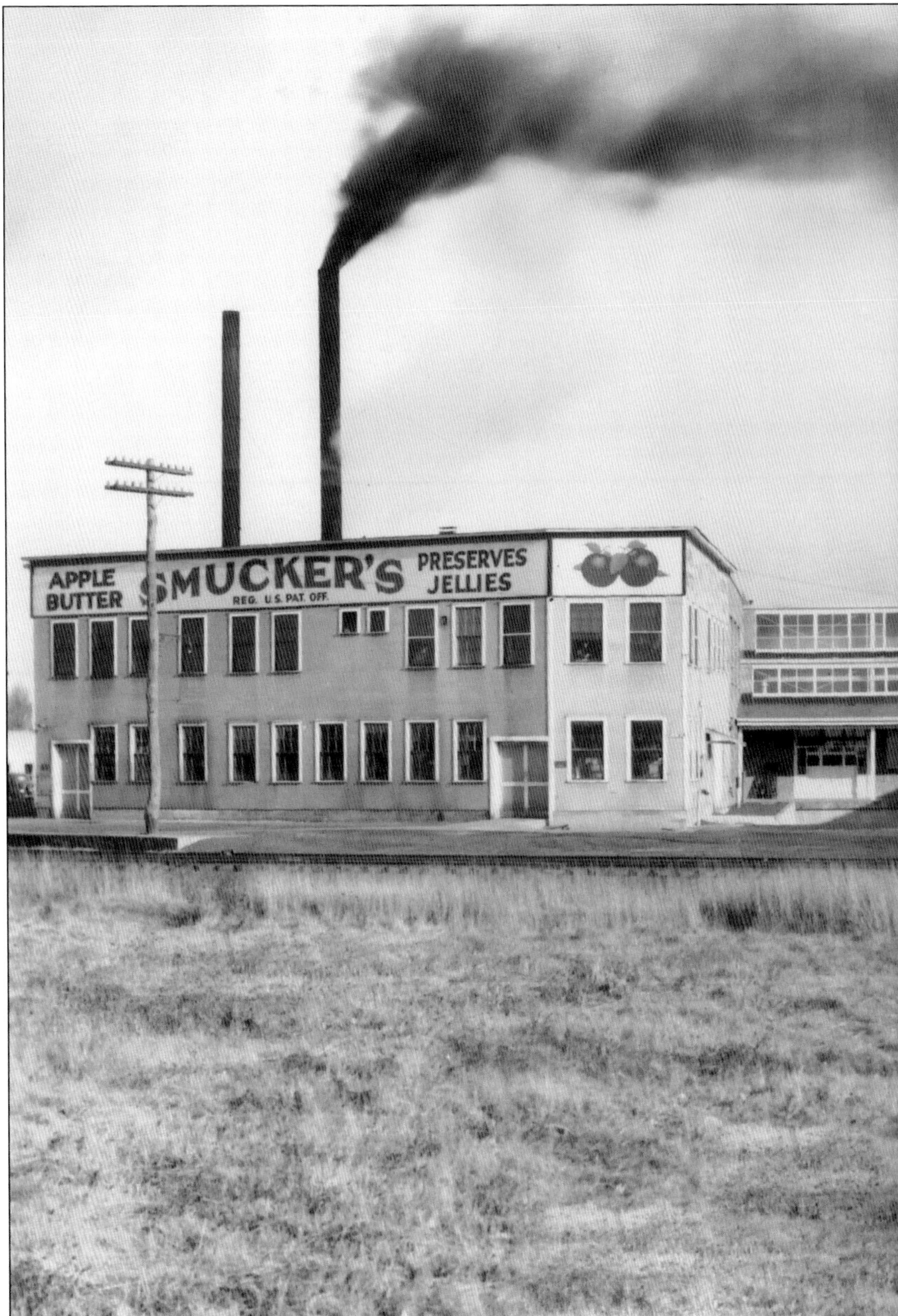
APPLE
BUTTER
SMUCKER'S
REG. U.S. PAT. OFF.
PRESERVES
JELLIES

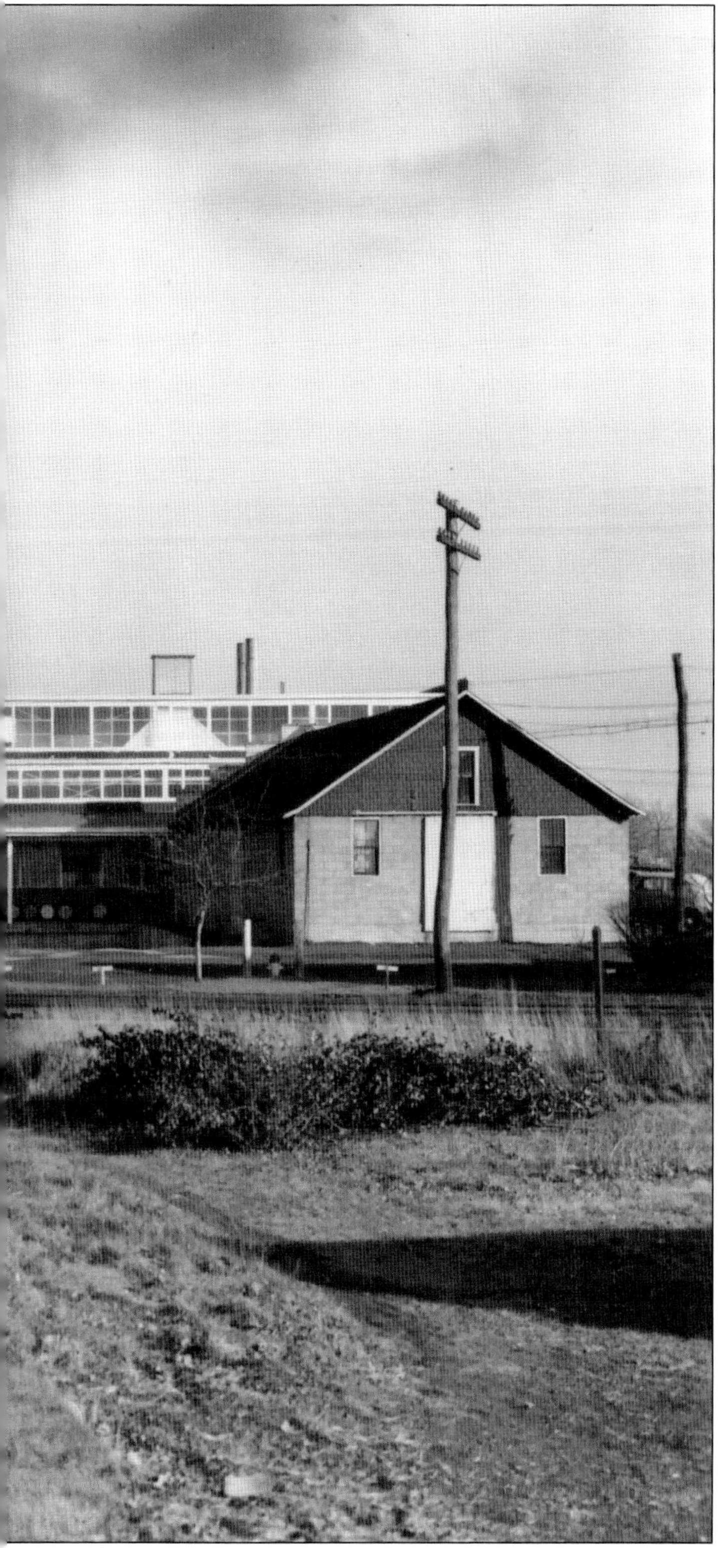

J.M. Smucker Company's factory and facilities are pictured here in 1920. The building on the left still stands and is a part of the factory today. It can be seen from State Route 57, located directly behind the Discovery Building.

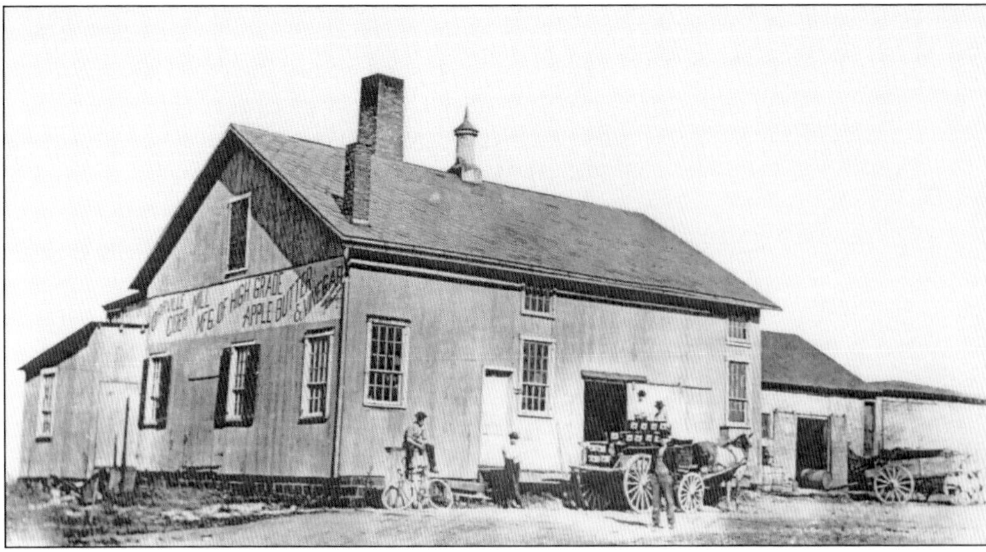

This is the building where the J.M. Smucker Company began its legacy. Jerome Monroe Smucker first made apple cider and apple butter and delivered it door to door via a horse-drawn wagon in 1898. Since it began, the business has acquired numerous other companies nationwide, developing into a multibillion-dollar company. Since 1998, the company has been featured in *Fortune* magazine's "100 Best Companies to Work for in the Unites States," ranking no. 1 in 2004.

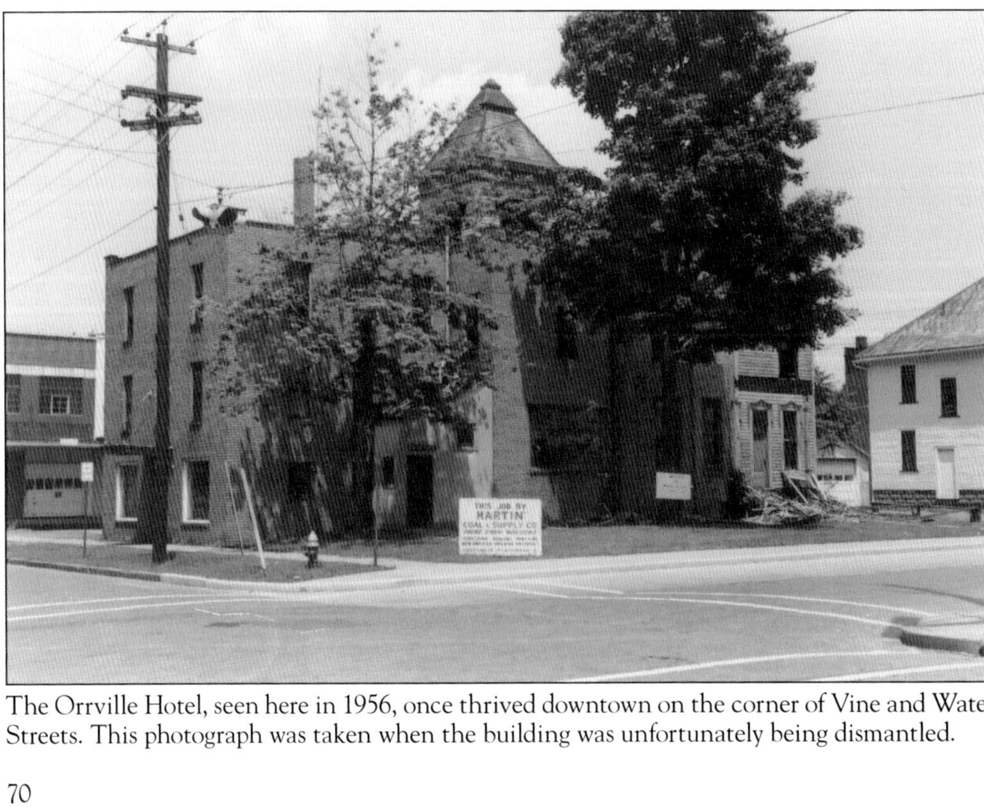

The Orrville Hotel, seen here in 1956, once thrived downtown on the corner of Vine and Water Streets. This photograph was taken when the building was unfortunately being dismantled.

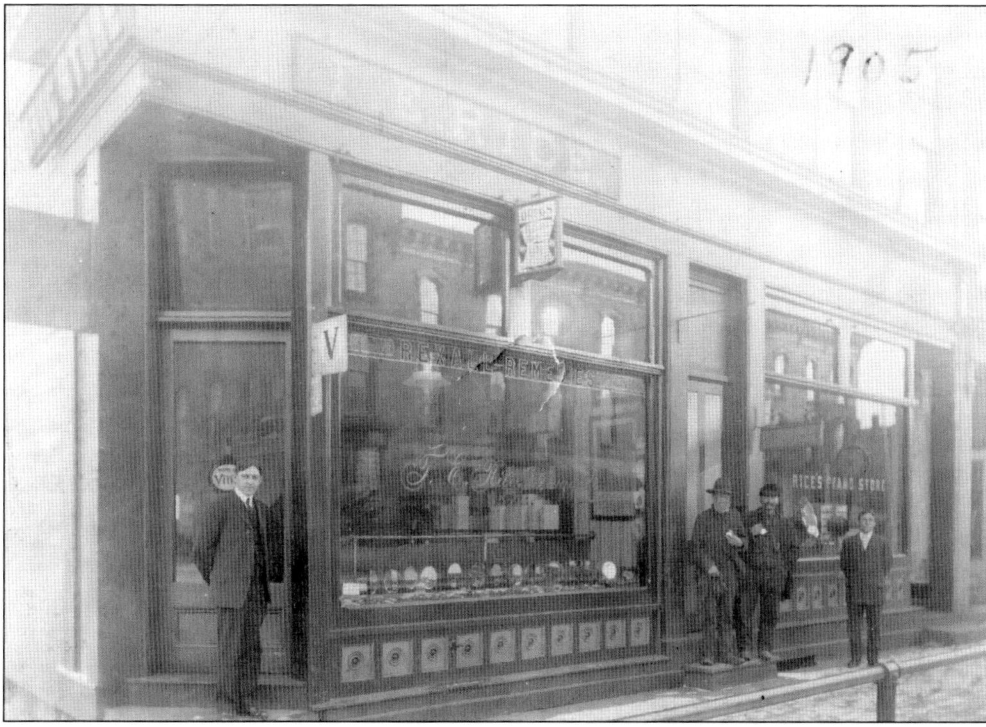

T.E. Rice Druggist's storefront is shown here in 1905. This location on the corner of Main and Market Streets was home to numerous drugstores over the years.

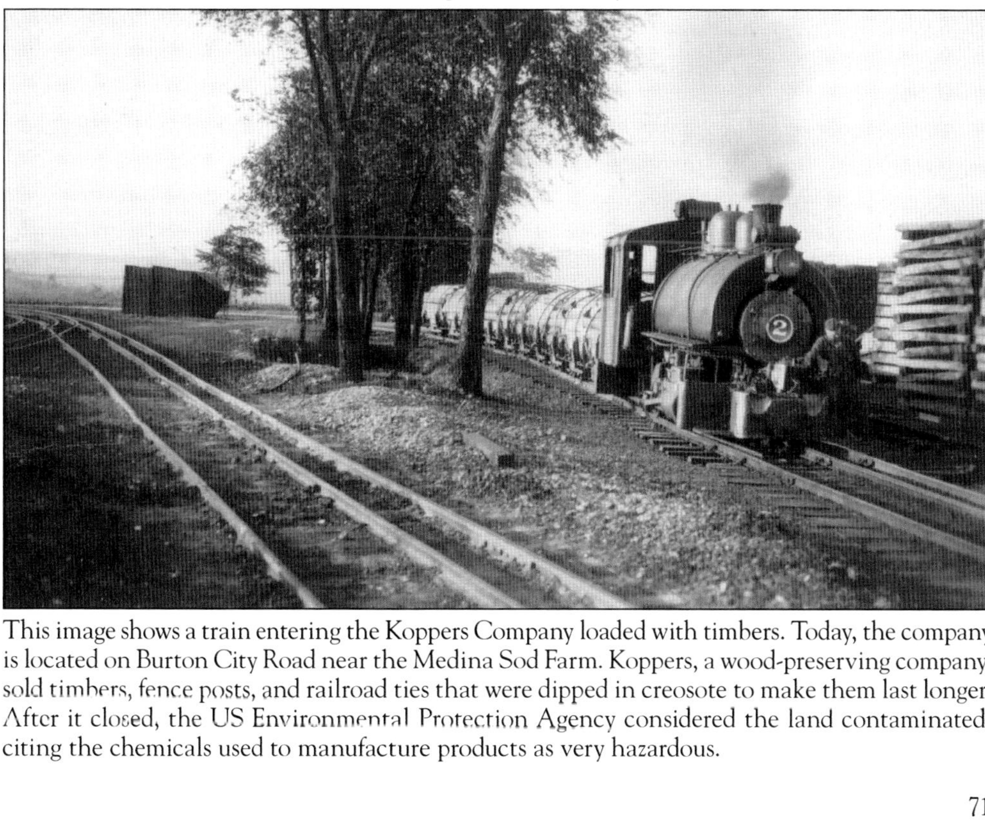

This image shows a train entering the Koppers Company loaded with timbers. Today, the company is located on Burton City Road near the Medina Sod Farm. Koppers, a wood-preserving company, sold timbers, fence posts, and railroad ties that were dipped in creosote to make them last longer. After it closed, the US Environmental Protection Agency considered the land contaminated, citing the chemicals used to manufacture products as very hazardous.

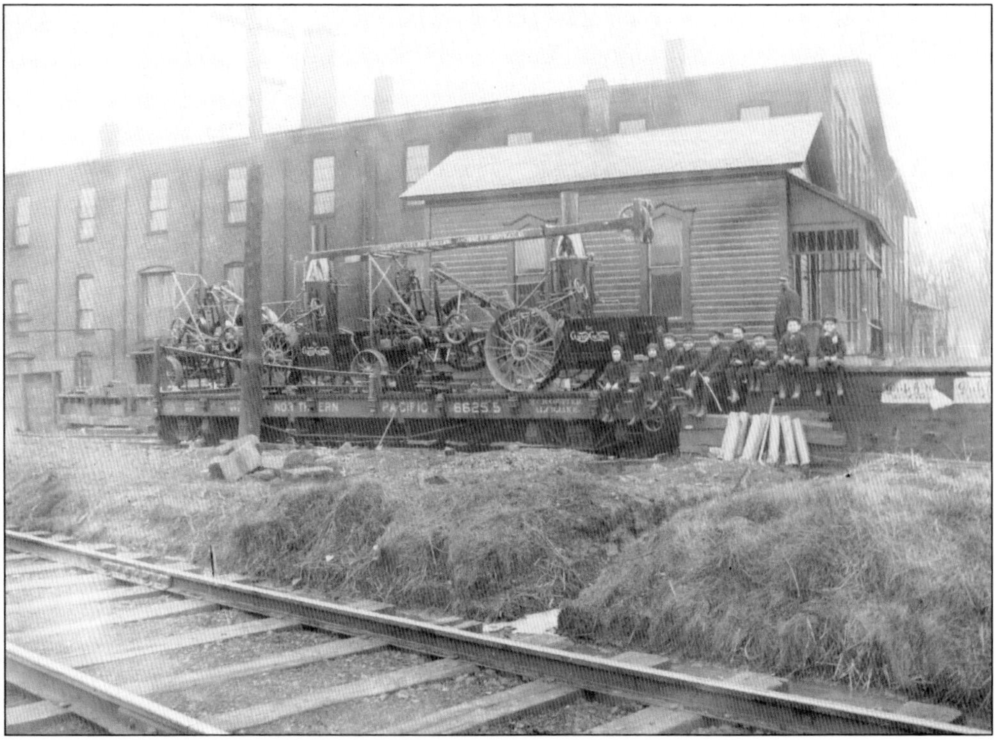

A load of Sanderson Cyclone drills is ready for shipment from its plant located on the corner of Vine and Market Streets. Numerous establishments in Orrville took full advantage of their location in proximity to the railroad; the closer businesses were able to ship all of their products directly on the line..

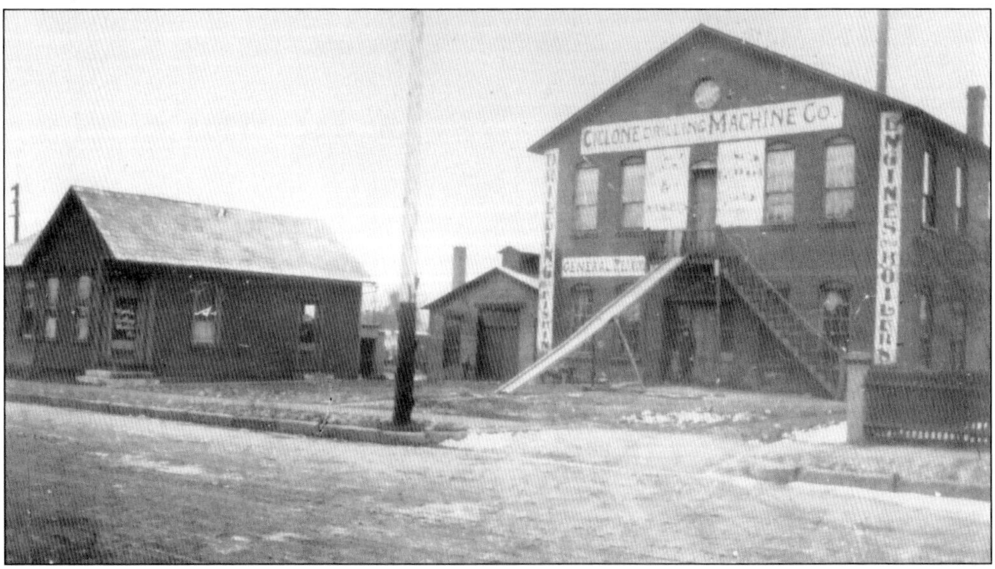

Pictured here in 1898 is the original Sanderson Cyclone shop in East Greenville, Ohio, located on Route 30. The business moved to Orrville in 1901, situating itself on East Chestnut Street. An advertisement from a local paper stated that the drills were used for "water well, oil and gas mining."

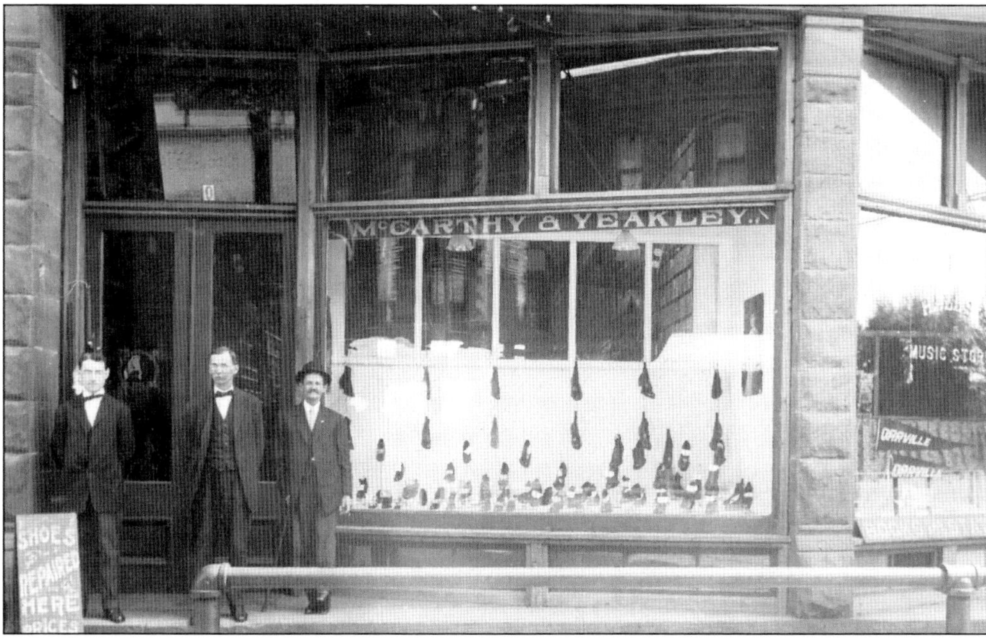

This photograph of the McCarthy & Yeakley Shoe storefront shows these unidentified men alongside a "Shoes Repaired Here" sign. Next door is Hall's Music Shop with Orville pendants for sale in the window.

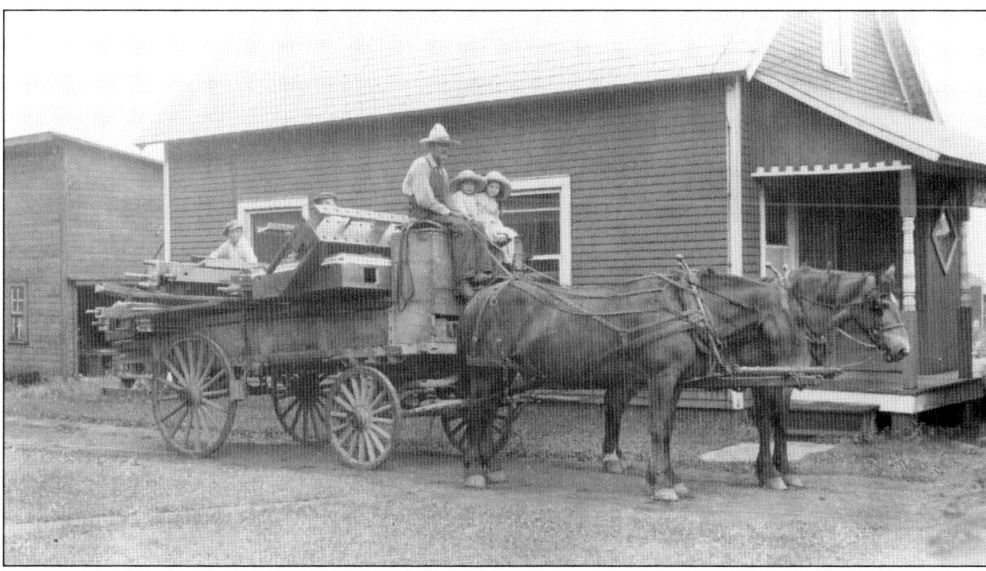

This Schantz pipe organ is being hauled to a freight car by Al Arnold. A.J. Tschantz began the business in 1873, mostly manufacturing parlor-style organs. The name was eventually changed to Schantz, and today, it is the largest and oldest pipe organ builder to still be under the original family's management. Company employees have traveled around the world to install, repair, and maintain pipe organs in various churches, cathedrals, and universities.

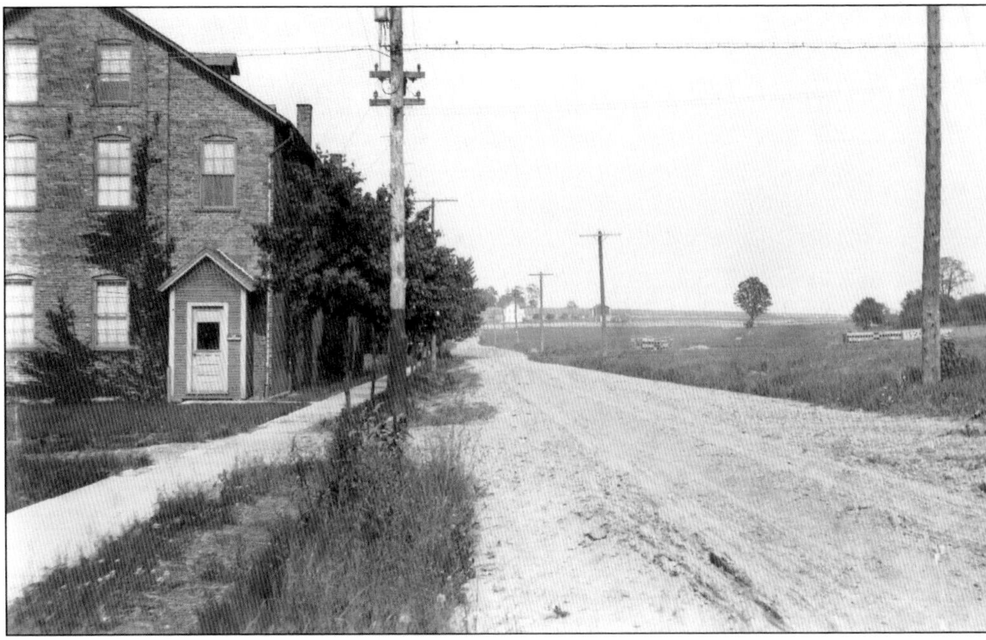

Since 1901, Schantz Organ Company, shown above, has been conducting all forms of business and manufacturing from the same building, now with some additions, located on the corner of Walnut and Oak Streets. This picture looks east on Oak Street; today, the street is lined with houses, and the company is nestled in a quiet residential part of town. The view below of the Schantz Organ Company faces west on Oak Street. A number of the residences lining Oak Street in the background still stand today.

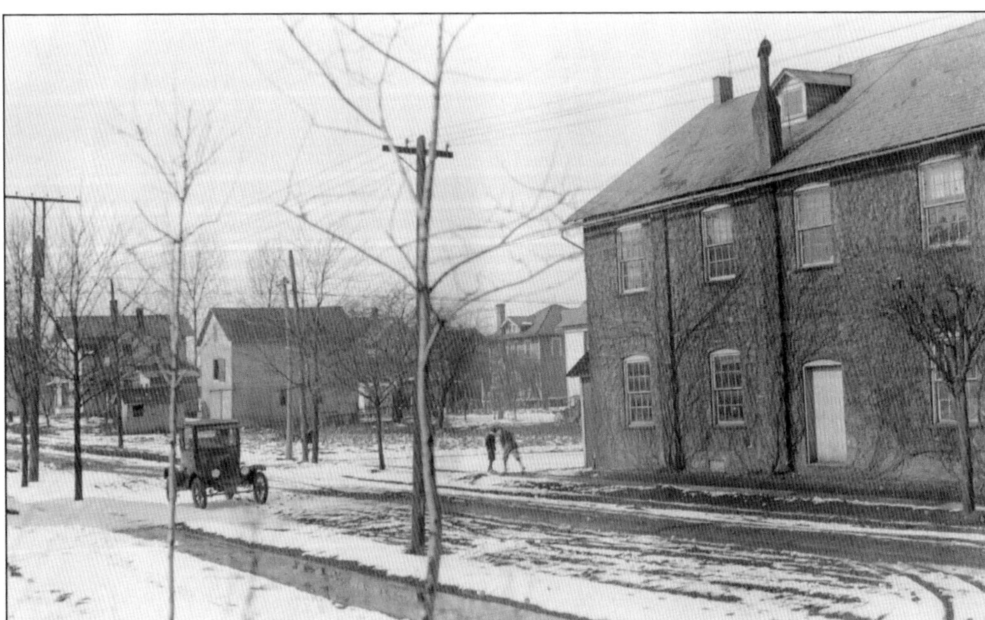

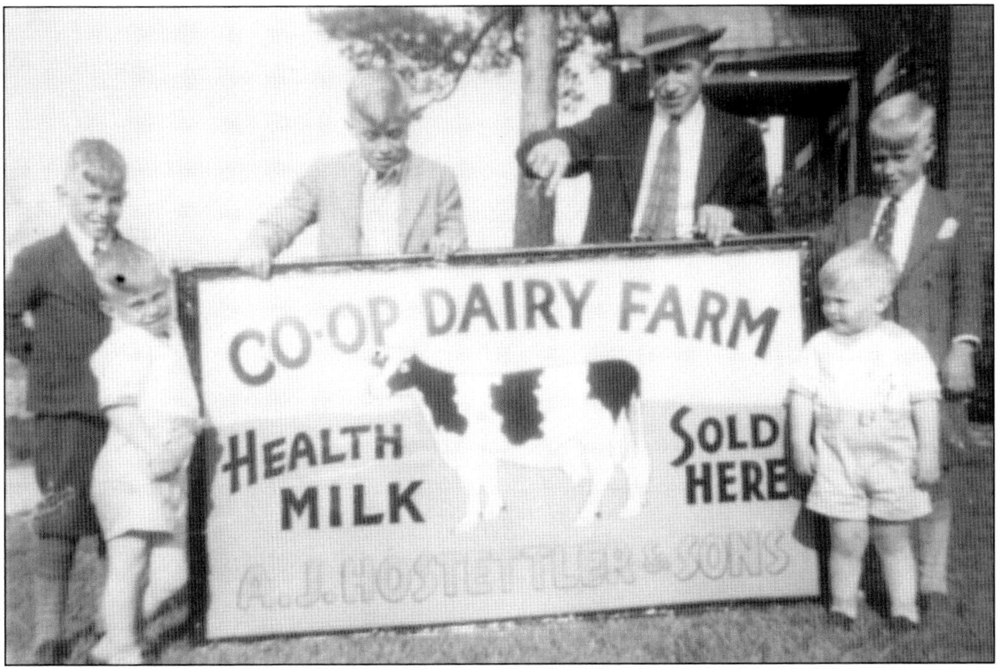

Ammon Hostetler and his sons, from left to right, Alvin, Ammon Jr., John, Homer, and Irvin, are seen here with the sign that hung in the pine tree in front of the family farmhouse on Hostetler Road. The last name on the sign is misspelled, and it was said that Ammon just never took the time to have it fixed. (Courtesy of the Irvin Hostetler family.)

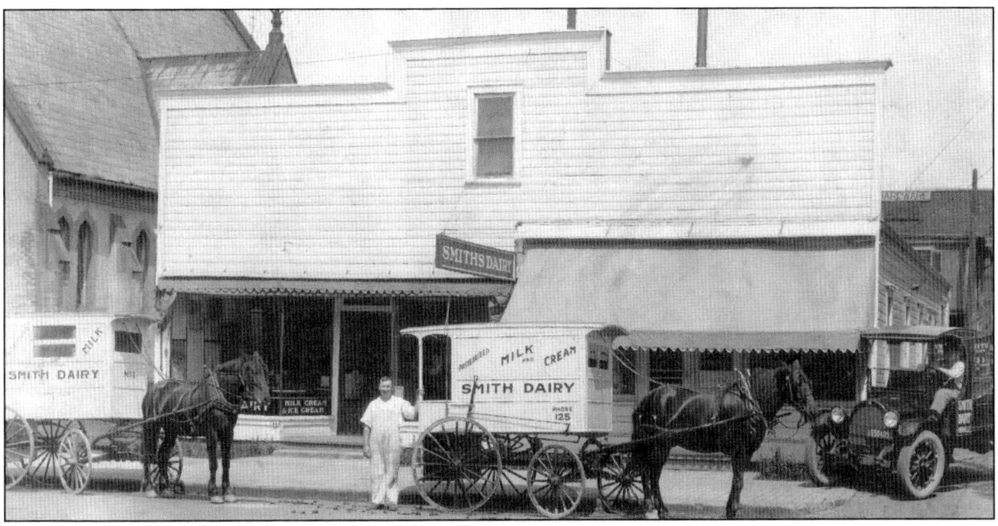

Gus Boss is seen with a Smith Dairy wagon in 1920. Gus was the brother-in-law of John and Peter Schmid, who partnered to establish the business in 1909. Originally set up in the basement of the Congdon Building on Market Street, they relocated the company in 1919 to the corner of North Vine and West Market Streets, seen here, next to the Lutheran church. Today, they have facilities downtown at the corners of Main and Church Streets and Church and Vine Streets, with corporate offices on Hostetler Road.

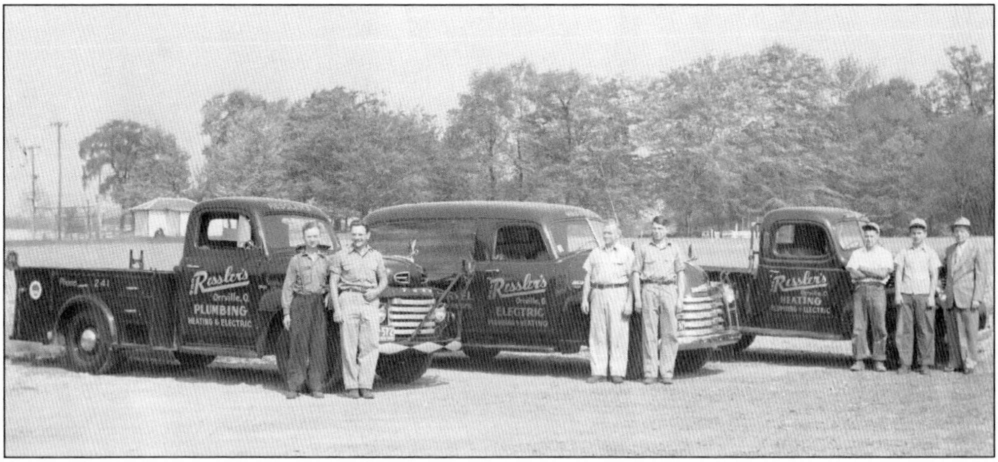

Taken in 1953 at Orr Park, this photograph is of Geo Ressler's Electric employees and work trucks. From left to right are George Ressler, Paul Kauffman, Henry Kauffman, Mahlon Zuercher, Arthur Shoup, Donald Ressler, and William Zarle.

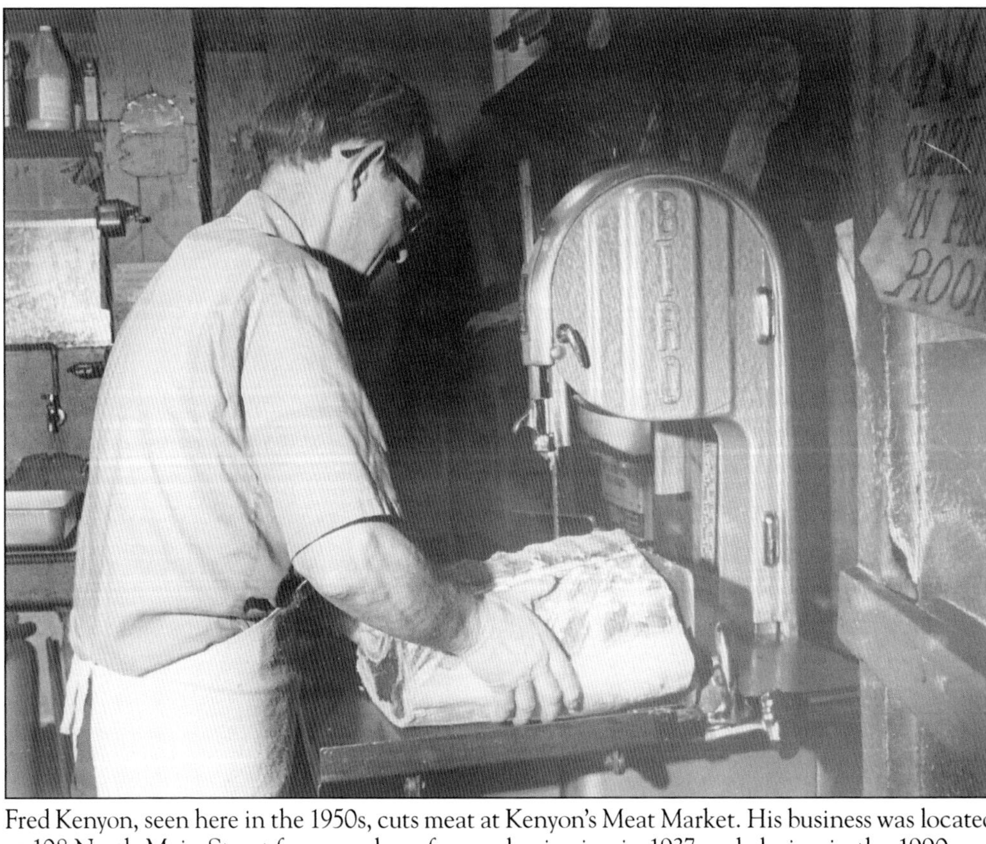

Fred Kenyon, seen here in the 1950s, cuts meat at Kenyon's Meat Market. His business was located at 108 North Main Street for a number of years, beginning in 1937 and closing in the 1990s.

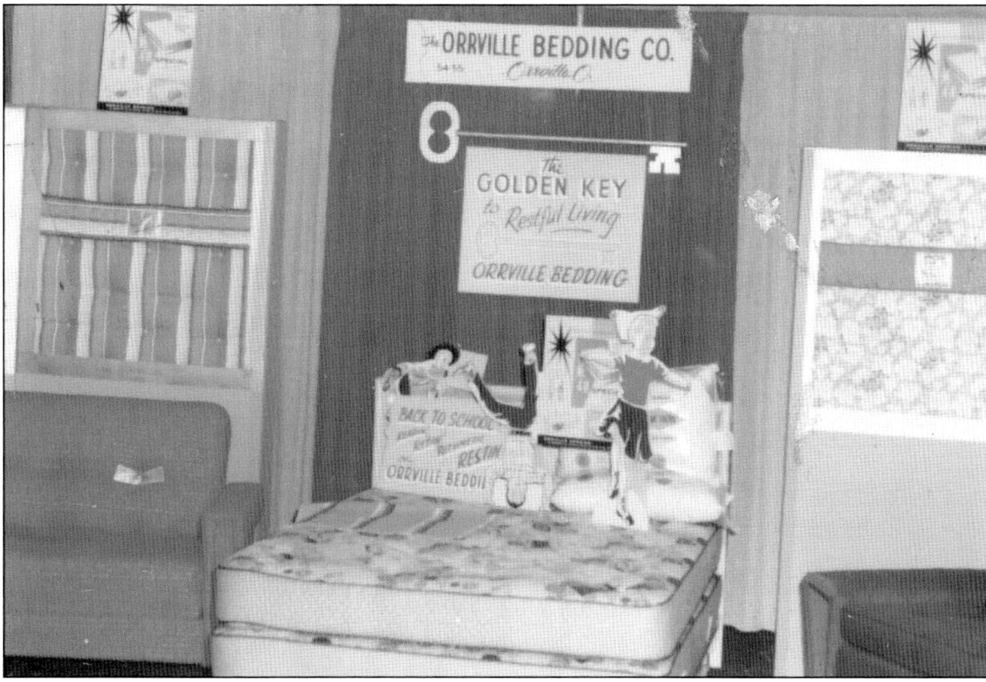

This is a photograph of an Orrville mattress from the Orrville Bedding Company taken at a mattress convention. The mattress factory was located between Market and Church Streets right along the railroad and adjacent to the Smith Orr homestead, and the longtime president of the business was W.J.S. Herbert. Today, the building is owned by the Smith Dairy Co.

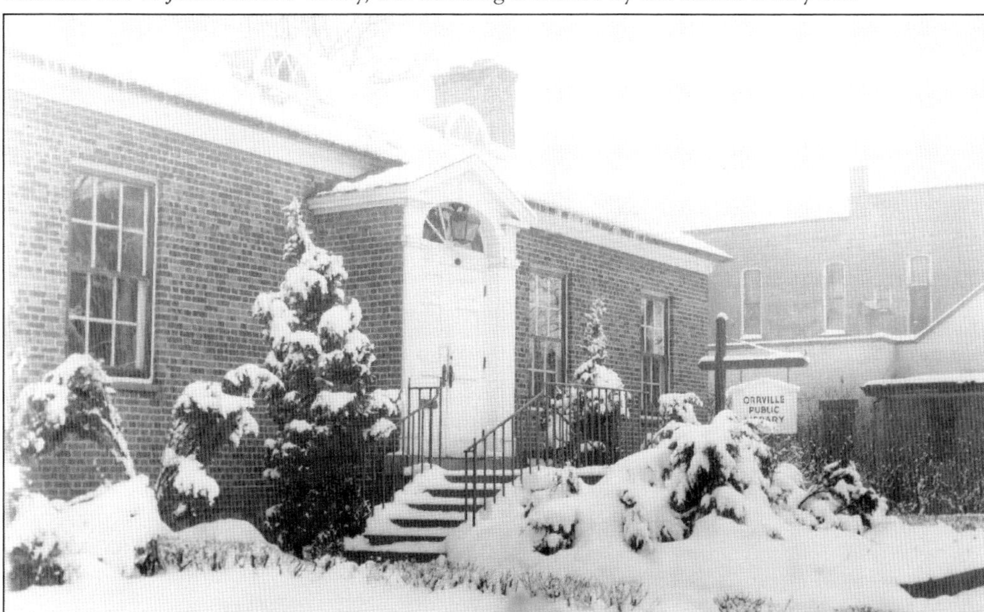

This section of the Orrville Public Library, built in 1941, can still be seen on North Main Street. Additions were made in 1977 and 2000, bringing the library to its current look. Today, the library is ranked second in the nation by the Hennen's American Public Library Ratings, which assesses small libraries across the country by how they serve their community and school system.

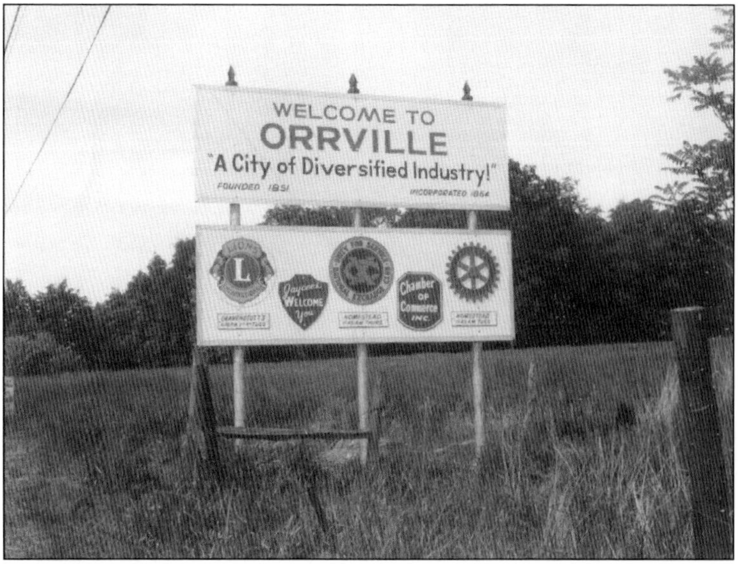

An Orrville sign greets visitors at the city's corporation limits with the tagline, "A city of diversified industry." That line was recently changed in 2011, and the Orrville Area Chamber of Commerce announced the new tagline, "Where Progress and Tradition Meet, Orrville, Ohio Thrive Here."

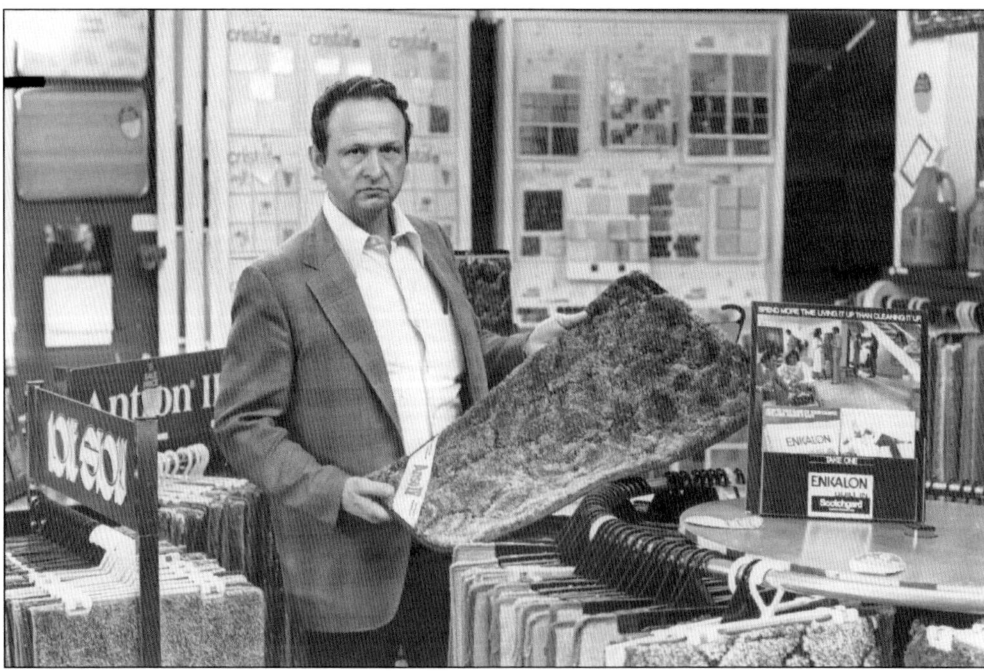

Pictured here is Dale Stroller, owner of Stoller Flooring, a longtime business in Orrville that opened in 1973. After a devastating fire in 2002 at its West Market Street location, the company relocated and is currently doing business just north of Orrville on State Route 57 across from White's Maibach Ford.

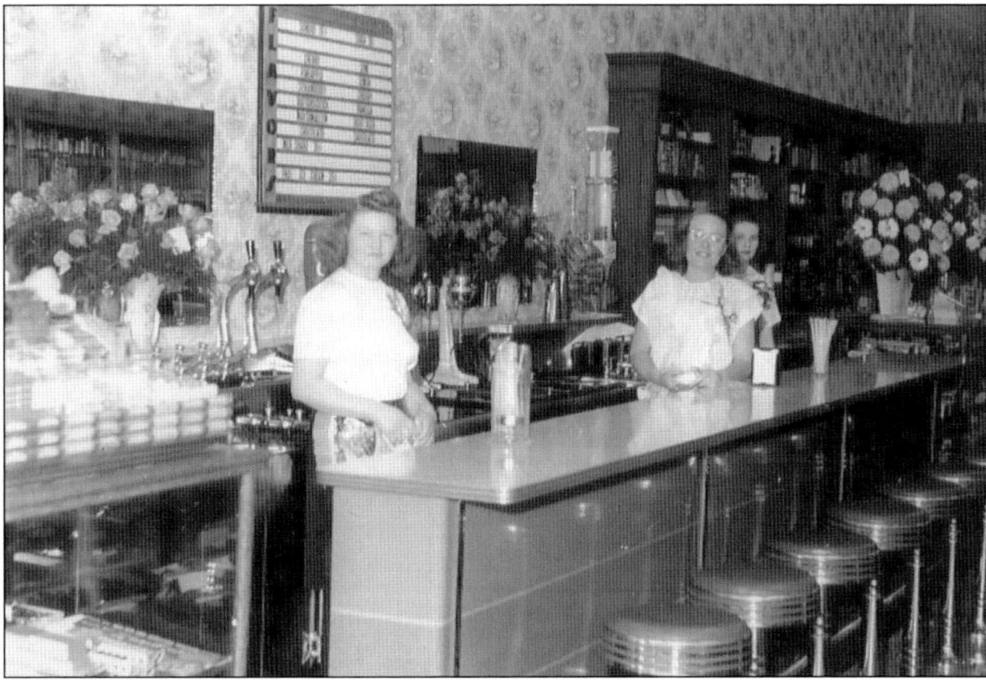

This photograph was taken inside Deitrick's Drugstore; the women are unidentified. The soda fountain was a local hangout after school for kids of all ages. The drugstore was owned by George Deitrick until he sold it to Herbert Sollenberger. Located on the east side of North Main Street, it was most recently Reynold's Drugs.

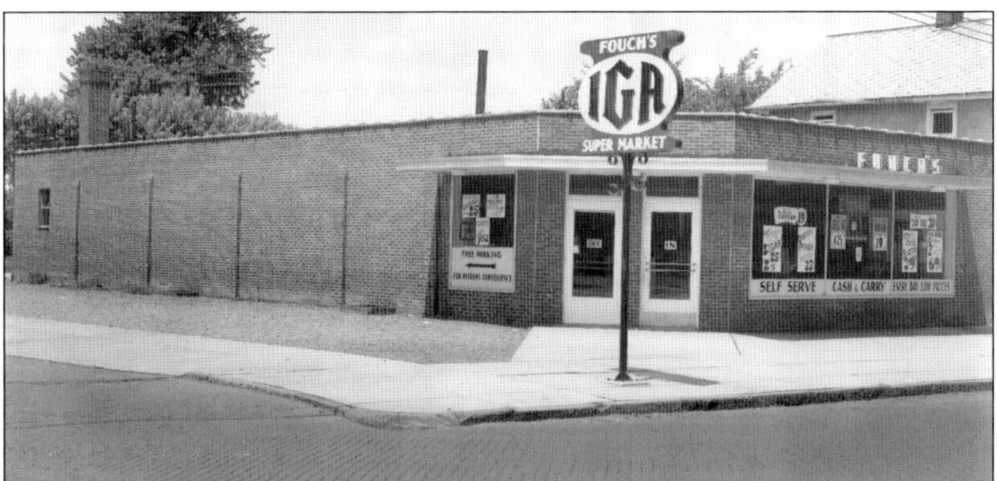

Fouch's IGA was owned and operated by the same Fouch family that once owned Fouch's Meat Market. The building shown here is on the northwest corner of South Main and Chestnut Streets. The structure, which later housed Smith's Grocery, is currently the home of the Bob Snyder Auto Exchange.

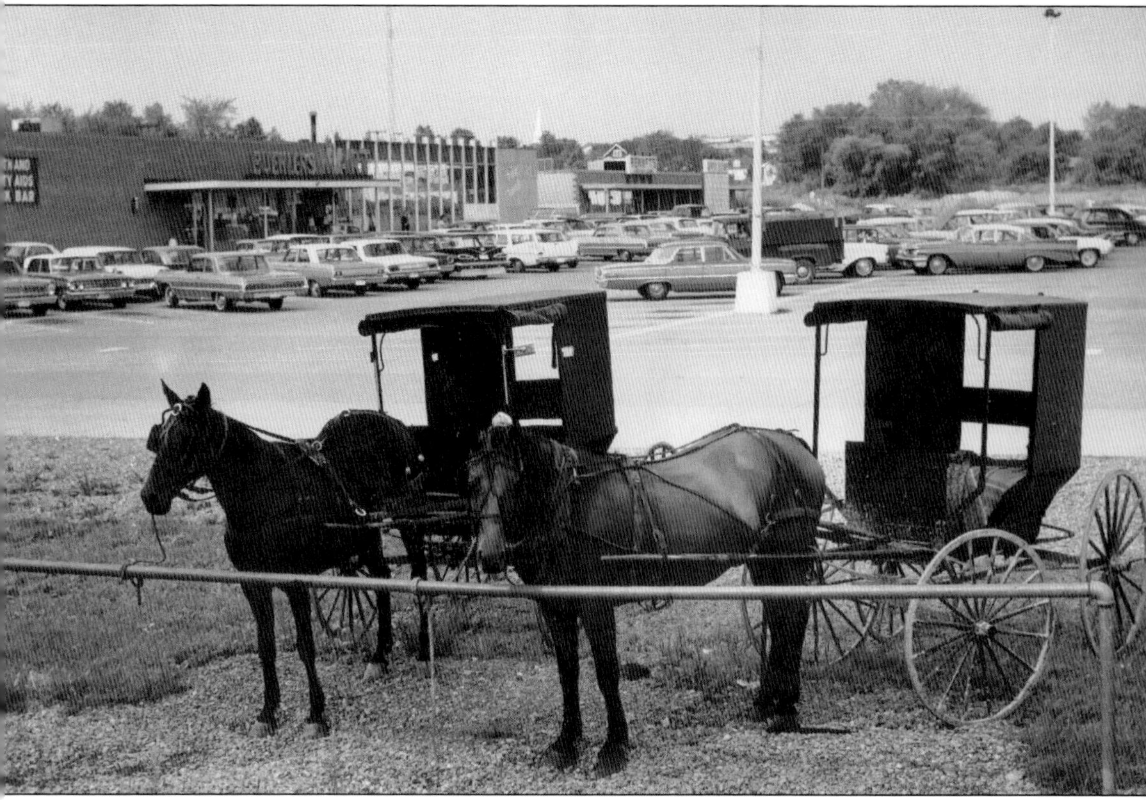

In this photograph, a couple of Amish buggies are parked at Buehler's on High Street. Buehler's grocery store opened in Orrville in 1959 and has been in the same location since then. Today, it has 13 stores in Ohio. Bennet's Appliance Center, seen to the right of Buehler's, was opened by Bennet Geiser in 1931. Selling appliances and specializing in repairs, the store has two locations in northeastern Ohio.

Five

Schools

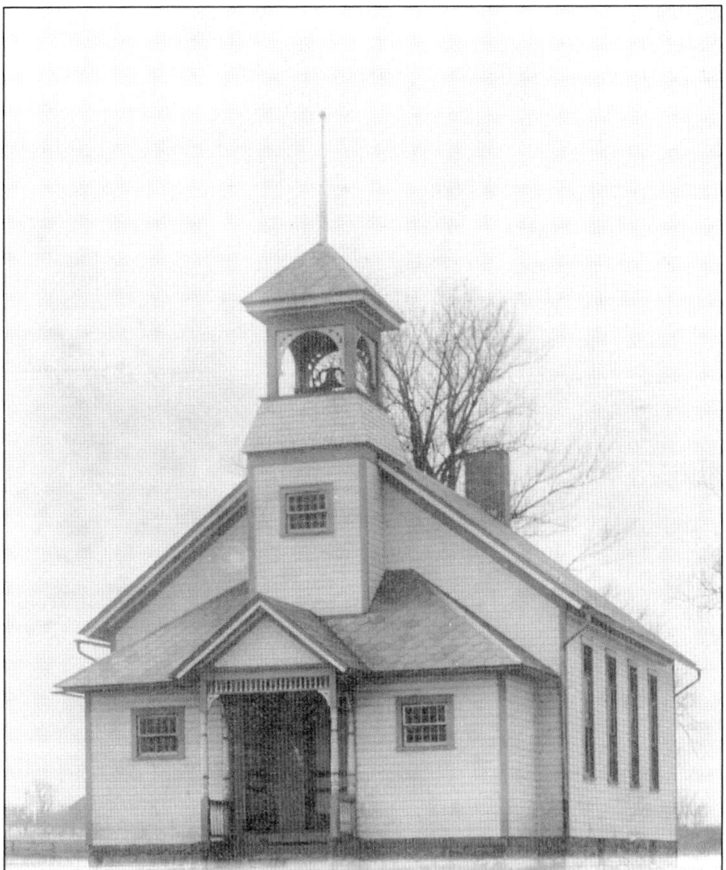

The Carr School was the first schoolhouse built in Orrville in 1851. It was a 20-foot-by-20-foot, one-room schoolhouse located on the northeast corner of North Mill and Church Streets.

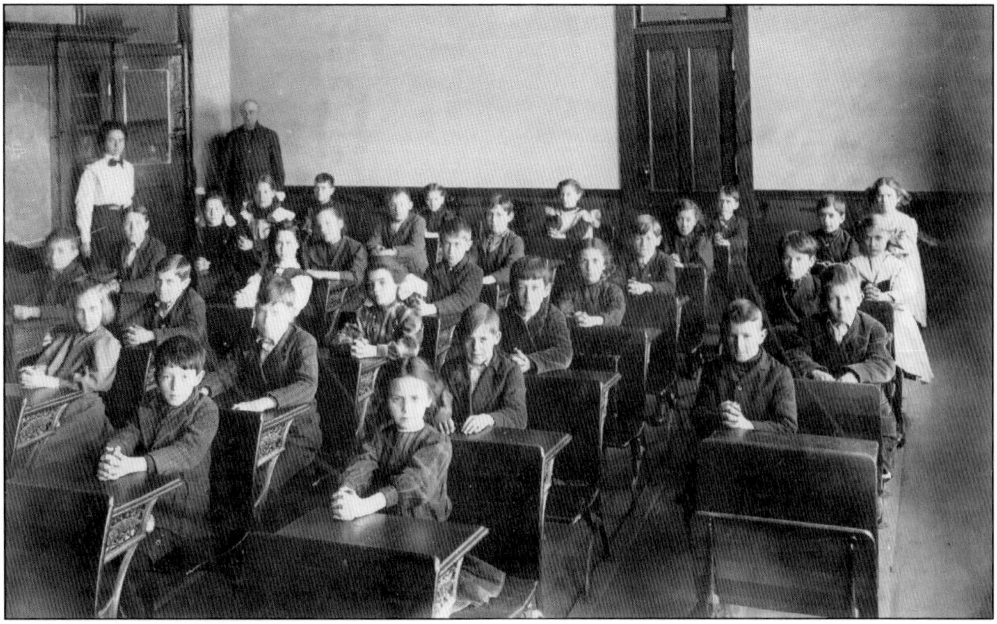

This photograph was taken in the one-room schoolhouse, or Carr School. The children and teachers are unidentified.

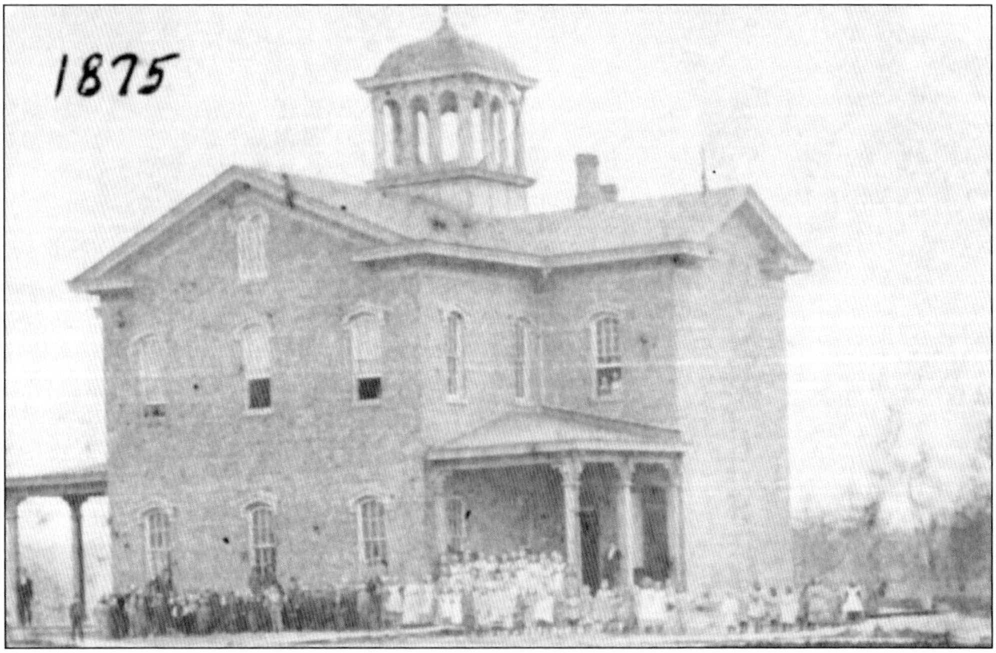

Walnut Street School, built in 1869 and 1870, only had three rooms. It sat on the southeast corner of Walnut and High Streets, and later, the high school was erected on that same land but on Church Street. This picture was taken 1875, before the 1883 additions of the north and south wings of the school. The building was razed in 1966.

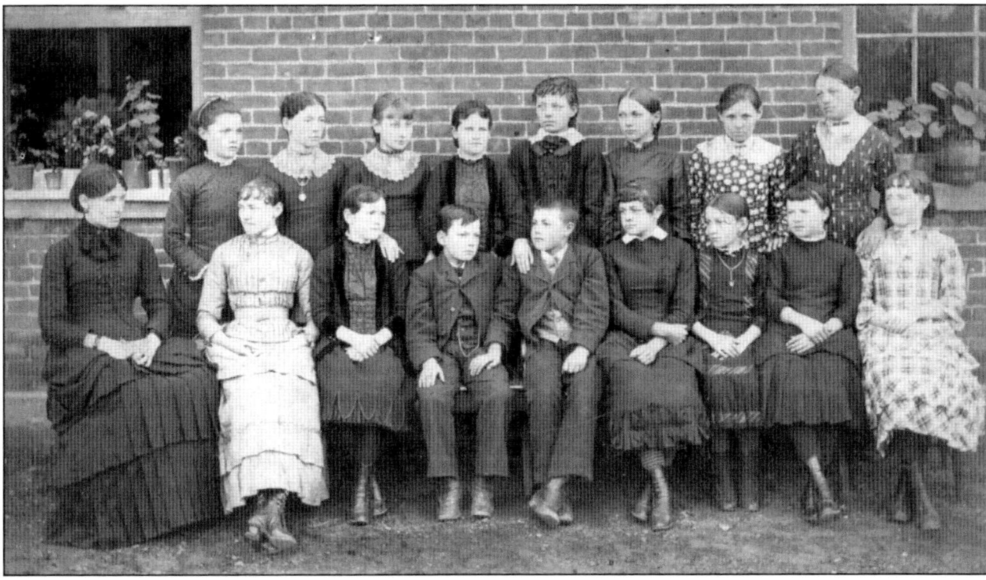

The students and teacher are unidentified in this photograph. This was a high school class in 1885. In 1896, the high school went from being a three-year school to an accredited four-year high school, and with that being said, there was not a graduating class in 1896.

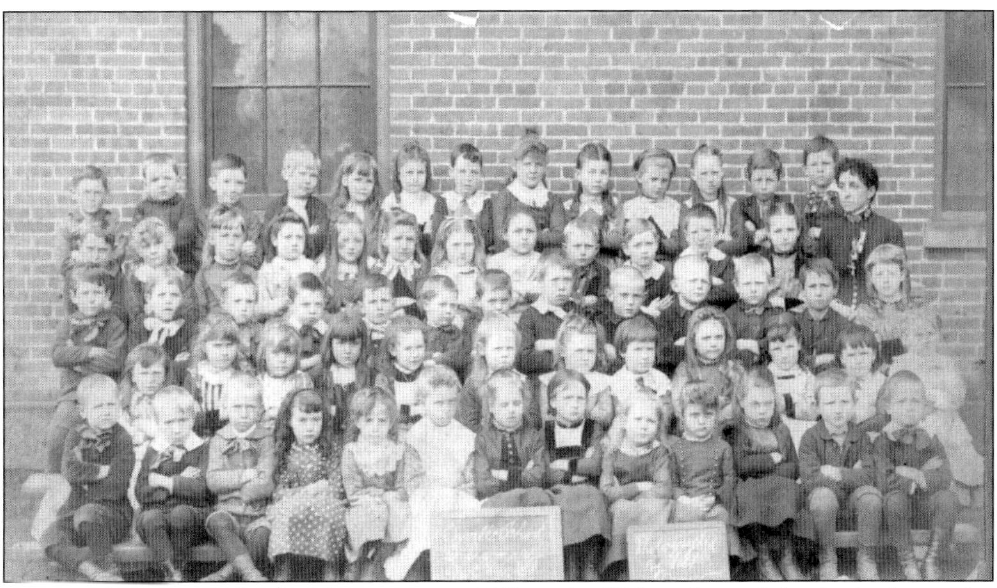

A group elementary school students poses in 1889 at the Walnut Street School, which was also known as the "Orrville School."

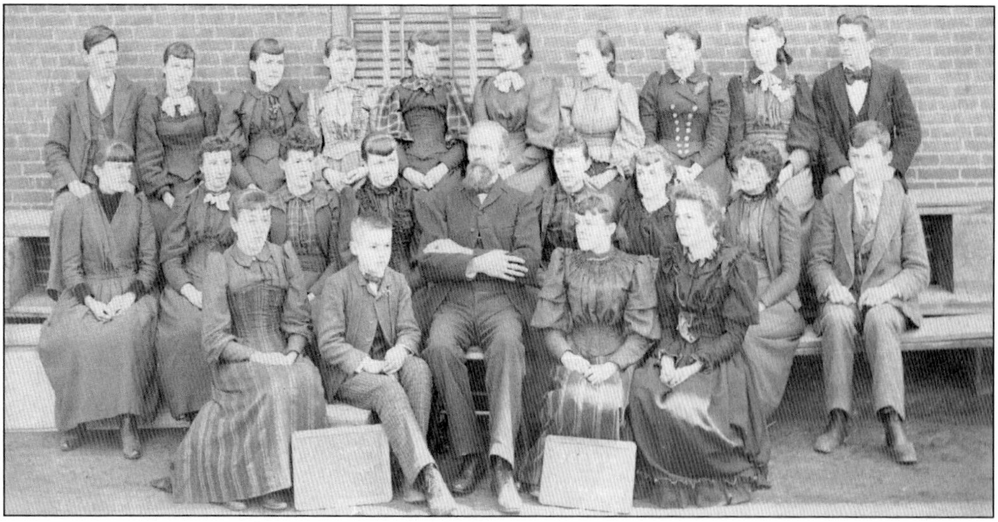

Here are 1893–1894 students of Orrville High School with Principal J.L. Wright in the center. Beginning in 1880, Wright was also the first superintendent. The first class to graduate from Orrville High School was in 1881, with two students receiving diplomas. Pictured here, but in no particular order, are Frank Koppes, Grace Boigegrain, Maggie Burnes, Laud Lee, Cora McArthur, Anna Taggart, Warren Wirth, Minnie Schantz, Bessie Wertz, Mabel Beck, Henrietta Blackwood, Anna Tiefenthaler, Russell McGill, Emma Arnold, Ida Fogel, Harry Shaffer, and Maude Miller.

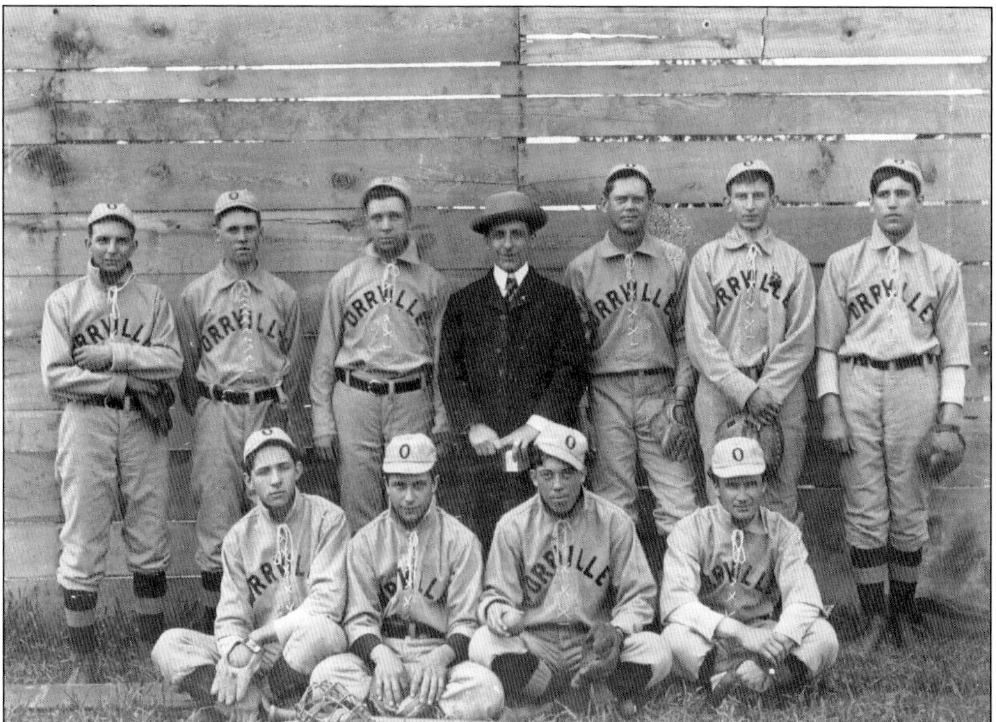

Here is the 1905 Orrville baseball team. Pictured from left to right are (first row) Bob Brenneman, ? Mathey, Charley Smith, and Ching Frey; (second row) Webb Airhart, John Drusell, ? Bancroft, Tom Rice, Peg Stevens, Karl Bricker, and Art Smith.

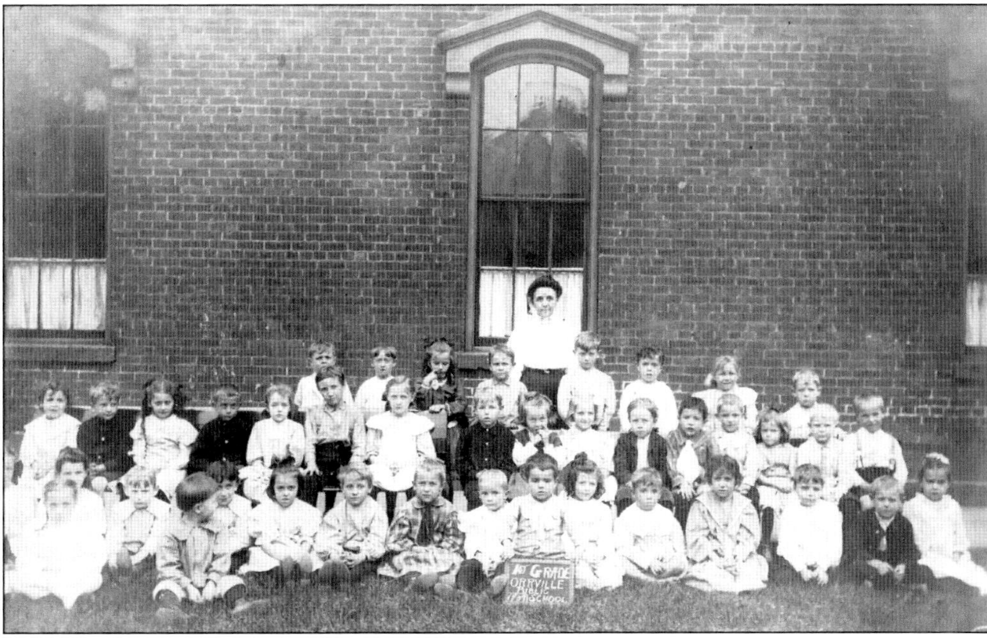

This class photograph was taken at Walnut Street School in 1907. The chalkboard that the child in the center is holding up reads, "First Grade Orrville Public Schools 1907." The Orrville Historical Museum is in possession of numerous class photographs, such as this one, from all four of the old elementary schools.

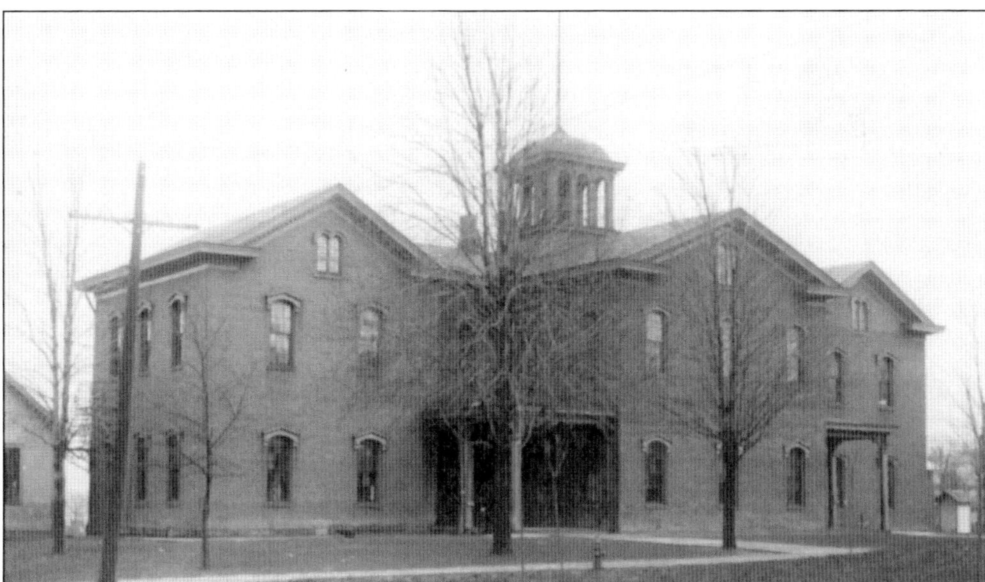

This is how Walnut Street School looked in 1911, complete with the north and south wings that were added in 1883.

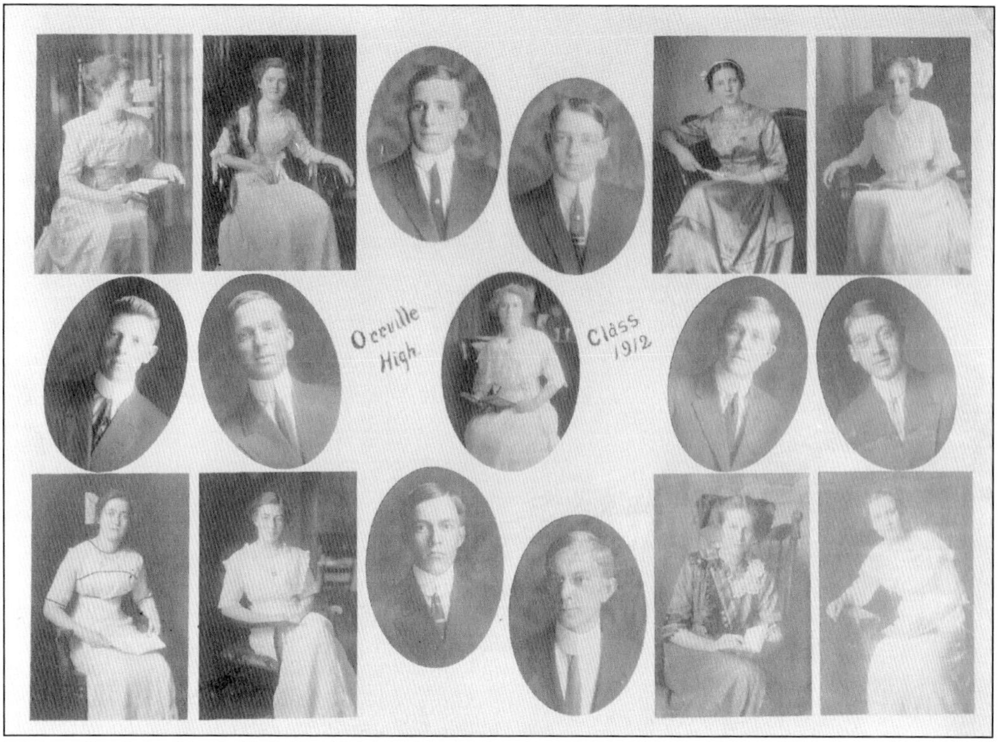

This is the Orrville High School class of 1912 composite. Early class composites are on display at the Orrville Historical Museum, with the composites from the 1960s to the present on display in the halls at Orrville High School. School yearbooks are also available for viewing at the museum, beginning with the *Red & Whites* from the early 1900s to the most recent graduating class.

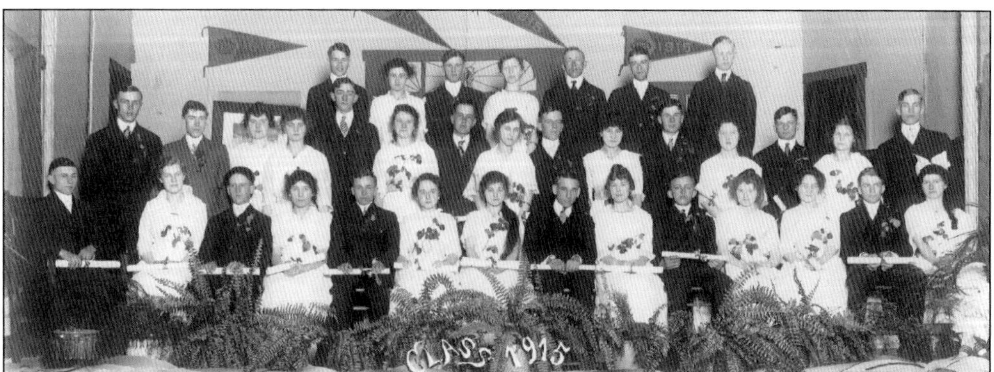

Pictured here is the class of 1915 at commencement in the auditorium of the high school.

Here is the 1917–1918 Orrville football team; members are, from left to right, (first row) Carl Wepler and Herbert Weaver; (second row) Harold Carson, Dewey Lytle, and Daniel Becker; (third row) Harry Kaufman, coach Herman Retzler, Harold Murray, Albert Lorson, Cleon Yoder, Harley Maxwell, Wayne Kimberlin, Elmer Weiss, Ralph A. Walte, Paul Kaufman, and Cecil Weible.

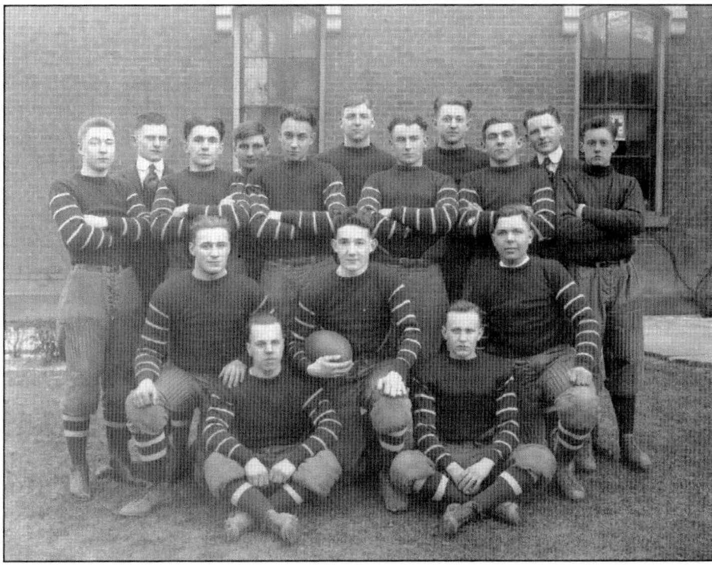

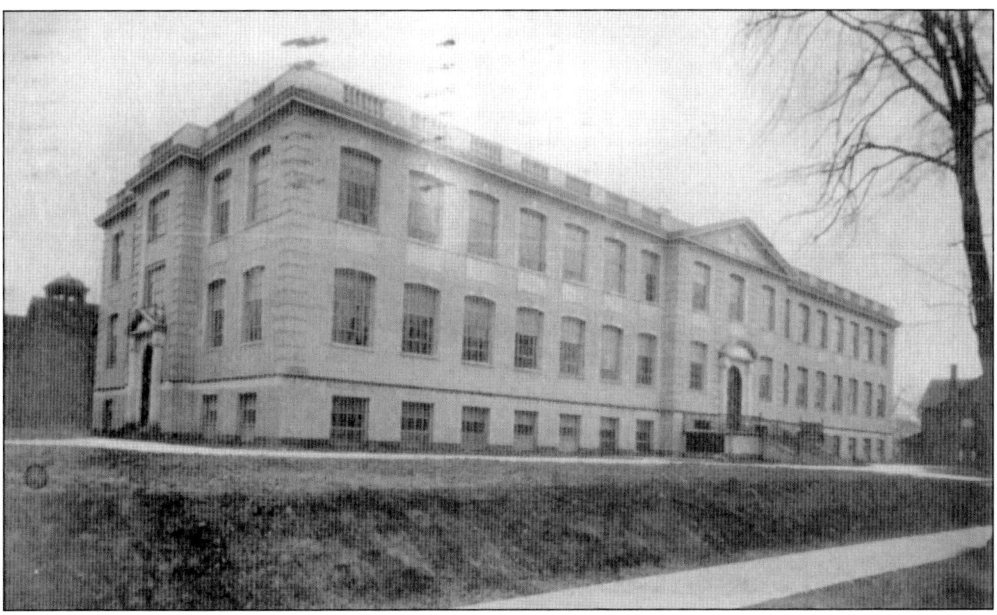

The Orrville High School, erected in 1921, is seen here with Walnut Street School in the background to the left. The structure was later the Orrville Junior High School after the new high school was built in 1955. Most recently, North Elementary School was housed there during construction of the new Orrville Elementary School on Mineral Springs Street. After the completion of the new elementary school, the building was razed in 2010. (Courtesy of Wayne Liechty.)

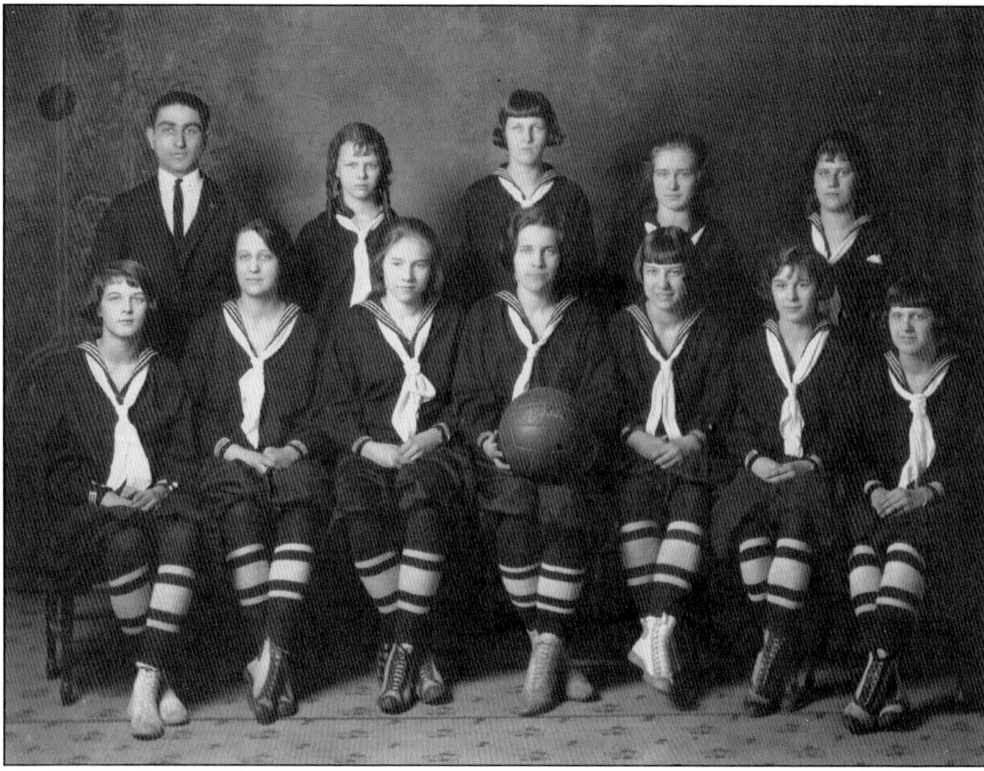

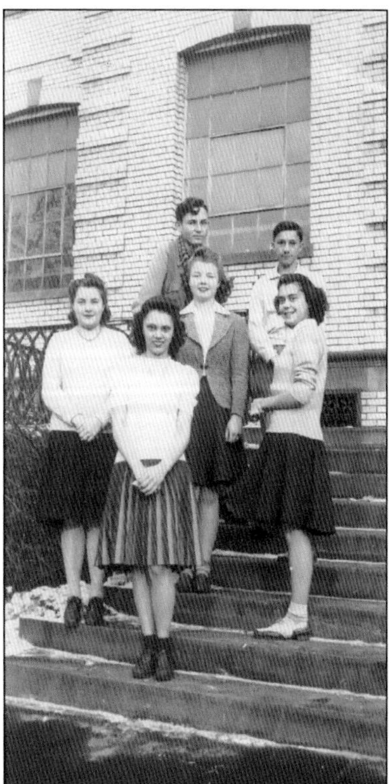

Pictured here is a 1920s girls' basketball team. Members from left to right are (first row) Hanna Royer, Helen Hodell, Ruth Ething, Catherine Irvin, Mary Kochl, Corrine Auble, and Geraldine Chapman; (second row) coach L.O. Weiss, Stella Stone, Dorothy Mushrush, Nina Burkey, and Treva McAfee.

On the steps at Orrville High School are, from left to right, (girls) R. Miller, Donna Schantz. Carolyn Warner, and Joan Most; (boys) John Waring and Jack Stands.

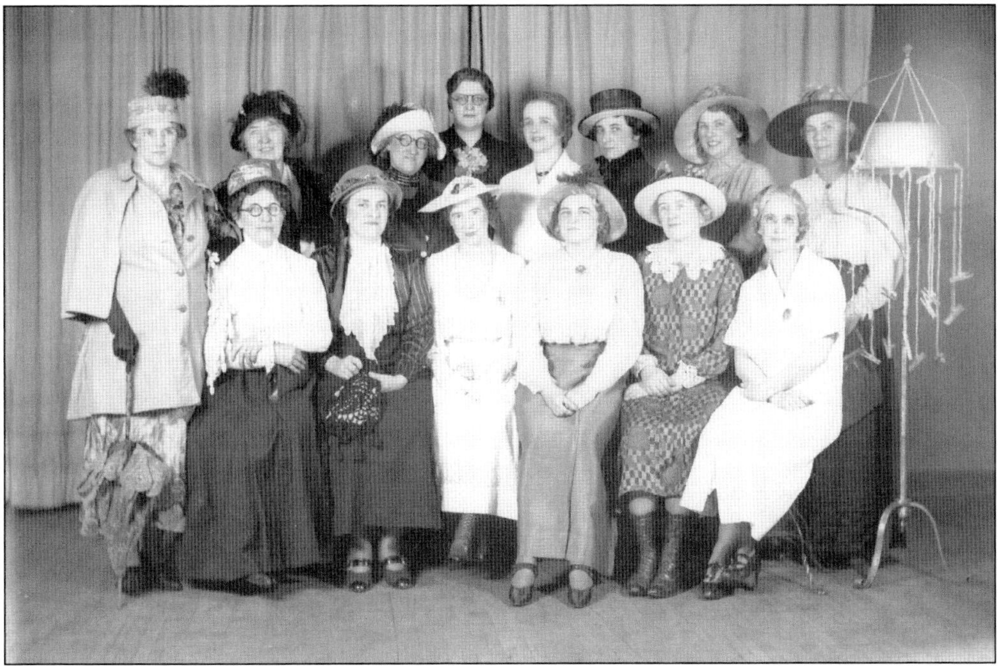

This is the Orrville Mother's Athletic Club for the 1937–1938 school year. From left to right are (first row) Mamie Huher, Alma Badertscher, Alma Elleworth, Betty Kinney, Margaret Weber, and Marie Crummel; (second row) Ruth Zarle, Lena Bartschy, Bessie Maag, Mae Kraft, Hazel Alleman, Maude Congdon, and Carrie Demlow.

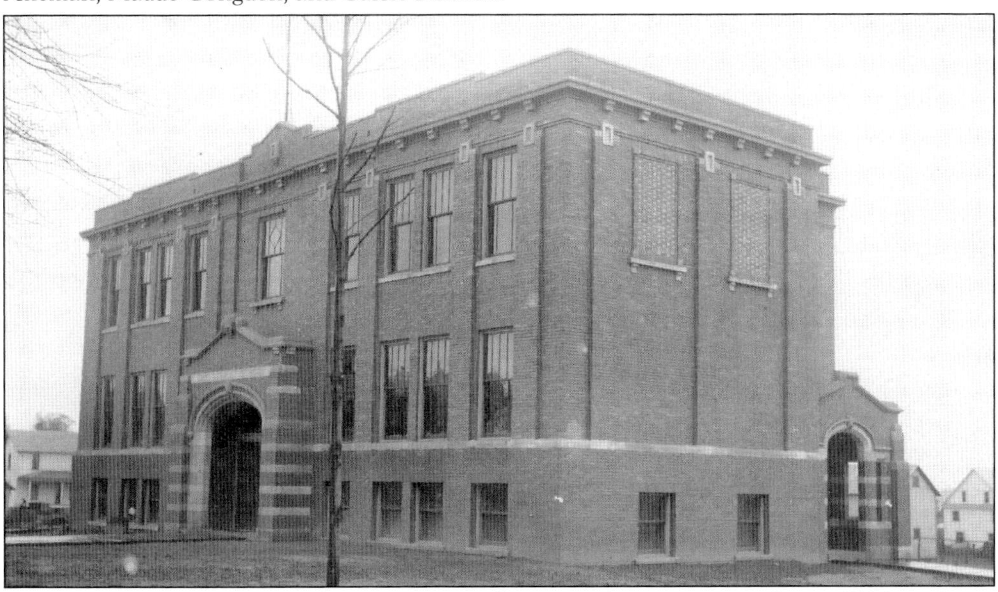

Oak Street Elementary School was constructed in 1908 due to overcrowding at Walnut Street School. The building housed kindergarten through sixth grade until elementary schools in the district went grade specific in the mid-2000s. At that time, the building became the fifth- and sixth-grade school. After the new Orrville Middle School, the home to fifth through eighth grades, was completed on Mineral Springs in 2008, Oak Street School was left empty, and the building was razed. It is currently single residential lots, with new homes being built in the school's place.

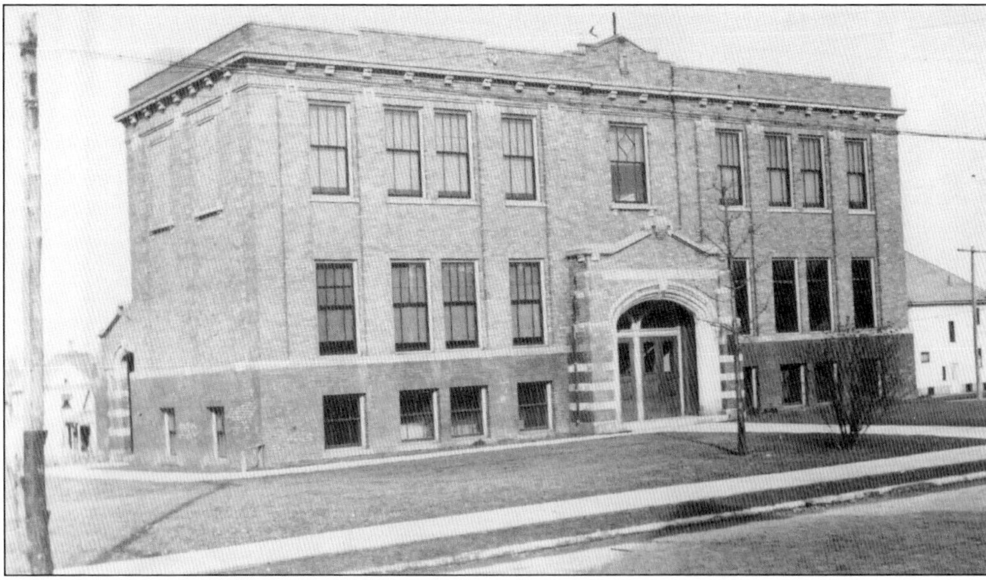

Above is a front view of Oak Street School, looking northeast from Oak Street. Below, the Oak Street School third- and fourth-grade classes are photographed at the entrance of the school in 1934.

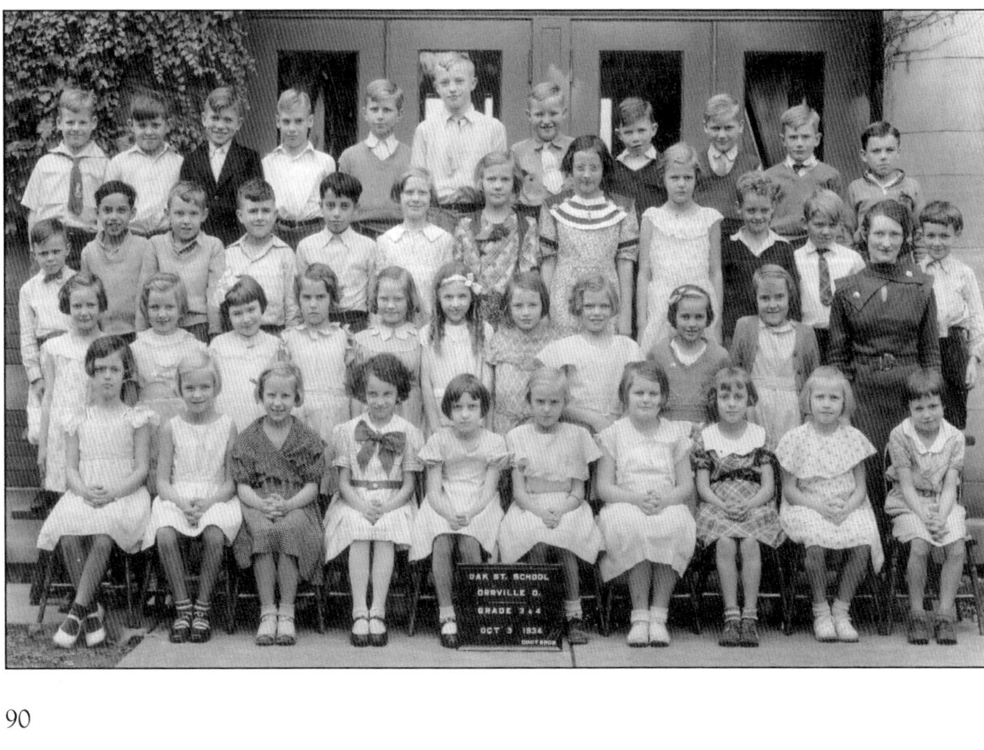

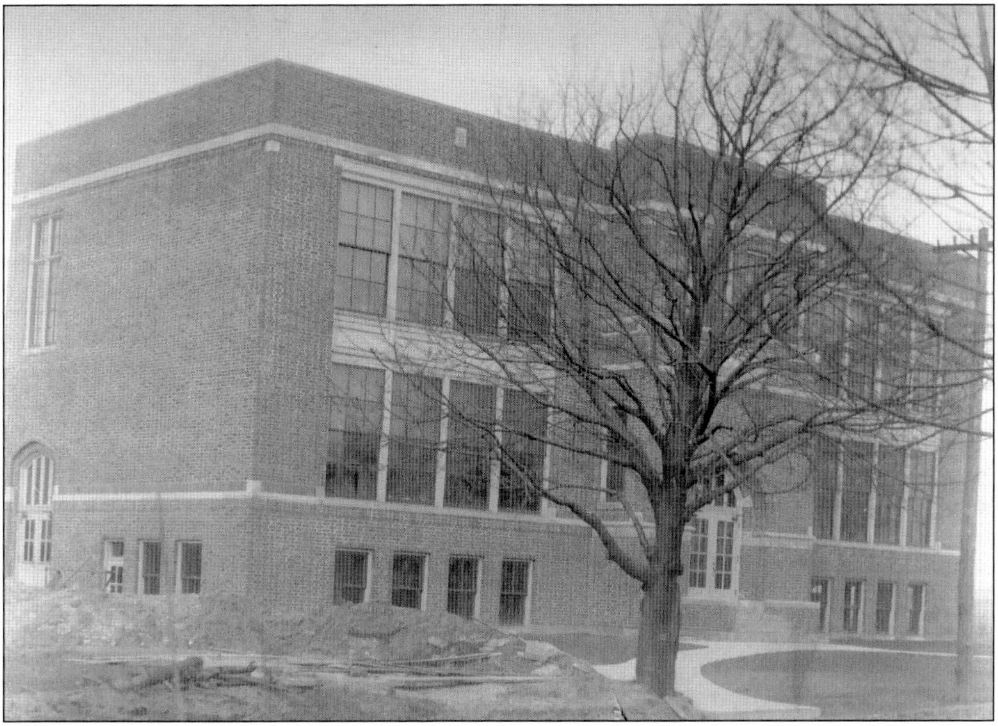

In the 1913 photograph above, construction finishes up on Maple Street School. The new elementary school housed grades kindergarten through sixth and was designed to offer the residents on the west end of town a closer schooling option. At the time, it was thought going to the south end of town to Oak Street School was too far. The students in the Maple Street School photograph below wear costumes for a class play.

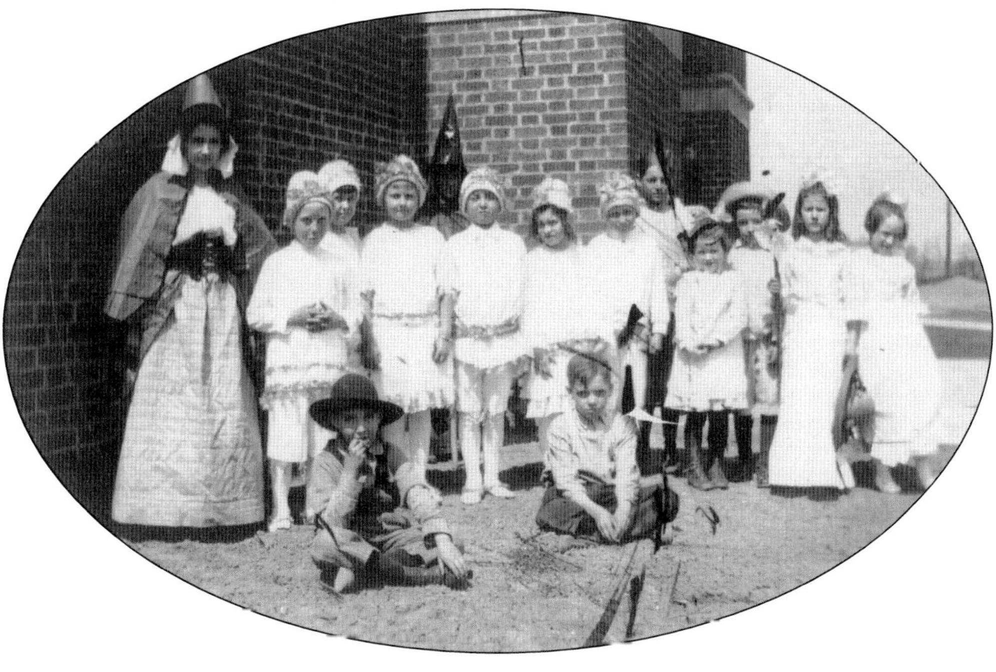

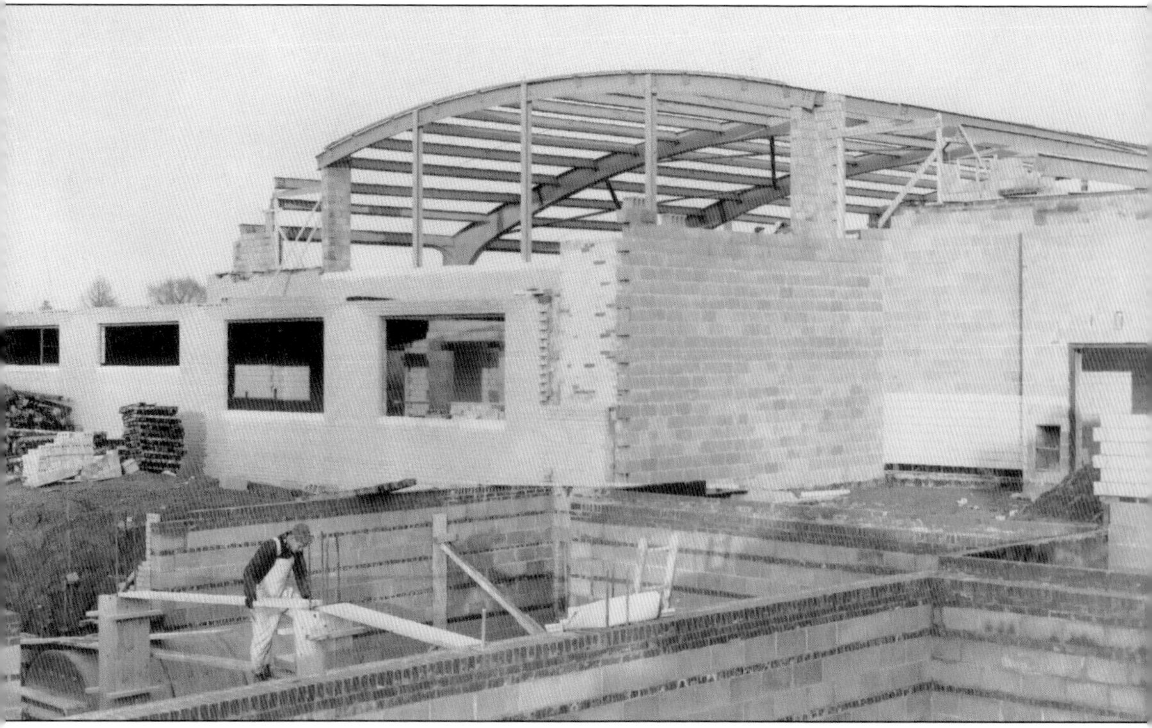

The construction of the new Orrville High School is pictured in 1955. The building houses ninth through twelfth grades. At the time of publication in 2012, construction is currently underway again on the property. The gymnasium and auditorium will remain, but another gymnasium will be added, and a new academic wing will be built to the north of the current structure.

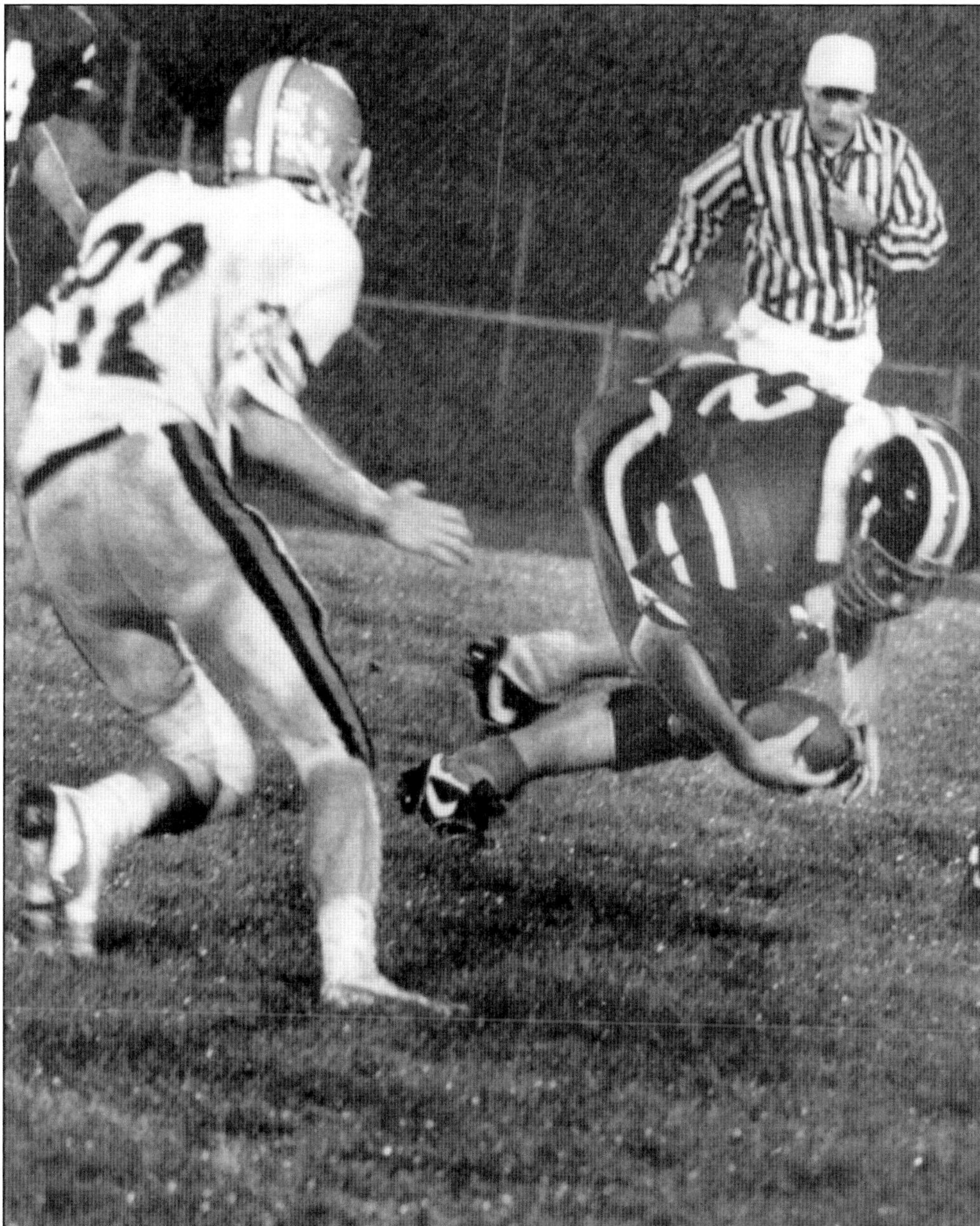

Orrville has always been a football town. This photograph of Ryan Neuenschwander was taken at Red Rider Stadium. The Orrville football team has gone to state playoffs 24 times, holding a record in Wayne County for the team that has been there the most. The Red Riders won the state championship in 1998.

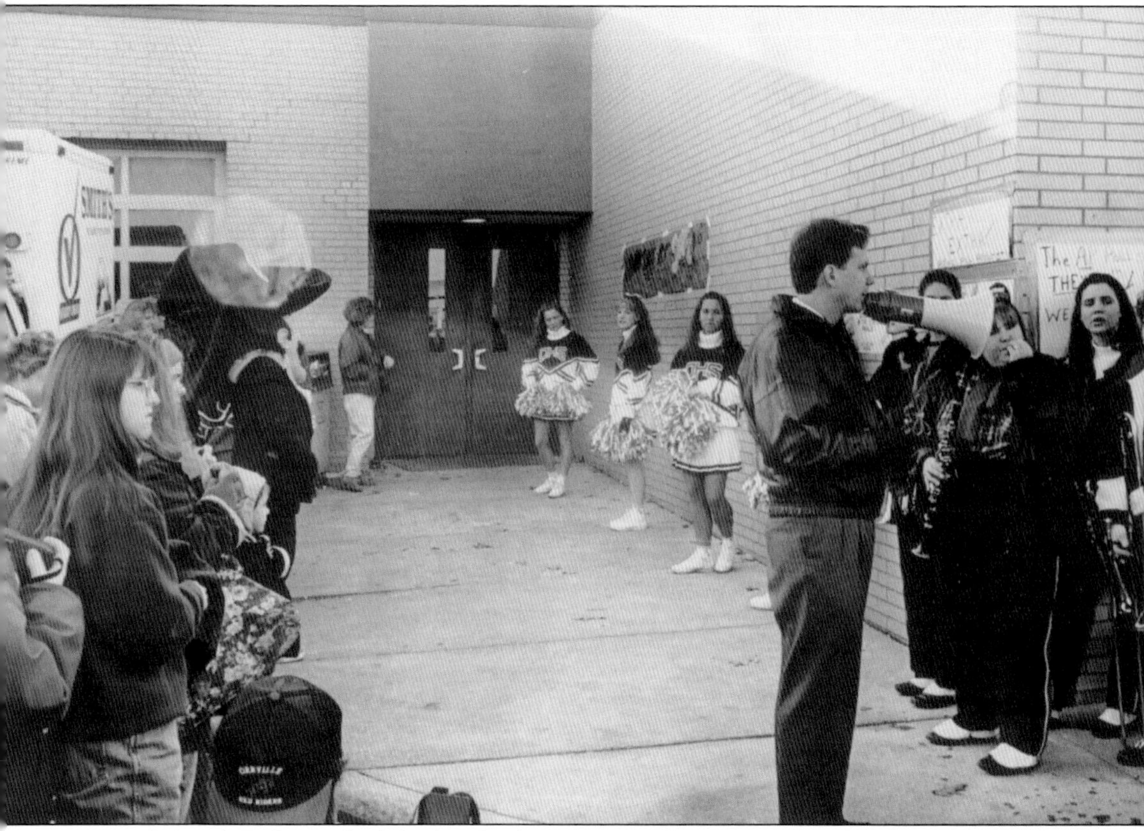

With Rowdy Rider on the left, cheerleaders prepare to form a tunnel at the door sometime during the 1990s. Longtime marching band director Dave Tibbitts gives the go-ahead to the band to begin playing the school's fight song, "Hoorah," as the football team readies for another victory.

Six

HOMETOWN HEROES

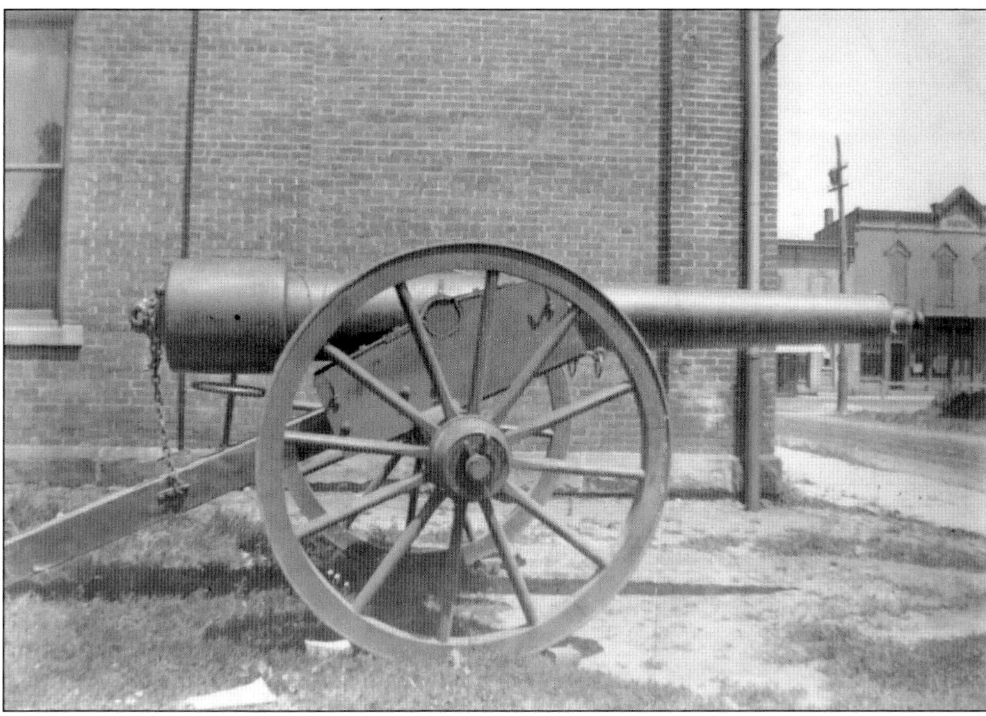

This Civil War cannon can still be seen at Crownhill Cemetery. It was used during the war and later put on display at the corner of Depot and Market Streets. It was then moved to city hall, and from there, it was transported to the cemetery. The base of the cannon was reconstructed recently so it will last longer as a piece of Orrville history. A total of 192 men from the Orrville area served in the Civil War.

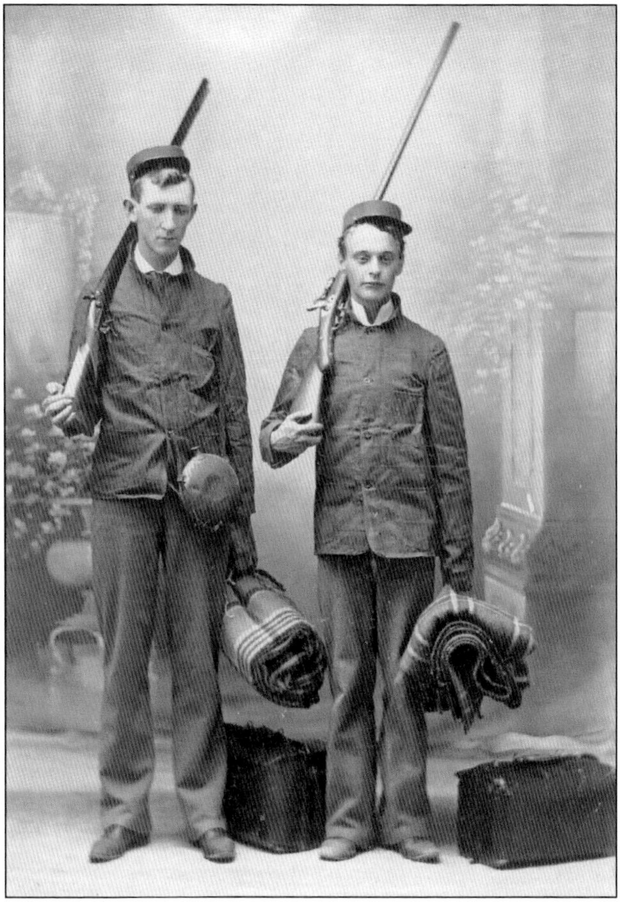

Ed Wirth (left) and Harry Taylor are pictured here, ready to leave home in 1887.

This photograph shows a train filled with soldiers departing from the Union Depot in Orrville for World War I in 1898. (Courtesy of Wayne Liechty.)

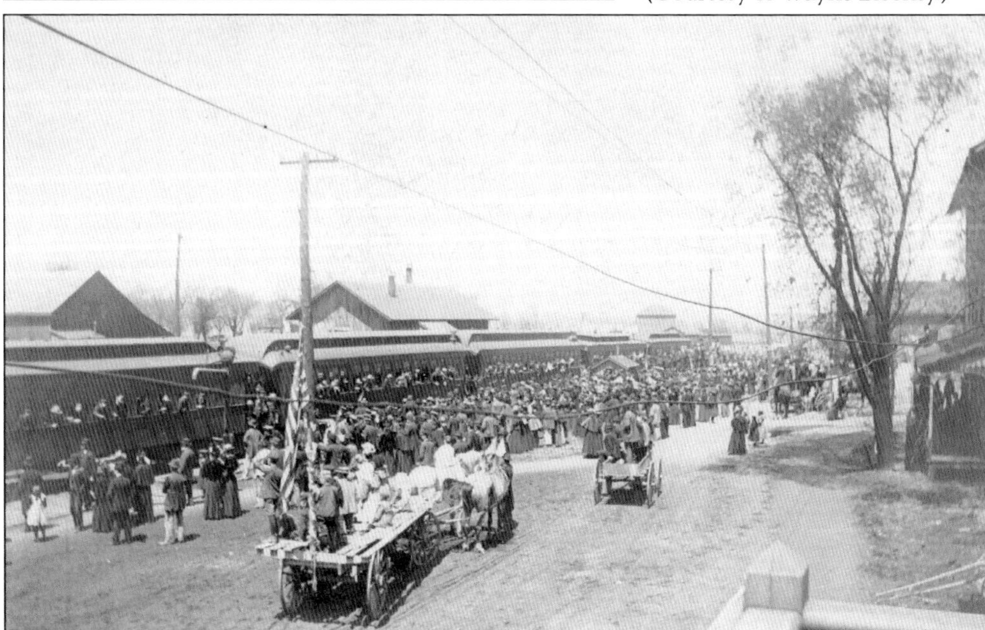

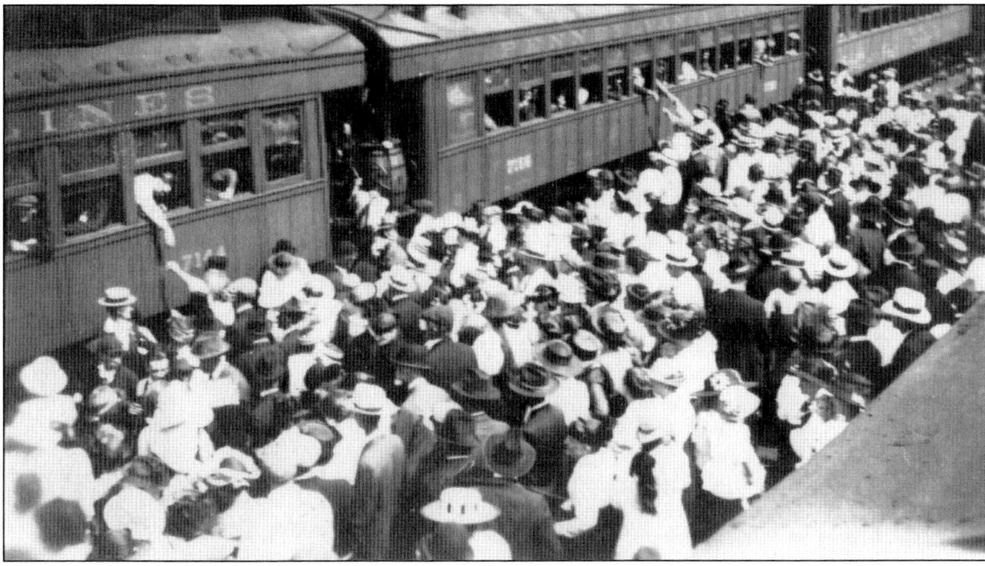

This is a closer view of World War I soldiers saying goodbye as their train leaves the depot.

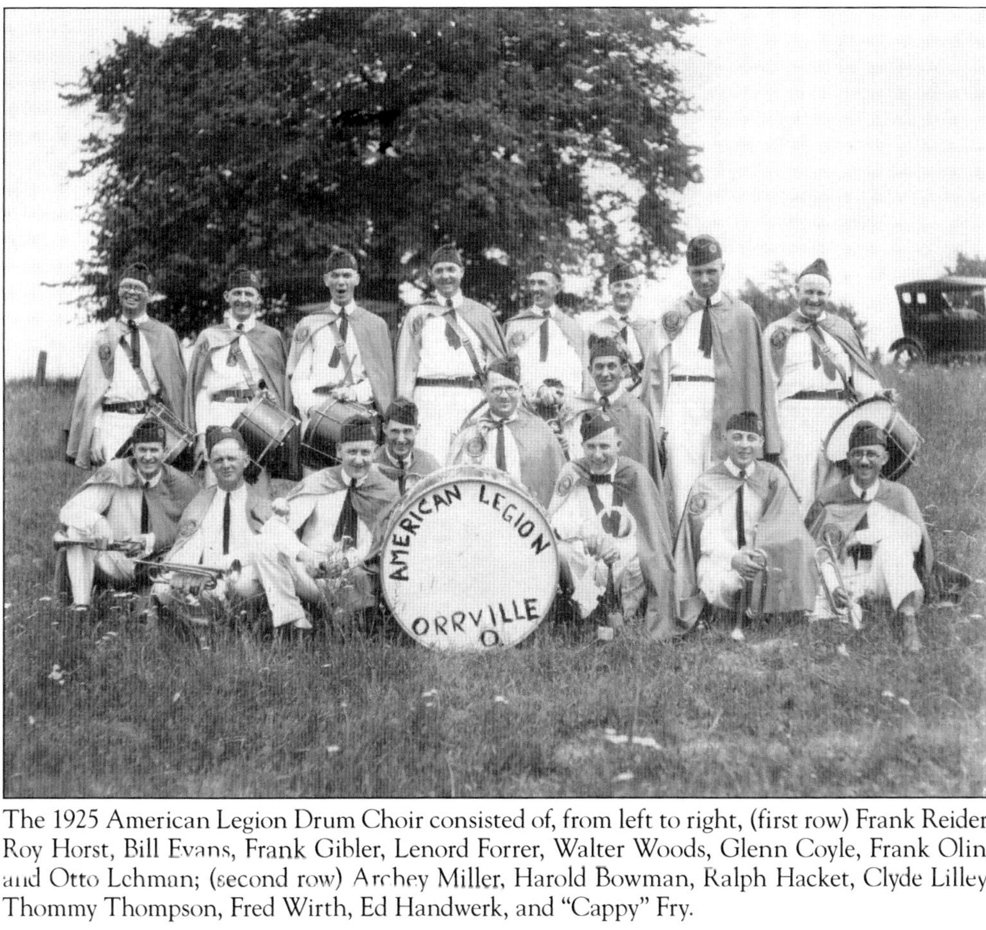

The 1925 American Legion Drum Choir consisted of, from left to right, (first row) Frank Reider, Roy Horst, Bill Evans, Frank Gibler, Lenord Forrer, Walter Woods, Glenn Coyle, Frank Olin, and Otto Lehman; (second row) Archey Miller, Harold Bowman, Ralph Hacket, Clyde Lilley, Thommy Thompson, Fred Wirth, Ed Handwerk, and "Cappy" Fry.

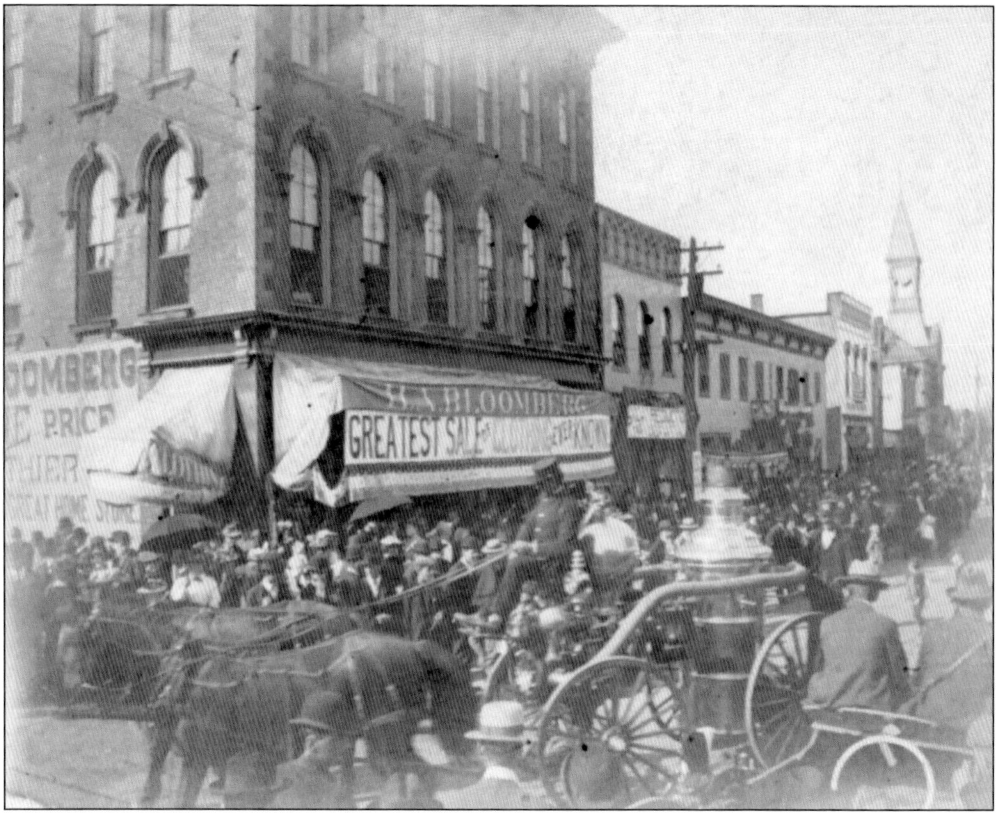

One of the city's first fire engines, driven by Sam Cook, turns onto Market Street from Main Street. The city had a group of men that fought fires with a bucket brigade, but an official department was not established until the great fire of 1872. Later that year, the volunteer fire department, known as the Dot Engine Company, was established with Norman Chaffin as the first foreman.

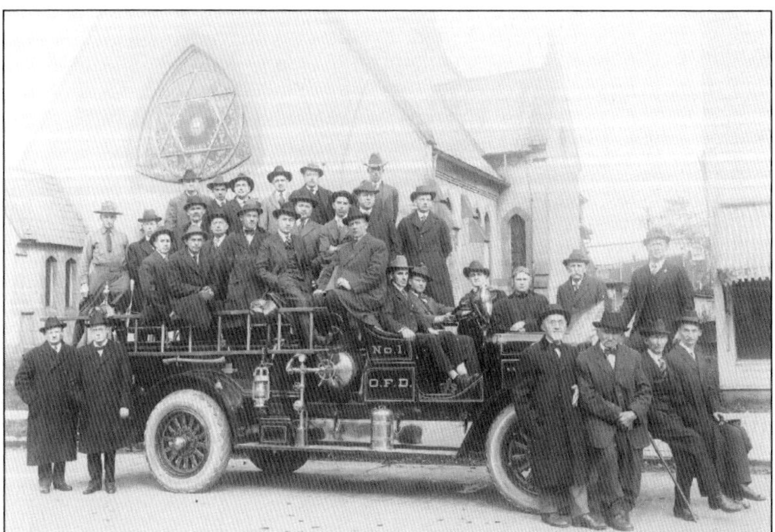

The members of the Orrville Fire Department are pictured in 1917. This image was captured on Vine Street in front of the Lutheran church. The Ahrens-Fox fire engine is on display at the Wayne County Historical Society Village.

A few members of the fire department observe a fire at Ulrich's Garage. This photograph was taken on January 18, 1930; it was six degrees below zero that day, and icicles can be seen on the windows of the building, as well as on the hat of one of the men pictured.

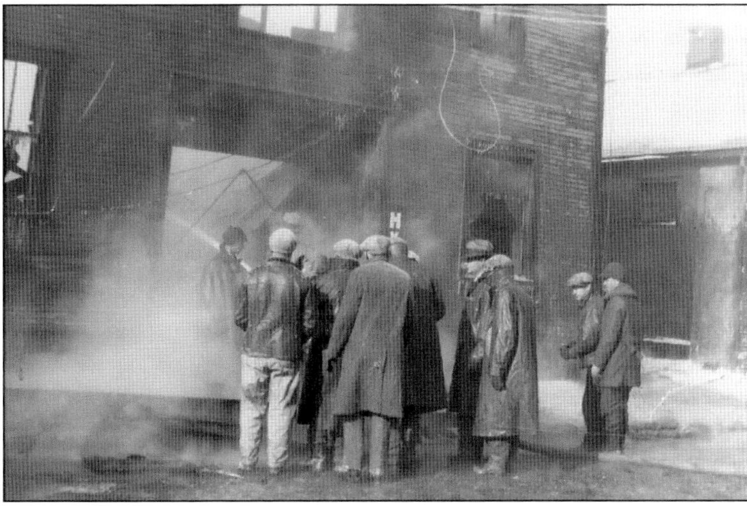

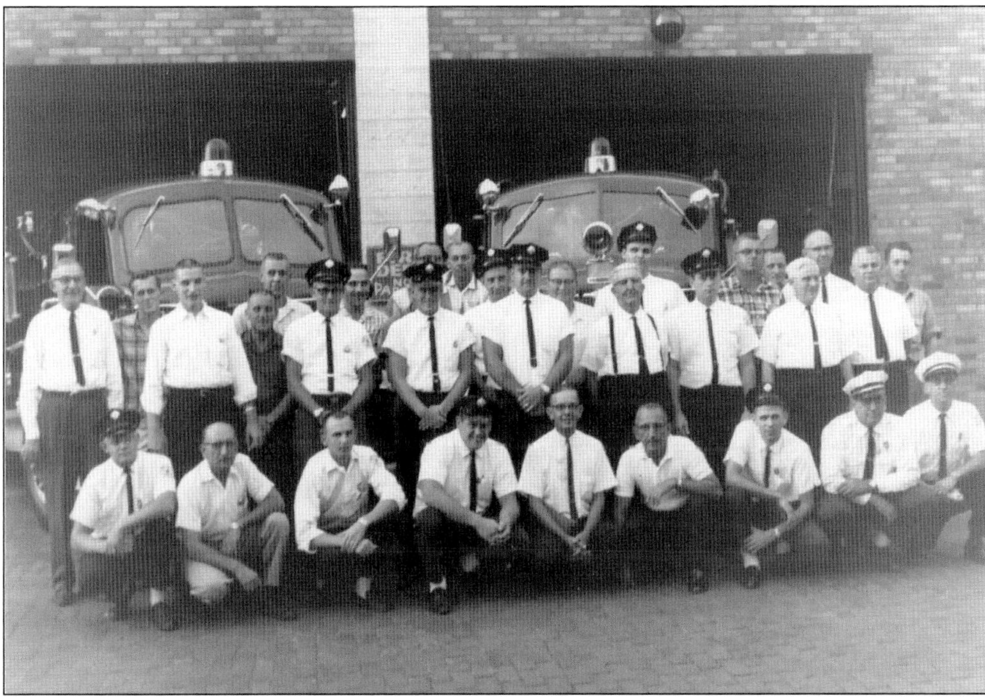

The Orrville Fire Department (OFD) poses in 1960. The department once housed its engines and ran all calls out of the back of the city hall on Water Street. From left to right are (first row) Roger Maiwurn, Kenny Mann, David Bishop, Gene Stuckey, Bob Maiwurm, Merl Saurer, Chester LeFever, Moss Martin, and Bob Stuckey; (second row) Art Lacey, Chuck Yehl, Dwayne Backstrom, Bill Earnsberger, Stan Stuckey, Earl Peters, Norm Garver, Ralph Eshleman, and Laird Null; (third row) Bill Stanford, Fritz Weaver, Russ Ballentine, Carl Moomaw, Doyle Hoffman, Roy Wade, Don Vandyne, Ray Forney, Charlie Herman, Ken Staley, Glenn Brown, Karl Bodager, Danny Markley, and Kent Staley. At the time of publication, Bill Earnsberger was still an active member of the Orrville Fire Department.

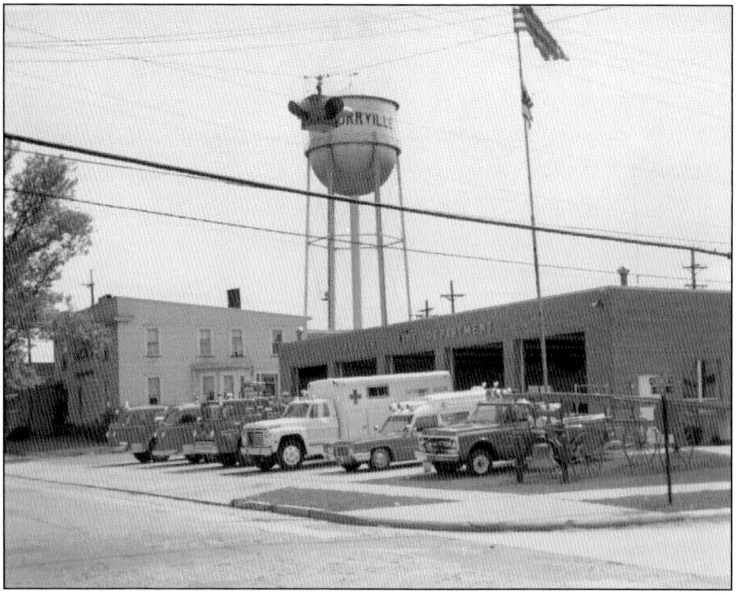

OFD Station No. 1 was dedicated in 1967 on the southwest corner of Vine and Church Streets and is still in operation today. This picture shows all the equipment the department owned at the time the new station was built. Station No. 2 was recently renovated and is located on Crownhill Road, just north of the cemetery. (Courtesy of Orrville Fire Department.)

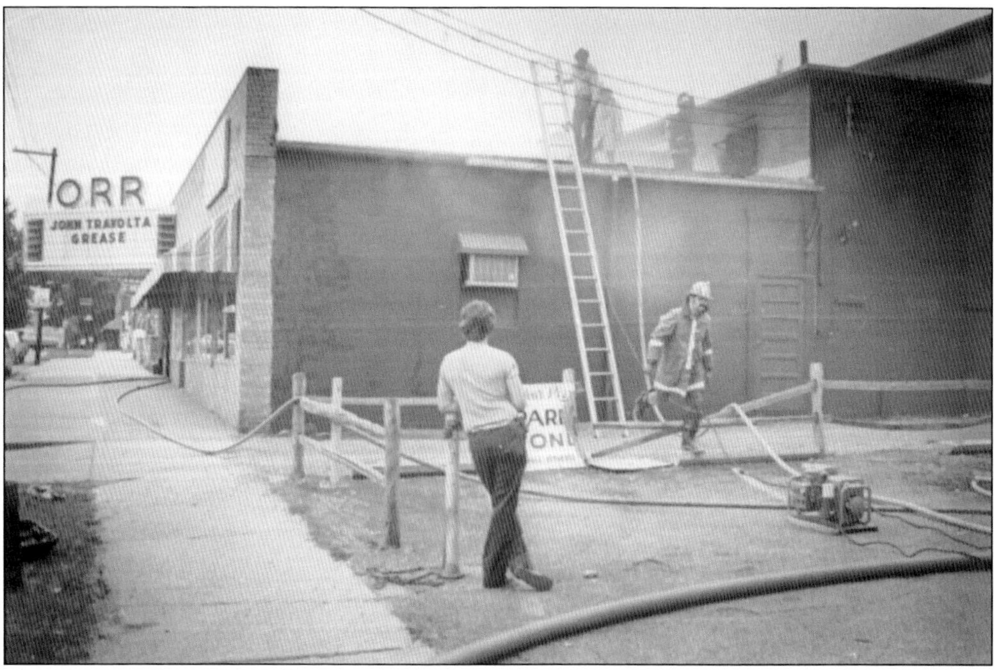

This photograph was taken during a fire at Orr Theater in 1978. The marquis advertises *Grease* with John Travolta, which was playing there at the time. (Courtesy of Orrville Fire Department.)

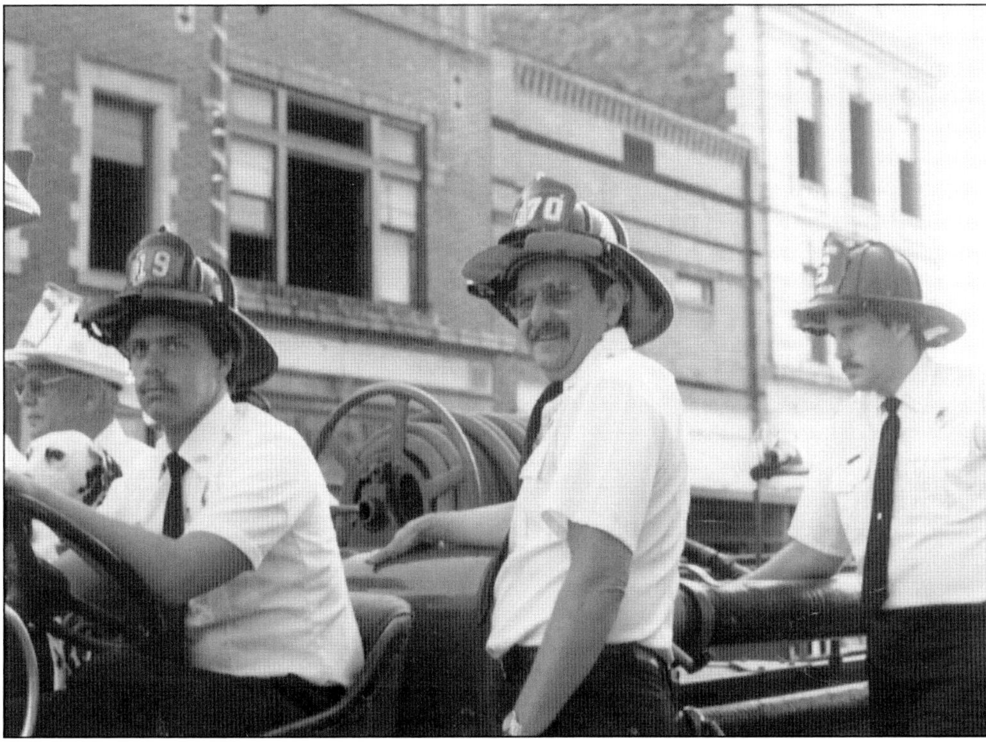

In this photograph, Chris Bishop (driving); his father, Dave Bishop; and Ron Dellafave take part in a parade downtown. The Ahrens-Fox fire engine was no longer used as a service truck but was still featured in local parades as a piece of Orrville Fire Department–owned Orrville history. (Courtesy of Orrville Fire Department.)

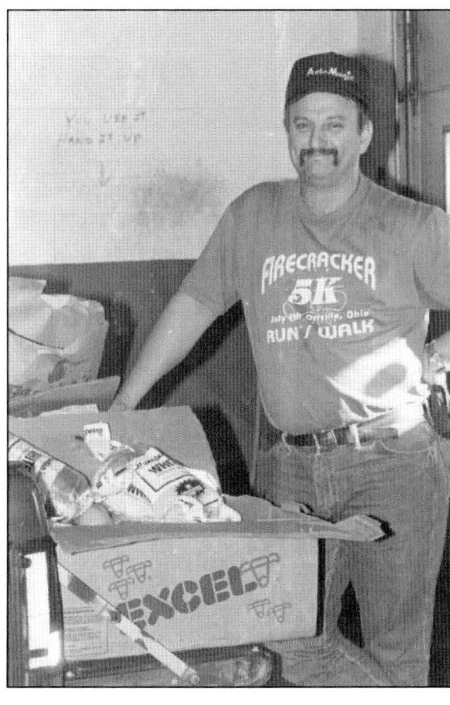

Jeff Lorson works the Orrville Fire Department's annual Christmas food drive. It is just one of the extra things the department takes part in to further serve the community. The food drive started in 1984 when the fire department and police department played a volleyball game against one another. Canned goods were collected at the game, equaling two to three cases, and a handful of families was fed that year. Since then, the food drive has grown exponentially. In 2010, about 350 families were fed, with over 35,000 pounds of food collected and $5,000 in cash donations given. The cash donations help to buy the perishable foods that are delivered along with the other goods collected throughout the community and in the schools.

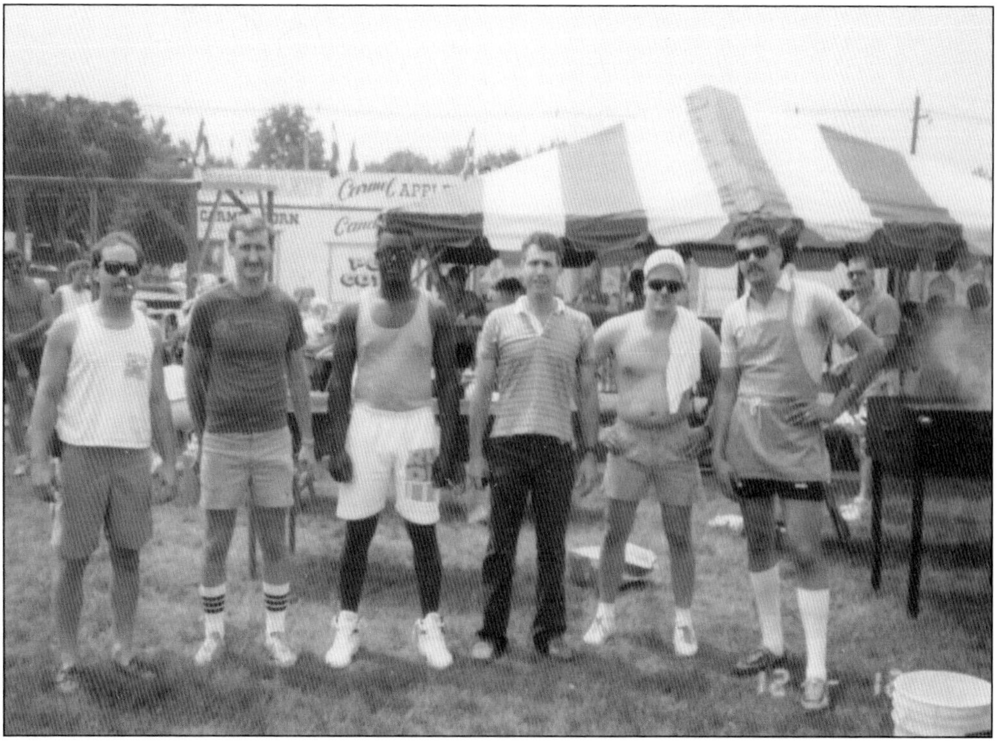

The Fourth of July carnival and fireworks presentation have been put on by the fire department each year since 1983. The Fire in the Sky fireworks show closes out the week's festivities. The display is put on by members of the department who have had special training in conjunction with Zambelli Fireworks Company. It is one of the largest shows put on in northern Ohio and draws crowds of upward 75,000 people. Working a rib cook-off in this photograph from left to right are Scott Maiwurm, Chuck Back, Reggie Winters, John Gresser, Tim Chomyak, and Mike Hostetler. (Courtesy of Orrville Fire Department.)

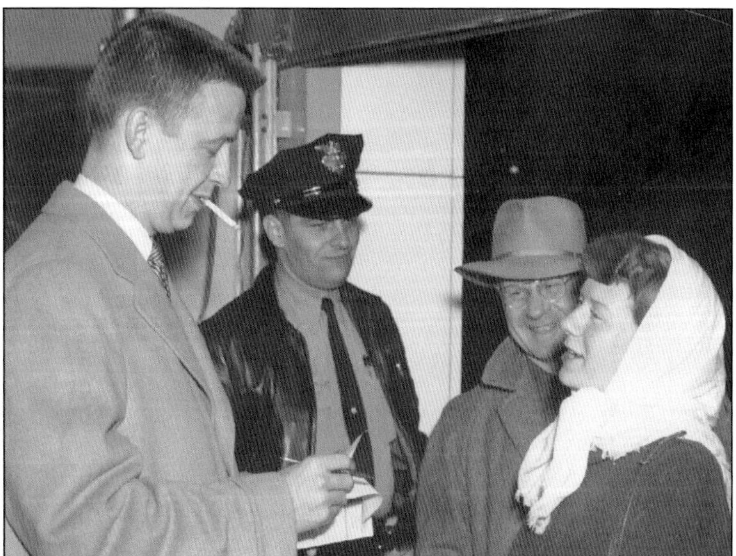

Here are a few of Orrville's finest at work. From left to right, Joe Finan and Bill Stocker collect a police statement from Bill and Susan Faulder.

Seven

Home Sweet Home

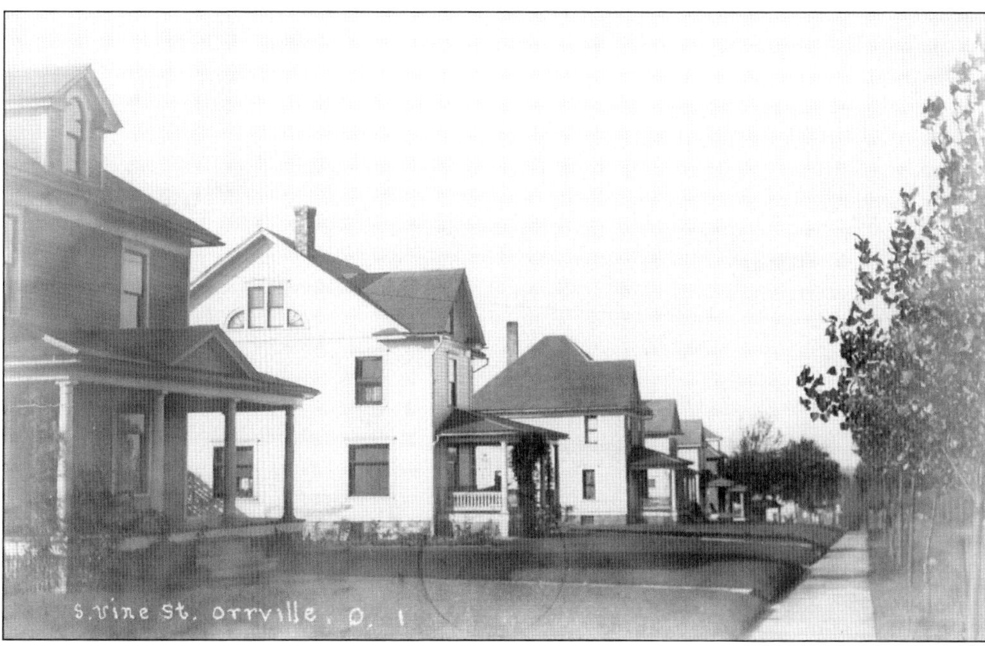

This photograph faces north from the corner of South Vine and Fike Streets. All of these homes still stand today. The exteriors look quite different, but the interiors still hold the original character. (Courtesy of Wayne Liechty.)

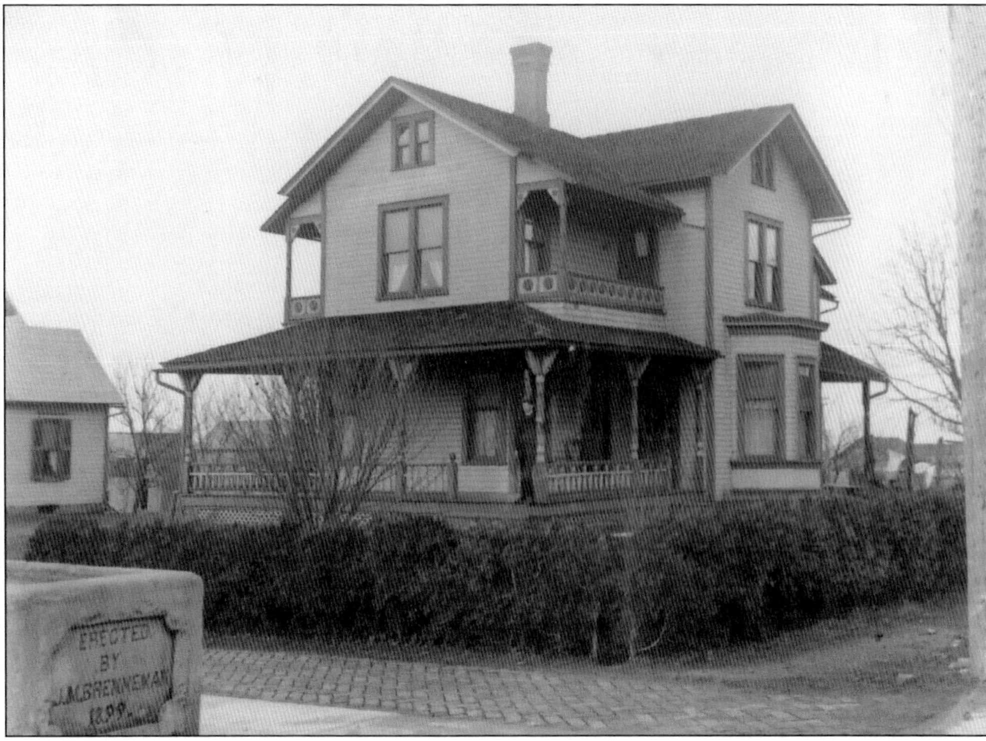

This house once stood on the northeast corner of South Main and Oak Streets. Built by J.M. Brenneman in 1899, the home was moved south of town onto the property where Mennonite Mutual Insurance is currently located. The structure was remodeled and rented out as a duplex. The insurance company no longer wanted the building, so they allowed the fire department to conduct training exercises there, and the home was burned down. The sandstone watering trough seen in the foreground is still on the corner of Oak and Main Streets in front of the gazebo and is used as a flower planter in the summer.

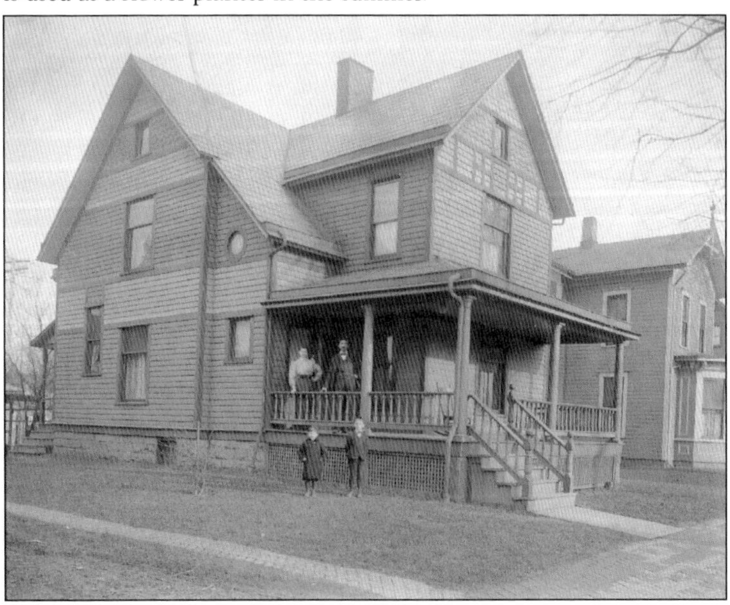

Built in 1901, the Charles Bowman house was located at 318 South Main Street. Later remodeled with business space added to the front, the home is still located on South Main Street on the east side, just south of Chestnut Street. In this photograph are homeowners Minnie and Charles Bowman and their boys, Ralph (left) and Harold.

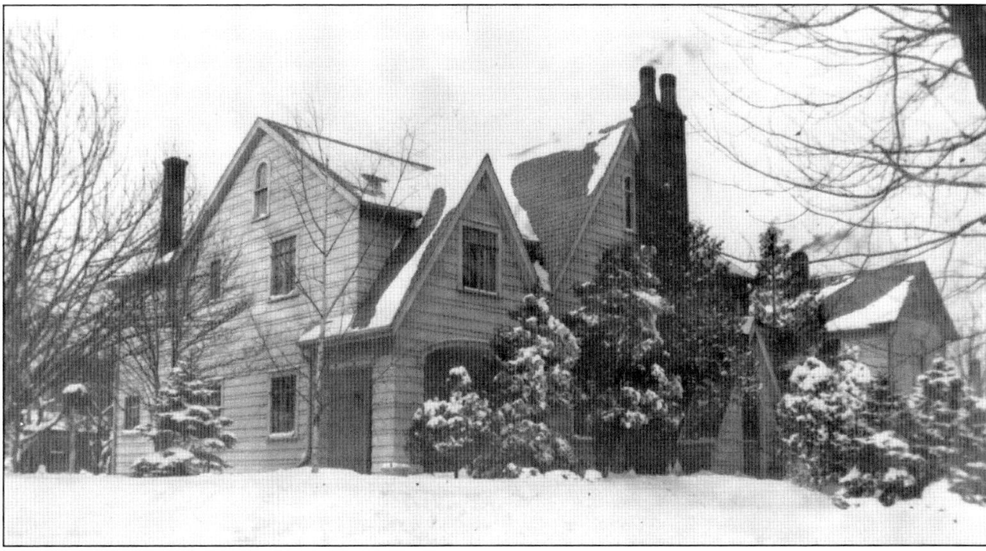

Originally built and owned by the D. Ed Seas family in 1926, the house at 721 South Main Street still stands today with many of the original characteristics remaining. The staircase has the original velvet-covered rope railings, and all of the matching light fixtures, which are detailed with horses, are still in use throughout the house. (Courtesy of Diana Morris.)

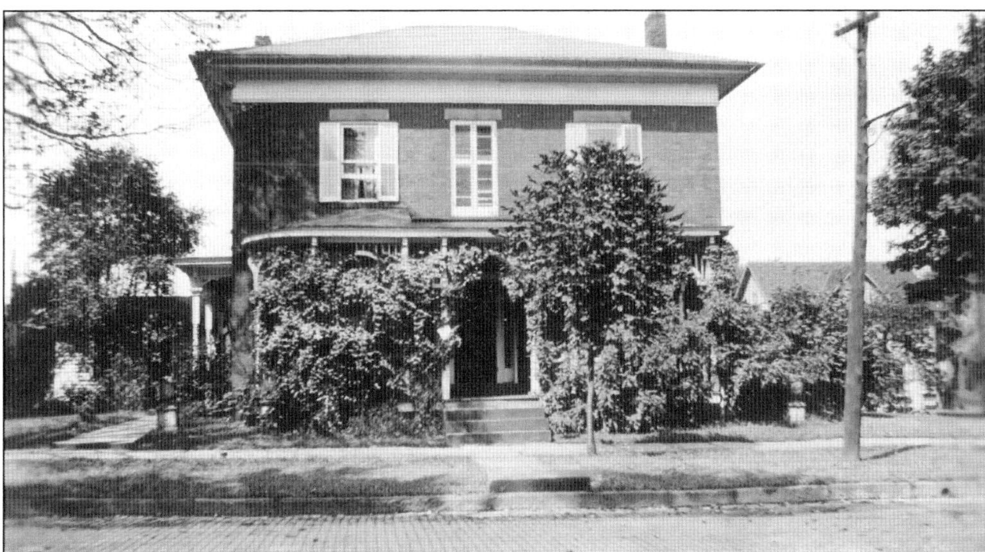

This home on East Market Street no longer exists, but the photograph shows that beautiful houses lined the street on the east end in 1922. This section of Market Street is now part of the business district, and parking lots are currently located under the overpass. Also seen in this photograph are the original brick streets that filled Orrville.

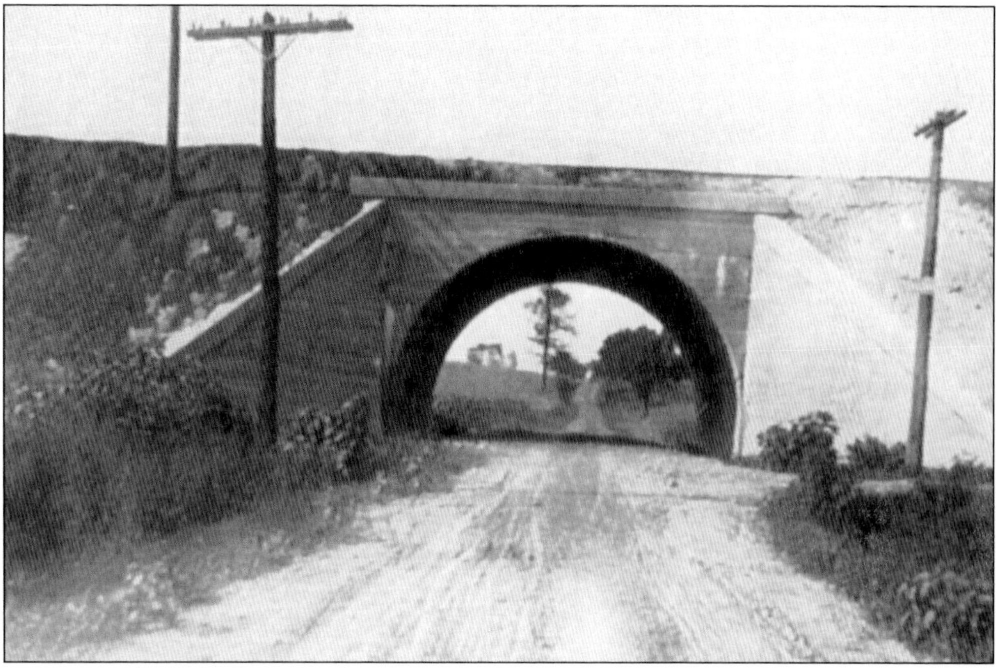

Known simply as "the bridge," it has been the victim of numerous high school students over the years. Students used to sneak out late at night to paint the bridge and leave their mark on the town. Crossing over South Crownhill Road, graduating classes once had an organized event of painting their class year on either side of the opening. That tradition no longer exists, as the bridge is owned by the railroad and painting it is illegal. Seniors at Orrville High School always find a way to leave a message of upcoming defeat during Wooster Week each year.

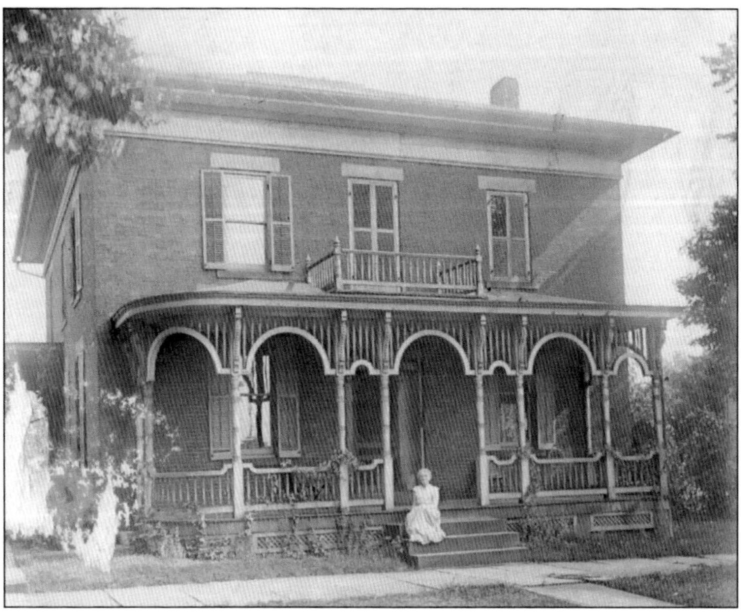

Built in 1860 by D.G. Horst, this is 237 East Market Street. The Horsts lived here from 1860 to 1886 before the home was sold to C.R. Beckley, who lived there from 1886 to 1905. The American Legion was then housed in the structure. When the home was torn down, the legion erected a new building on the site in 1960 that remains on the same property today.

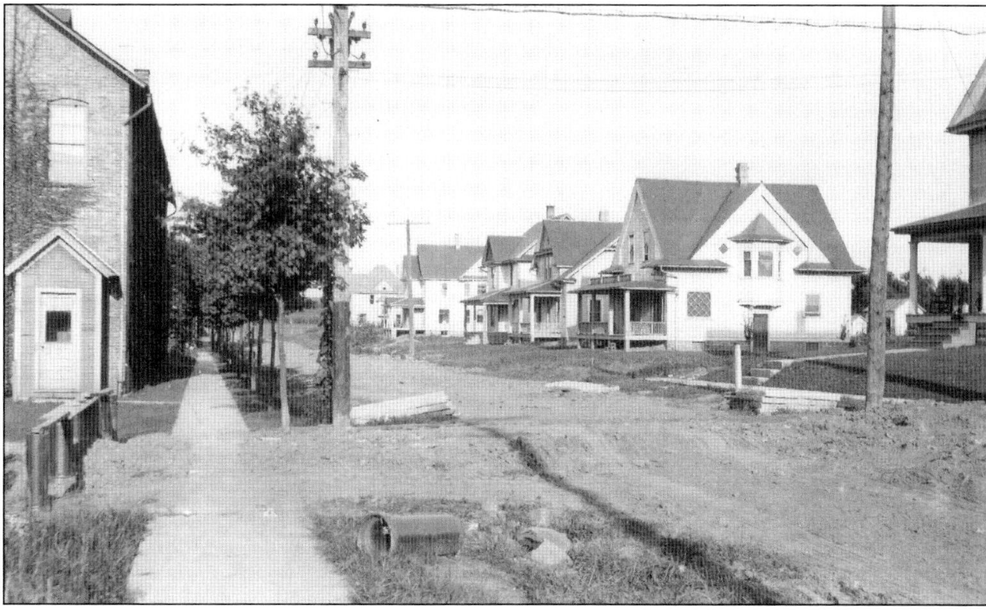

Here is East Oak Street as it looked in 1916. The Schantz Organ Company can be seen in the left corner of the image. Walnut Street is being paved for the first time in this photograph, which will cover up the dirt street that lines the neighborhood.

This home, located on the northeast corner of Church and Walnut Streets, faces Church Street. The children on the porch from left to right are Marie Myers, Hazel Wear, and Ethel Tracy. The home was torn down, and the original Orrville High School was then constructed on this site.

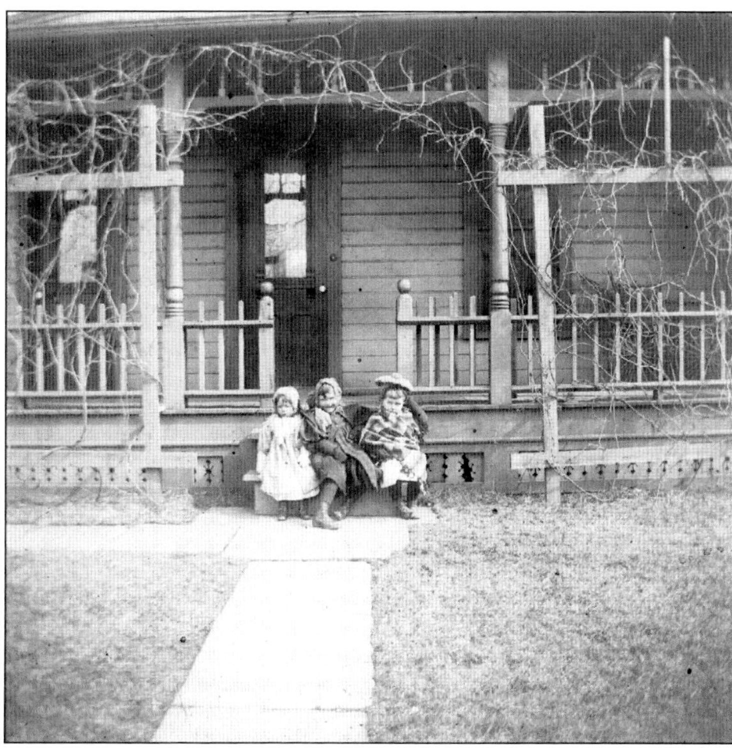

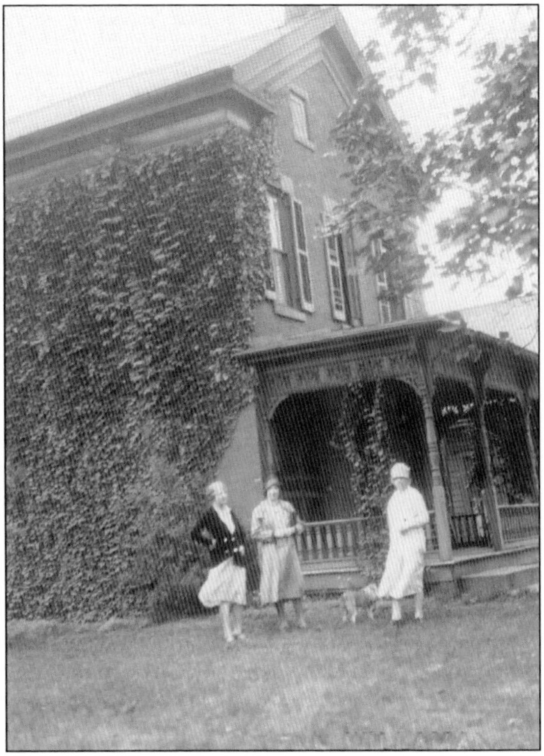

The home of John McGill was located on the southwest corner of Market and Vine Streets. Pictured from left to right are Alfa Baughman, an unidentified woman, and Lill McGill. Runion's Furniture Annex currently sits on this property.

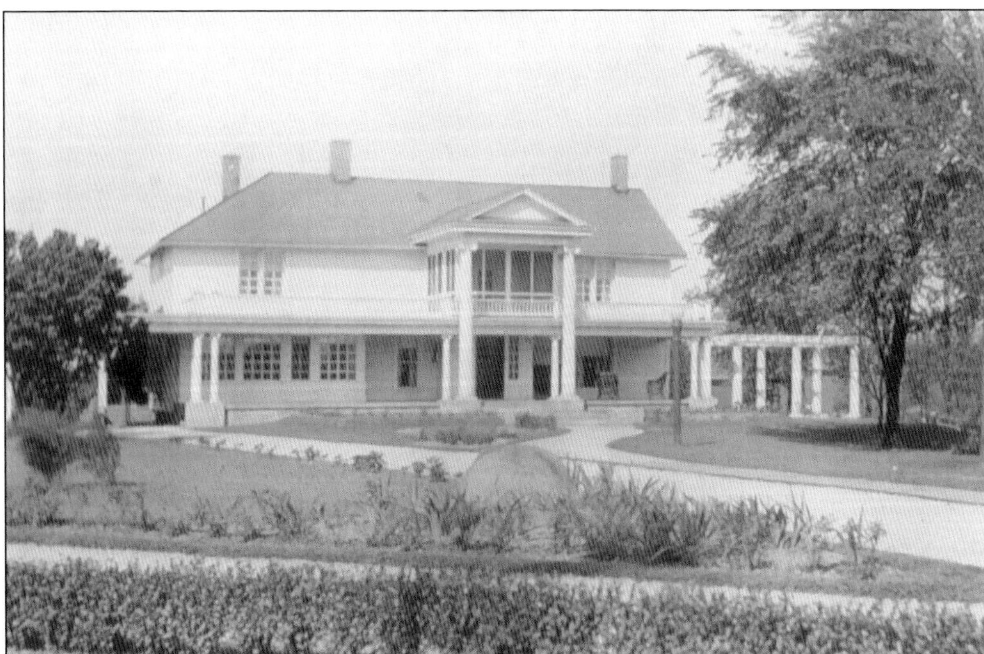

The house at 365 West Market Street, also known as the Smith Orr homestead, was originally built by Christian Horst in 1840 as a log cabin. After being remodeled and added onto a number of times, the home looks today as it did here in 1926. It is owned by the Orrville Historical Society and operated as a museum and banquet and party facility.

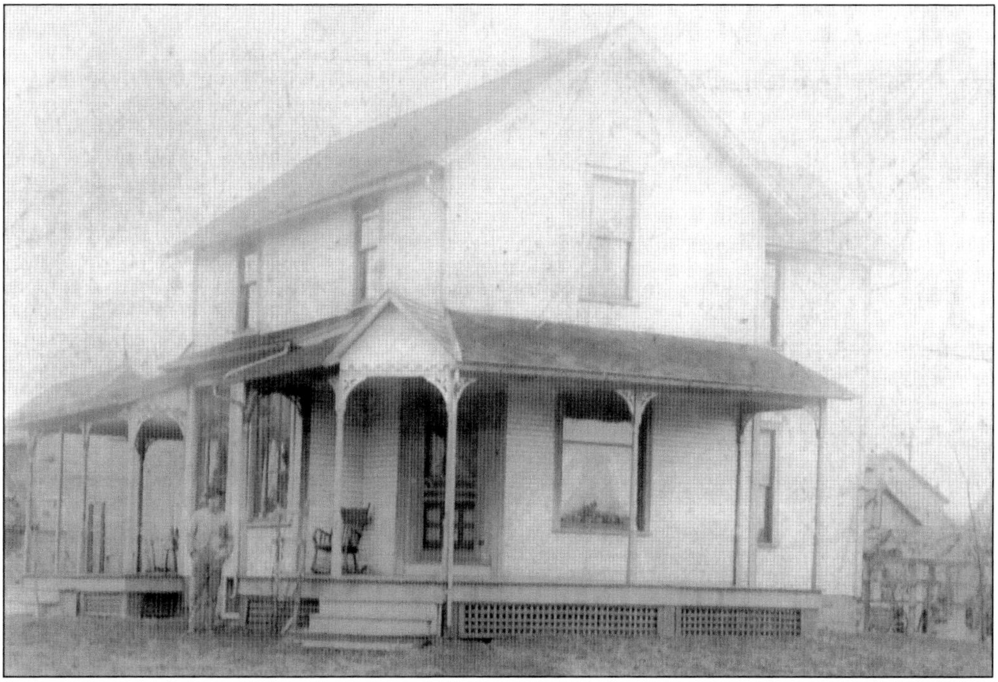

The Starn family farmhouse, seen here, still stands on the corner of Arch and Walnut Streets. (Courtesy of Alison Wagner.)

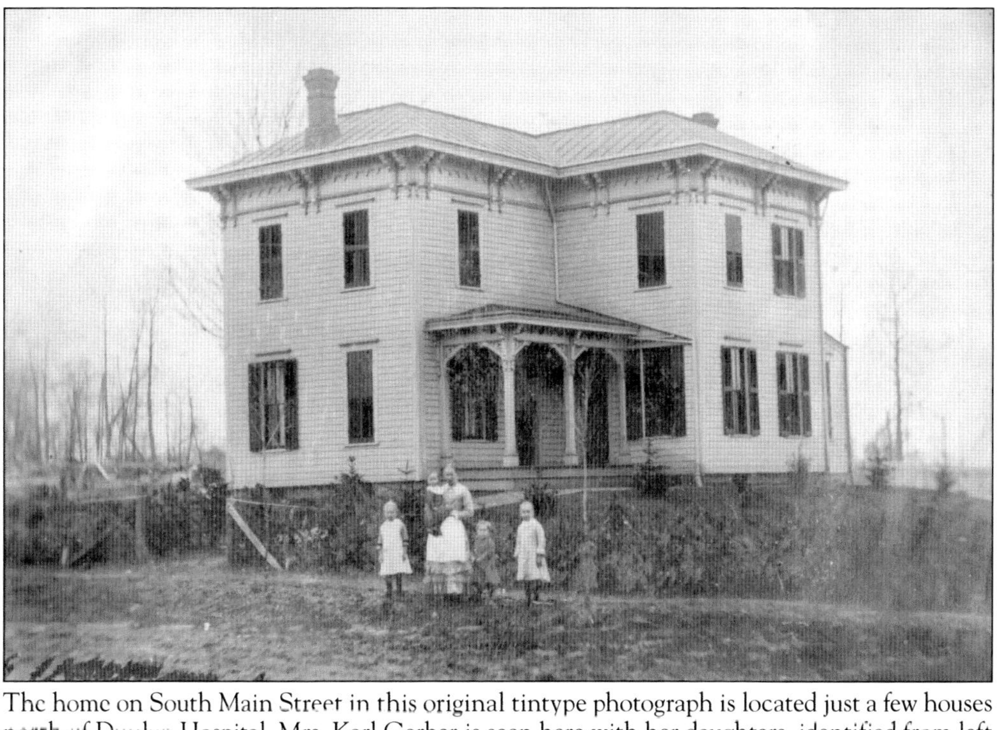

The home on South Main Street in this original tintype photograph is located just a few houses north of Dunlap Hospital. Mrs. Karl Gerber is seen here with her daughters, identified from left to right as Clara, Emma, Millie, and Lydia.

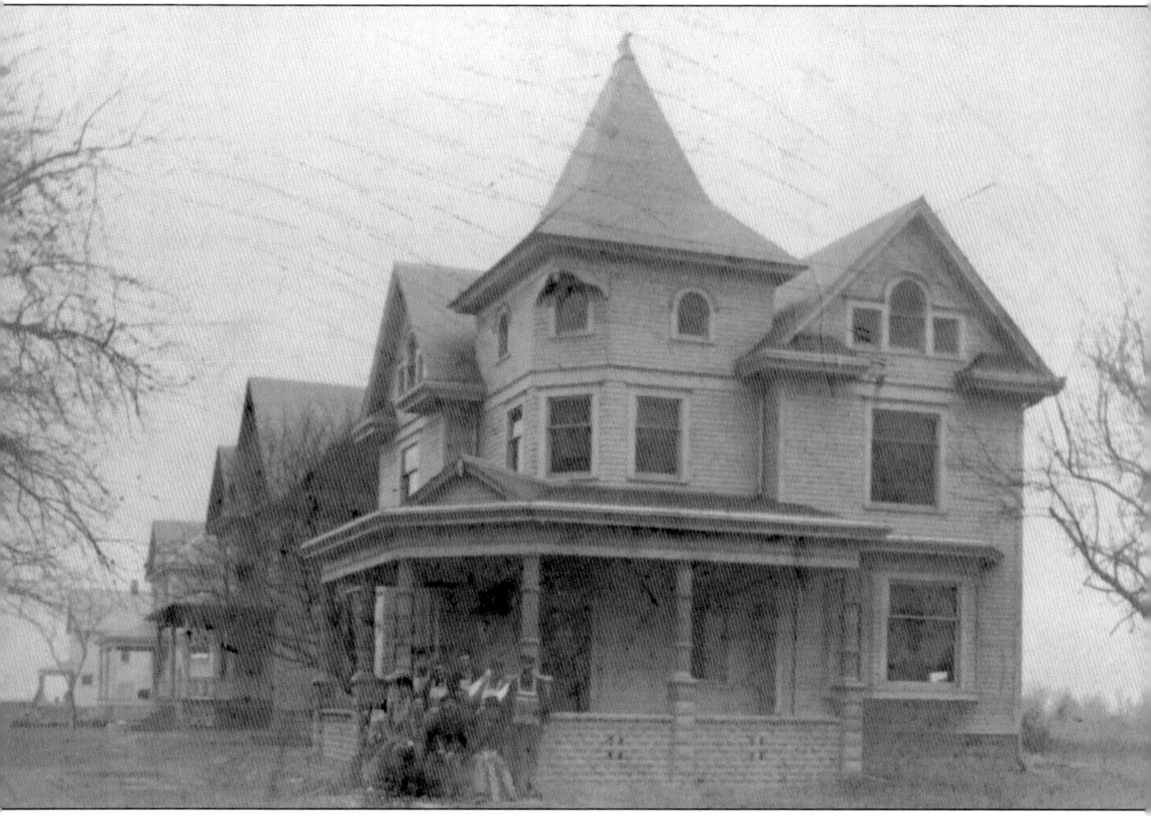

Construction had finished on this home in 1900, and the crew that built it poses for a final photograph. The home still stands at 805 South Vine Street on the corner of Fike and Vine Streets.

Eight

Houses of Worship

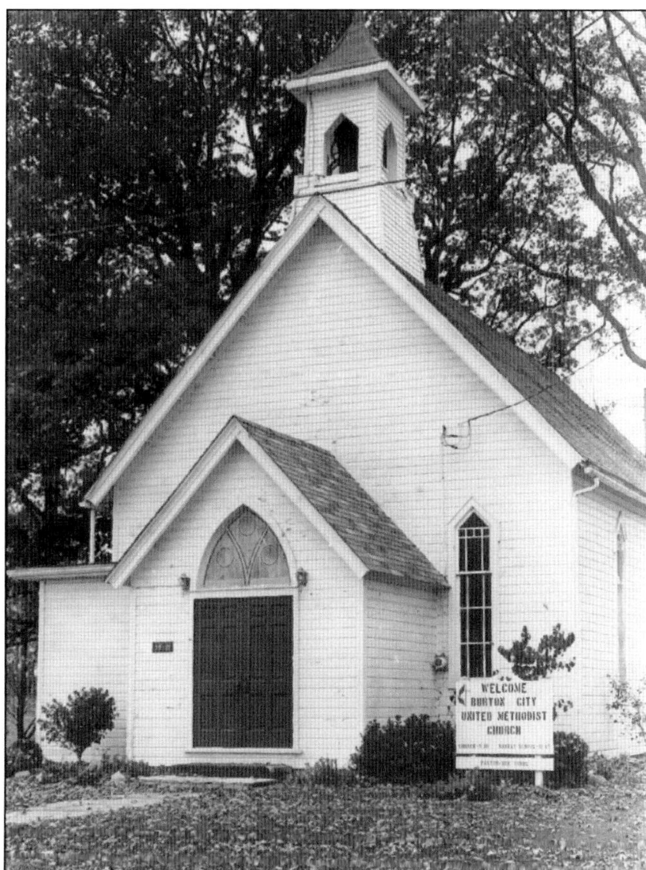

The Burton City Methodist Church, located at 3448 Mount Eaton Road, still enjoys an active congregation today.

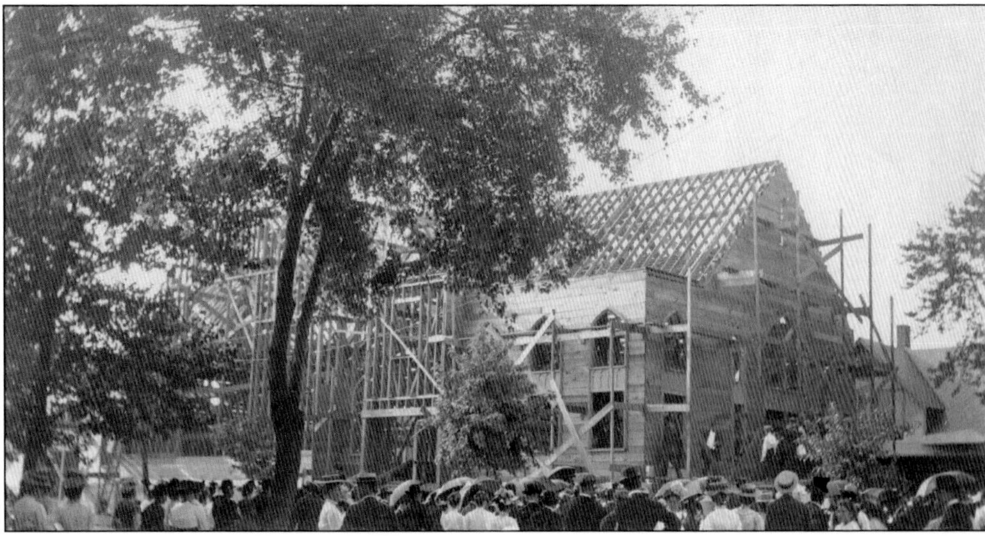

Above, the Reformed church on the corner of Main and Church Streets undergoes construction. The first cornerstones were poured on August 16, 1908, and the building was completed the following year in 1909. The church and its original stained-glass windows remain. Today, it is the Christ United Church of Christ. Pictured below is the completed Reformed church. It looks the same today except for a few additions to the west, as well as a new entry way enclosing some of the stained glass on Main Street. (Above, courtesy of Wayne Liechty; below, courtesy of Orrville Historical Society Archives.)

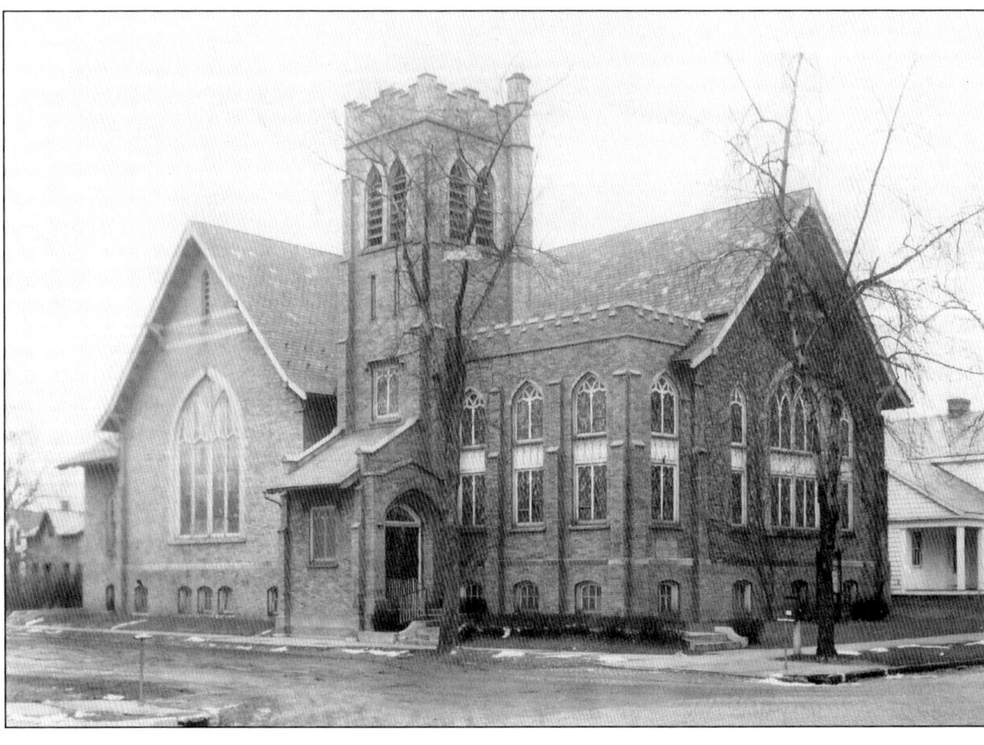

Rev. Delaine McGhee is seen here at the St. Luke Methodist Church, which once stood on Church Street. It stood on the corner of Church and Walnut Streets directly across from the old junior high school and the Orrville Public Library. Today, the library parking lot is located there.

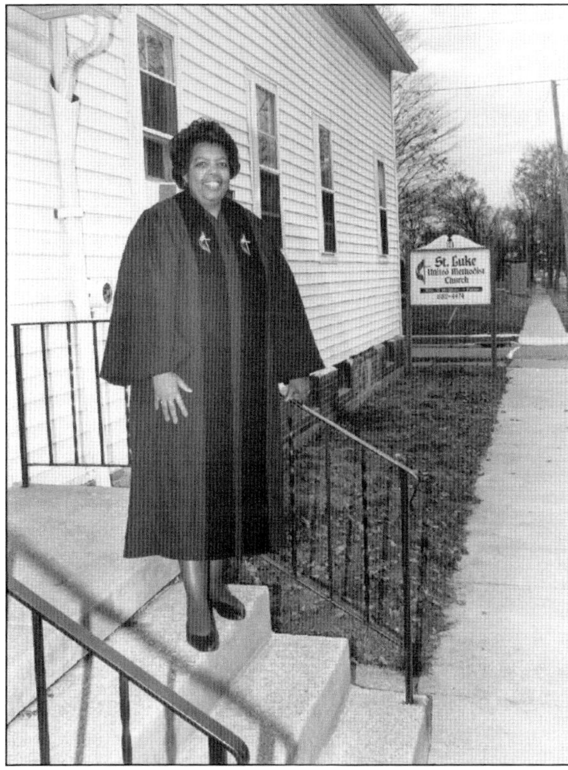

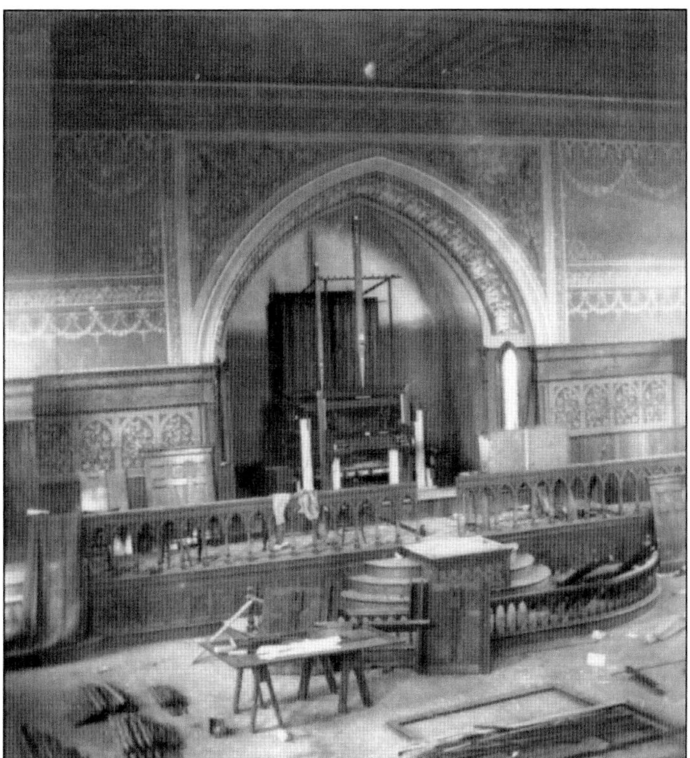

A Schantz Organ installation takes place at the Reformed church in the early 1900s. Every organ in the churches in Orrville is a Schantz organ.

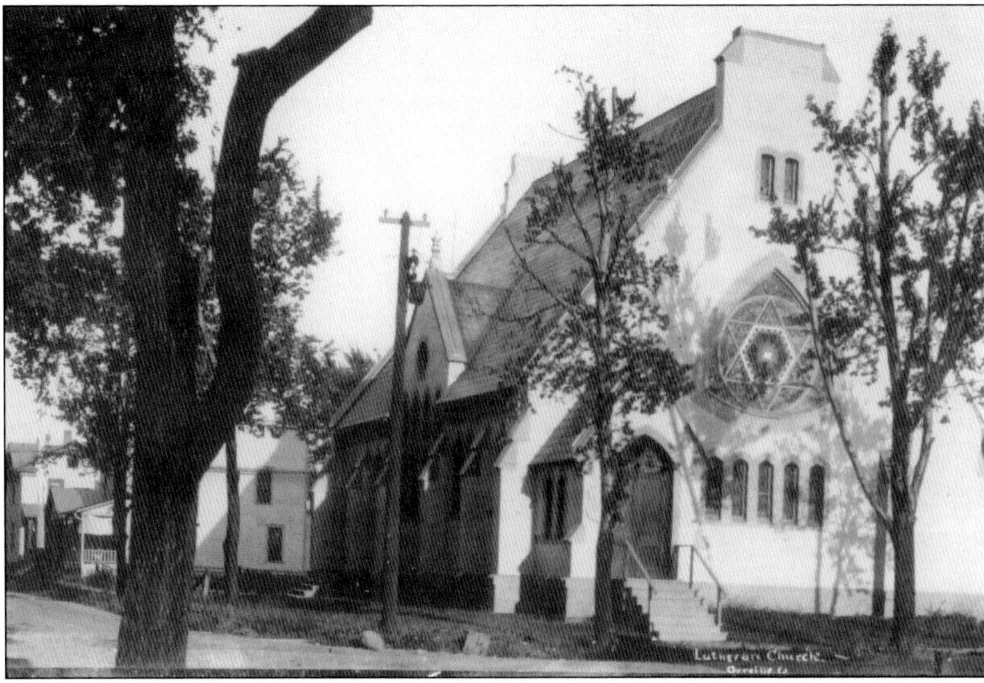

The Lutheran church on the corner of Vine and Water Streets once had its entrance on the west end of the building, off of Vine Street. This photograph was taken in 1930, and though additions have been made since then, much of the original stained glass remains. Today, the church is known as the Augsburg Lutheran Church. (Courtesy of Wayne Liechty.)

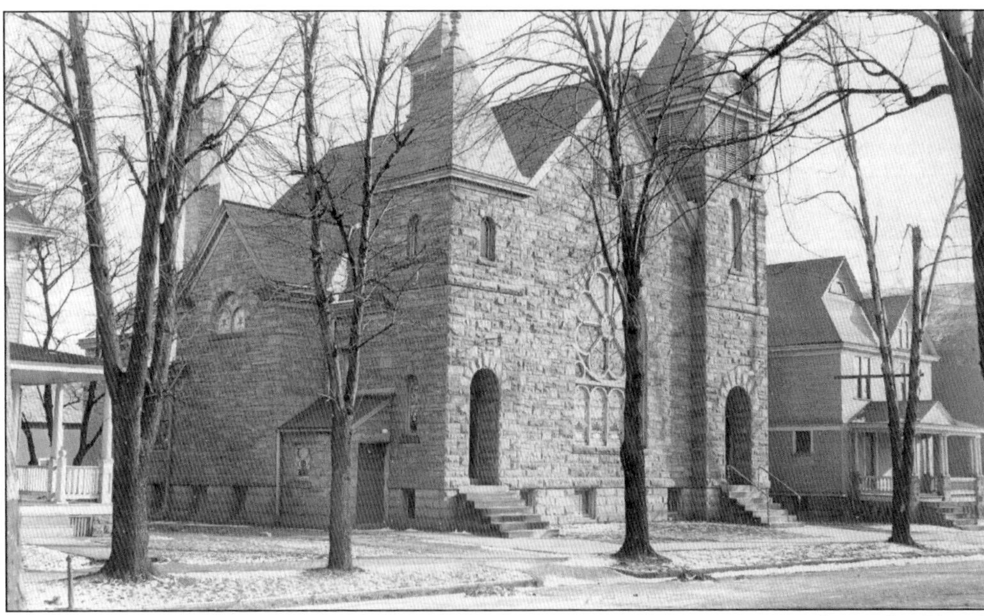

Here is the Methodist Episcopal church on North Main Street in 1906. Known today as the Church of Christ, it still stands, along with its parsonage, directly across from the Christ United Church of Christ. The center arched, stained-glass window has since been bricked over, but many of the other stained-glass windows have remained in the building. (Courtesy of Wayne Liechty.)

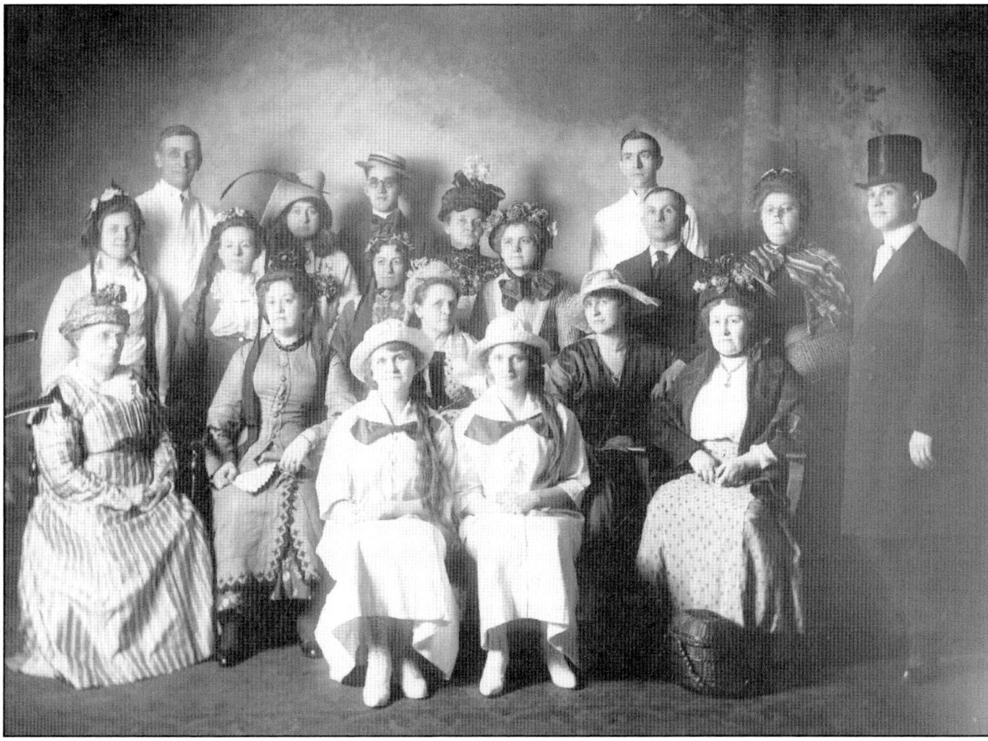

The Methodist church put on a play in 1917 in the old town hall. Some of the people included in this image are ? Weaver, ? Meins, ? Brenneman, Ethel Emrich, ? Steiner, Maria Davis, ? Baker, ? Kraft, ? McIntyre, ? Gambee, ? Cook, Harrold Stambaugh, Blanche Beck, and ? Brenneman.

The New Hope Christian Church on North Walnut Street is still active today. It was the longtime home of the Orrville Friendship Meals, which were served on a weekly basis to those less fortunate in the community.

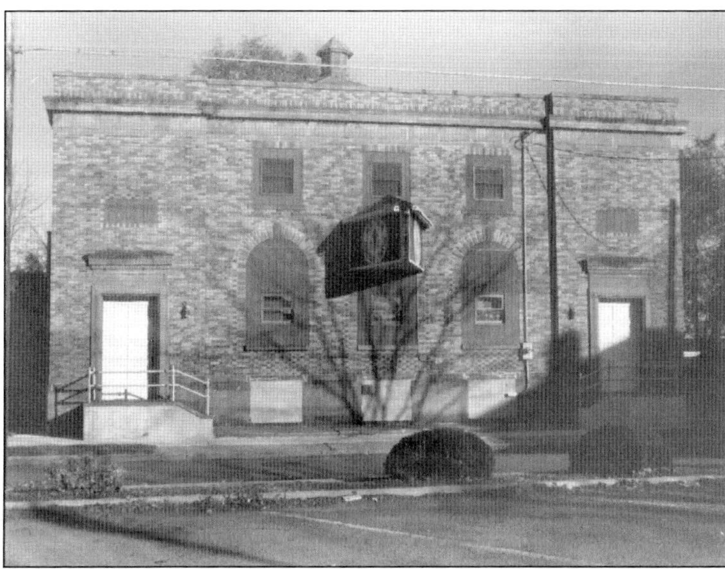

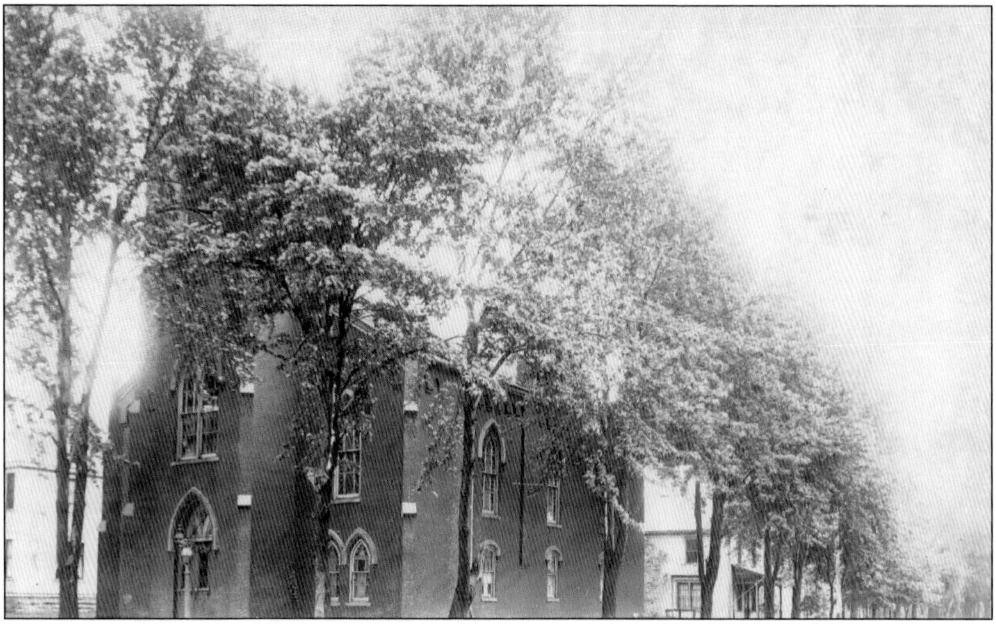

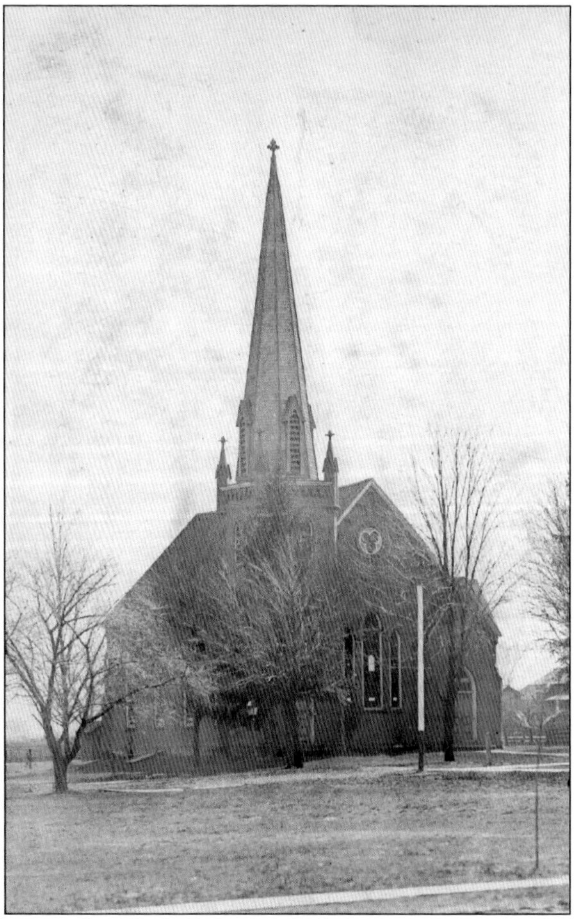

The Presbyterian church is pictured on the northeast corner of Main and Church Streets. The church was razed in the 1990s, but one of the beautiful stained-glass windows was incorporated into the interior architecture of the remodeled Orrville Public Library. Today, the property is a part of the library's parking lot.

Here is an early photograph of St. Agnes Catholic Church on Oak Street. The church is still there, but it looks much different today than it did then.

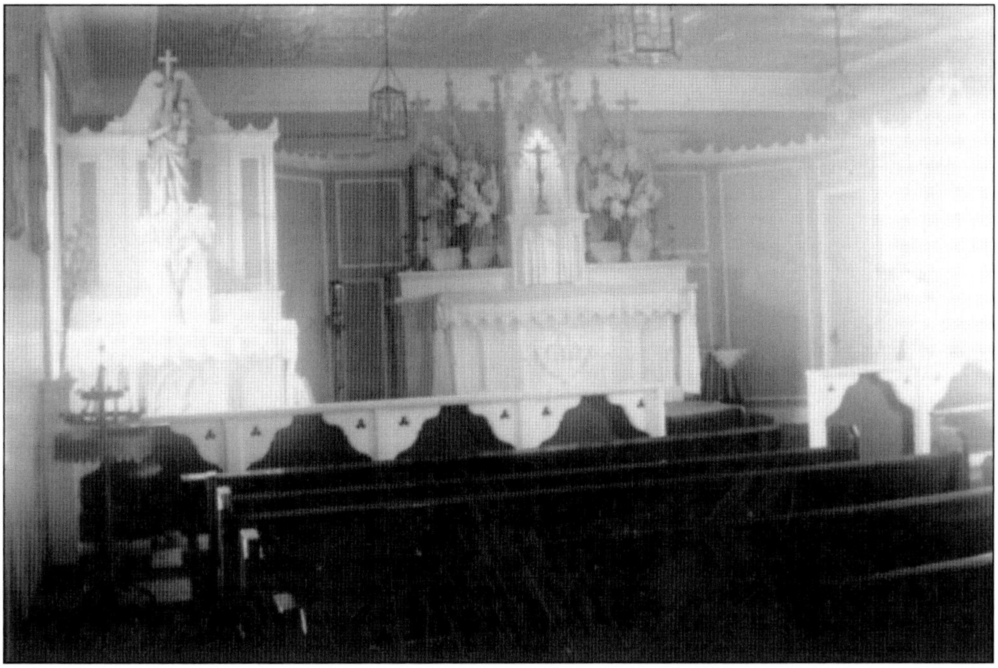

This interior photograph of St. Agnes Catholic Church was taken in 1940. Much like the exterior, a lot has changed over the years; however, the church still sits on East Oak Street on the south end of town in a quiet residential neighborhood.

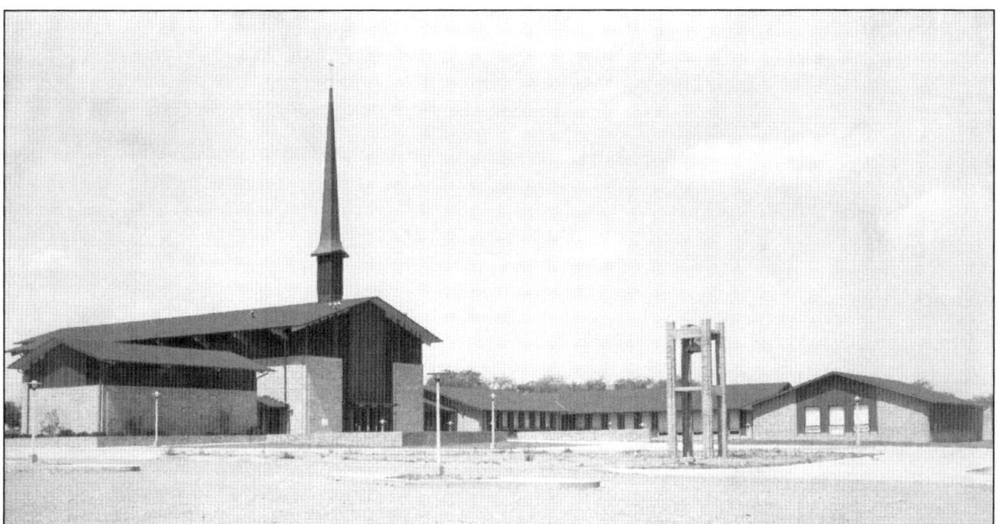

Pictured here is the Trinity United Methodist Church on North Crownhill Road. The first group of Methodists met in Orrville in 1852. Over the years, they have used a number of churches and locations of worship until the current church was built in 1969.

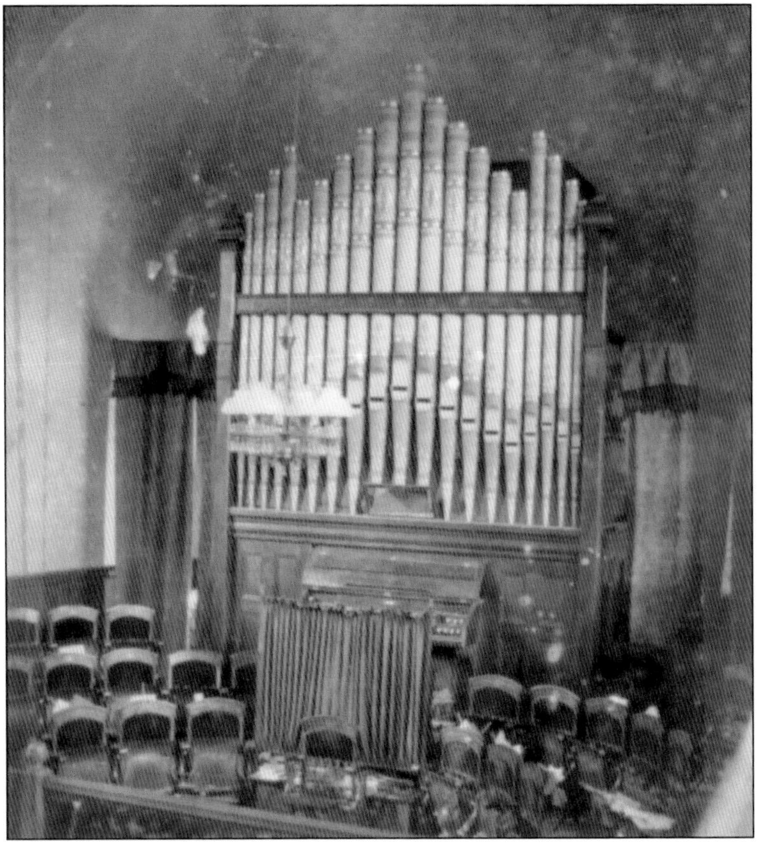

This is a photograph of a finished Schantz organ in the Old Reformed Church. The church was only used for a few more years after this was installed before the Reformed congregation moved to their new church, which was built in 1908 on the corner of North Main and Church Streets.

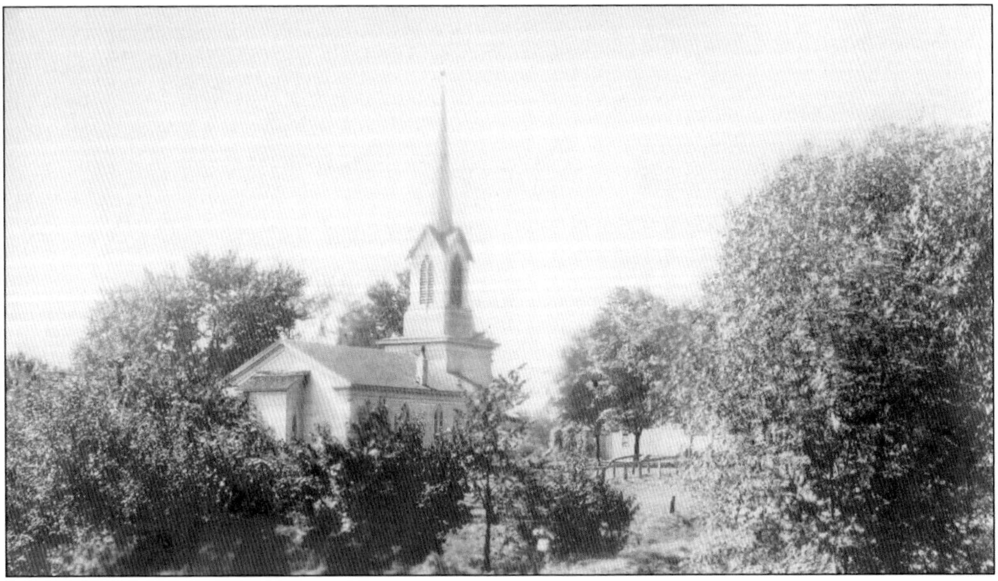

The Union Church, the first church in Orrville, was built by the United Brethrens in 1854 on the southeast corner of Church and Mill Streets. Reverend Belton was the first pastor of the nondenominational church, which had Methodists, Disciples, and Presbyterians in attendance. This photograph was taken in 1905.

Nine

Hustle and Bustle

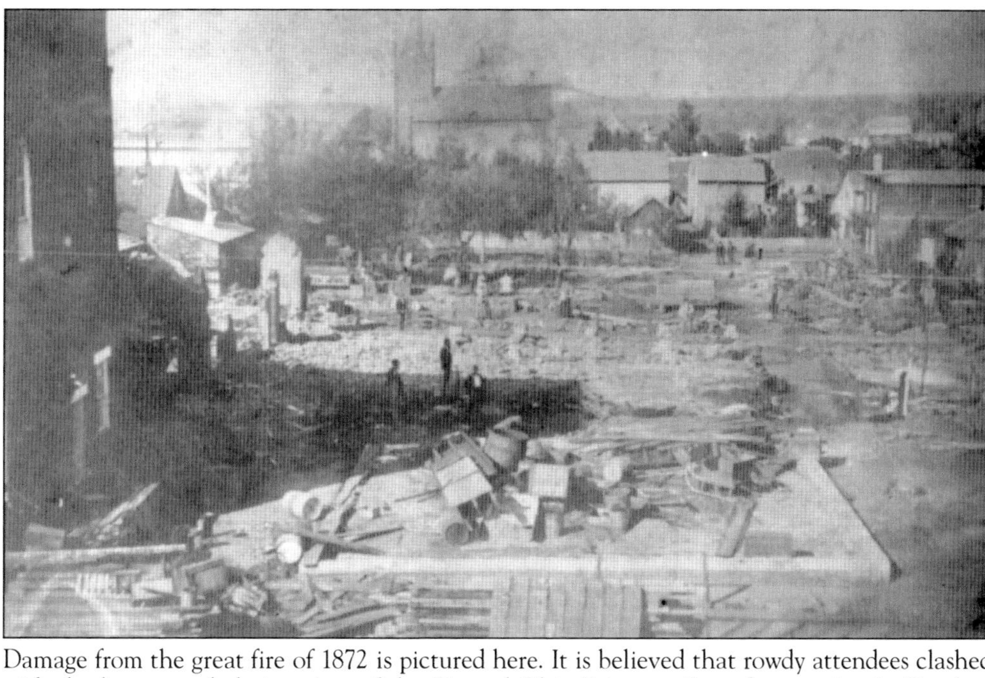

Damage from the great fire of 1872 is pictured here. It is believed that rowdy attendees clashed with the law around closing time of the Central Ohio Fair on a Saturday evening in October. Taking their escapade further, they proceeded downtown and ignited the fire that decimated much of the area. The blocks from Market to Church Streets and Main to Walnut Streets were a total loss.

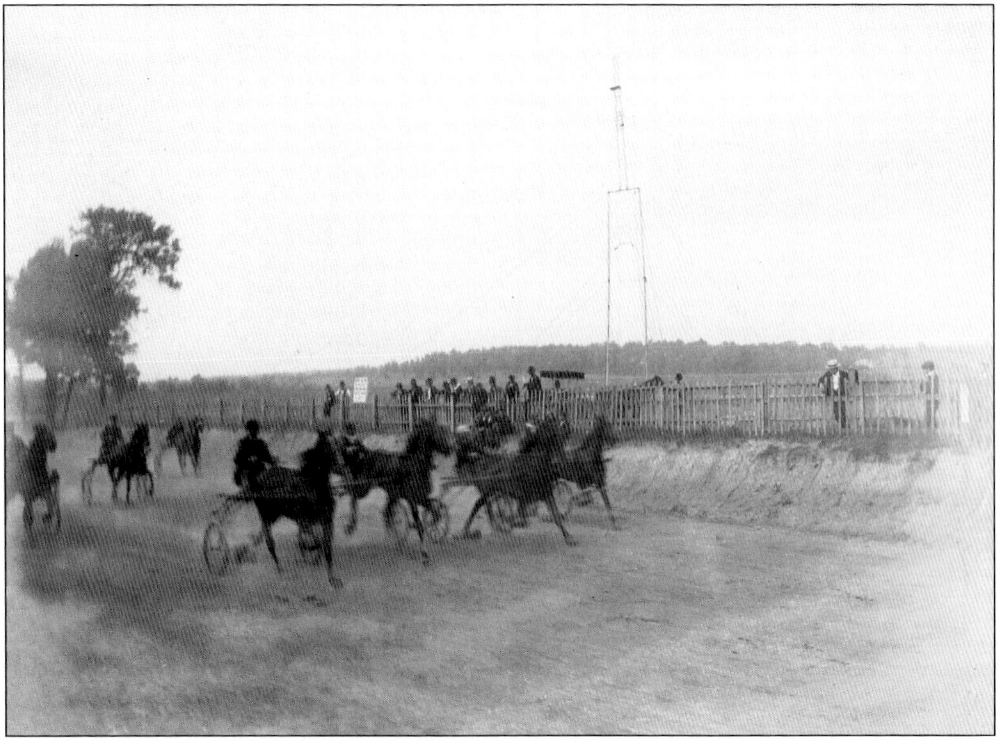

Horse-and-cart races take place at the Central Ohio Fair in 1898. Orrville was home to the fair from 1868 to 1907, and Joseph Snavely ran it; the fair ended after his death. Located east of town and just north of Orr Street, the fair advertised "unusual amusements." Those amusements included sideshows, eating booths, foot races, the Orrville Silver Cornet Band, a men-only "girlie show," and a half-mile racetrack and grandstands. The buildings on the ground included an agricultural exhibit hall, arts building, and two large horse barns. Exhibits included bantam roosters, guinea pigs, dried elderberries, pumpkins, cattle, and needlework. It was the largest fair in Ohio and featured special excursion trains that ran into town for it each year.

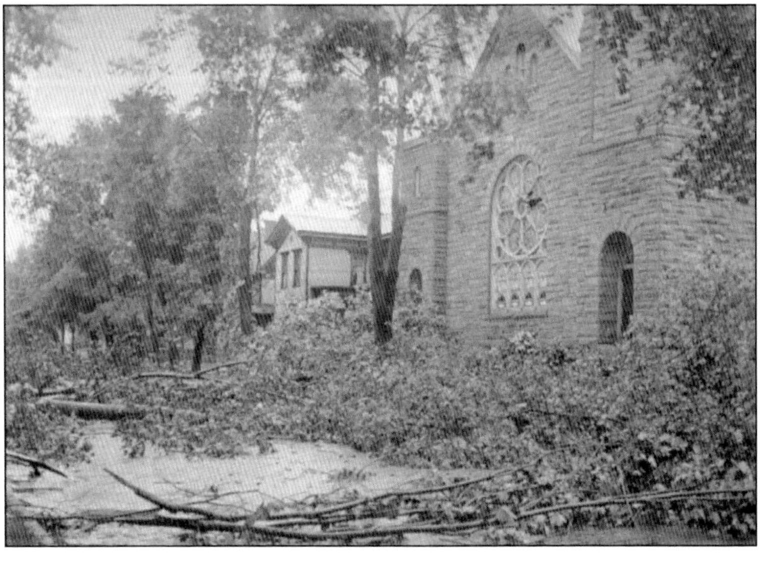

A cyclone came through Orrville on July 25, 1907, leaving quite a mess in its wake. This photograph was taken on Main Street, right in front on the Methodist church. (Courtesy of Wayne Liechty.)

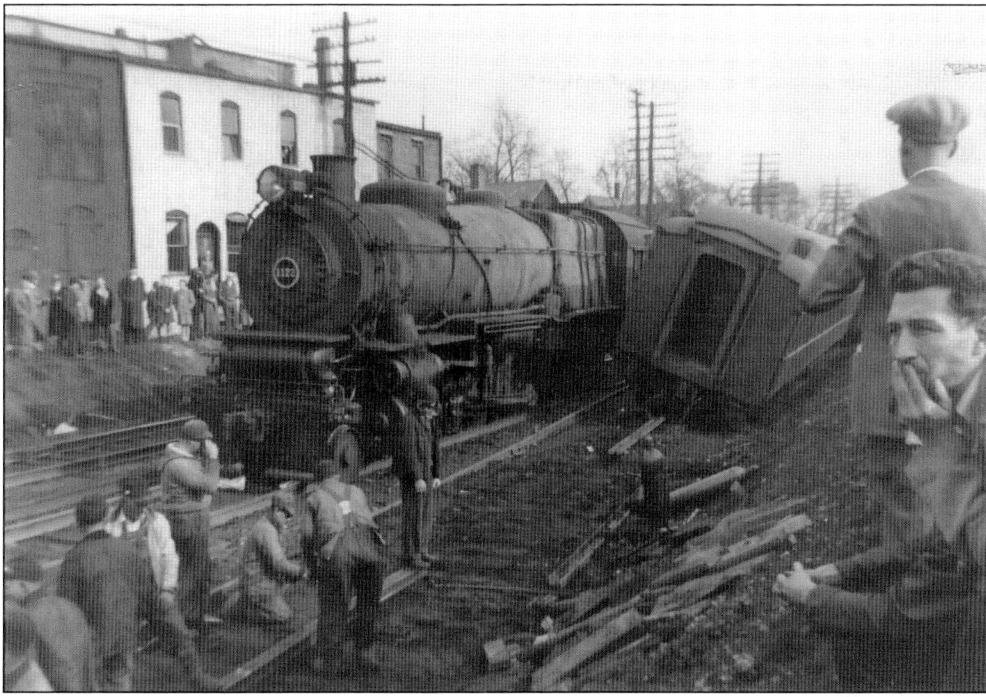

This train accident attracted quite a crowd in 1910. These tracks were located downtown, just east of Main Street. Today, this would be between the chamber of commerce and Ming-Hing Chinese restaurant.

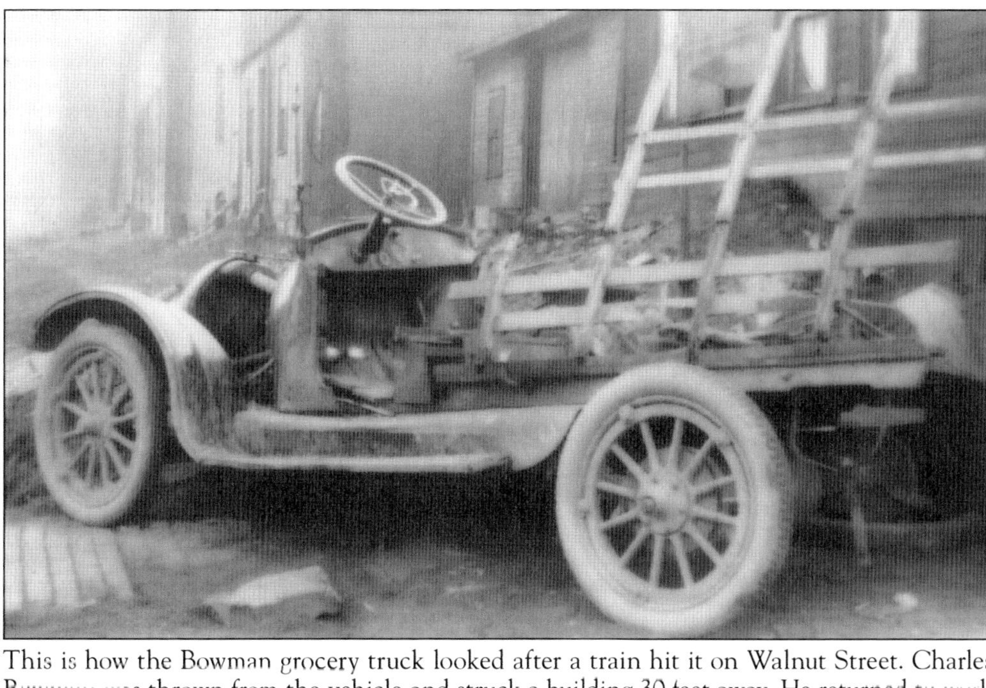

This is how the Bowman grocery truck looked after a train hit it on Walnut Street. Charles Bowman was thrown from the vehicle and struck a building 30 feet away. He returned to work at his grocery store about a month later.

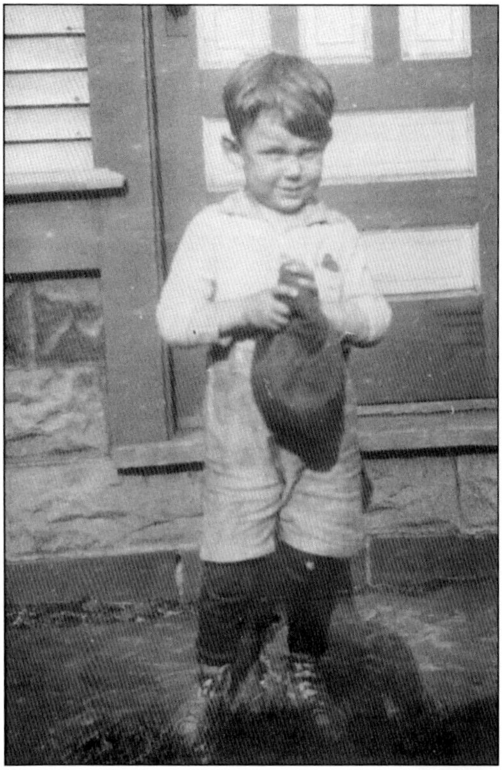

On December 28, 1928, four-year-old Melvin Horst, seen here, disappeared. The news made national headlines, people were accused, stories were told, and yards were dug up in the search of the missing child. No one was ever charged, the child was never found, and what happened to him remains a mystery today.

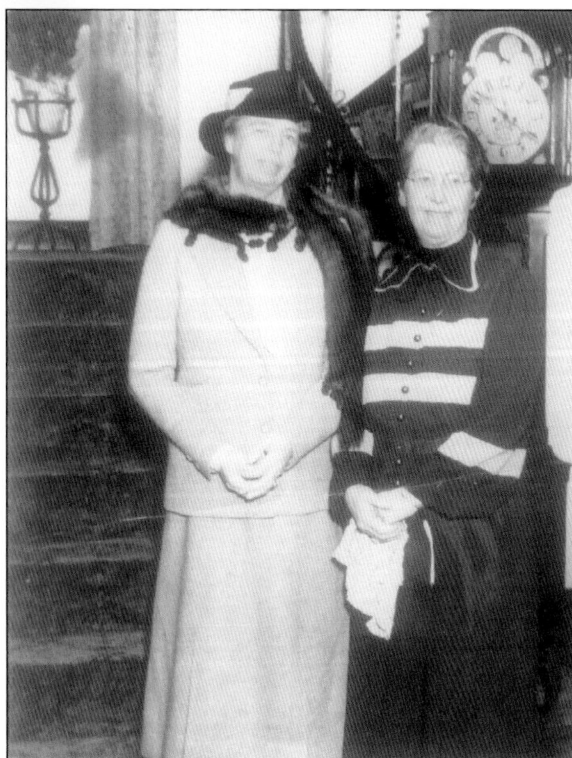

First Lady Eleanor Roosevelt came to Orrville in 1938. Traveling from Akron via automobile, she arrived around 10:00 a.m. on a Wednesday. This photograph was taken at a reception for the women of Wayne County at the home of Mrs. D. Ed Seas on South Main Street. Roosevelt then boarded a train bound for Fort Worth, Indiana, at 11:21 a.m. All schools were dismissed 45 minutes early for lunch to see her off at the depot. Her stop in Orrville wrapped up a three-week tour throughout the country, which helped to raise money for the charities she was involved with. (Courtesy of Diana Morris.)

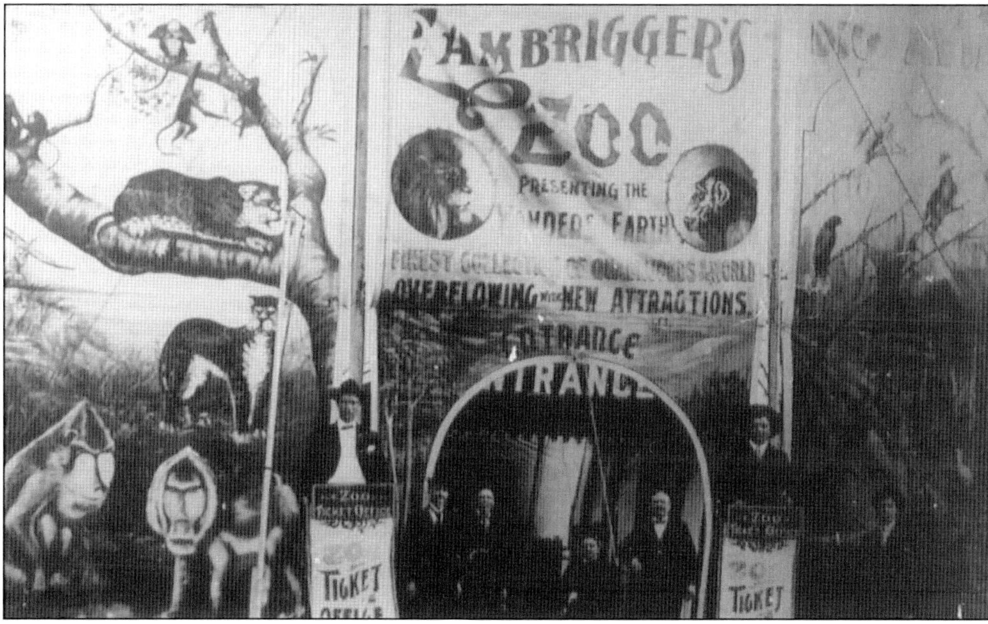

This photograph was taken at the entrance of Gus Lambrigger's Wild Animal Circus and Human Freak Show. It is said that the show boasted a 600-pound man, who in reality weighed 250 pounds.

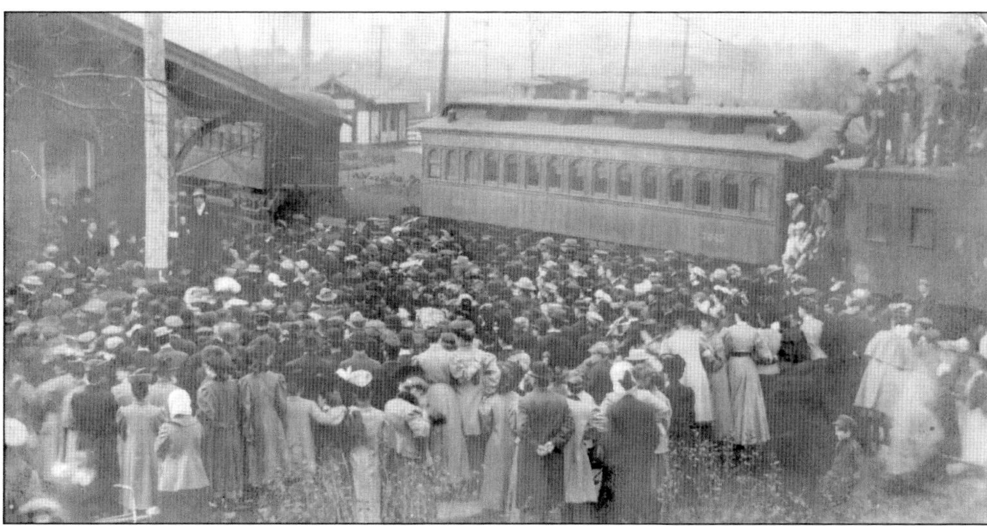

Pictured here is W.J. Bryan's reception at the Union Depot during his campaign for president of the United States. He ran and was defeated by President McKinley in 1896 and 1900. (Courtesy of Wayne Liechty.)

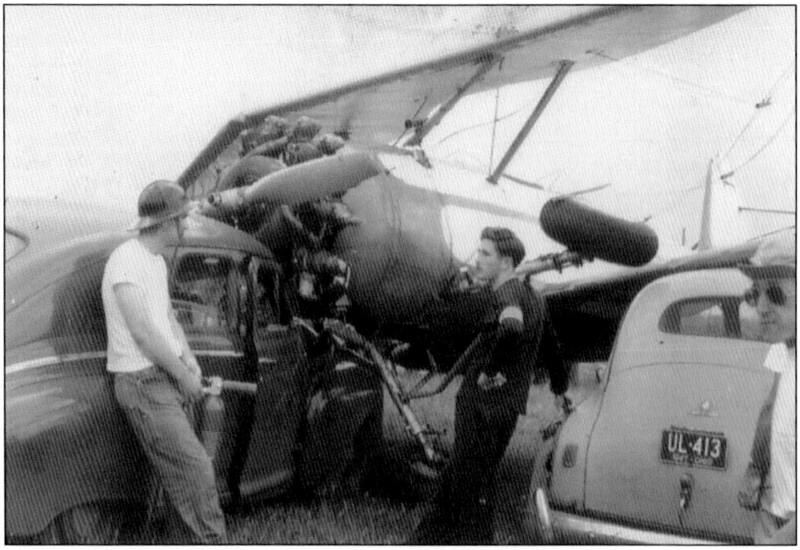

A biplane crashed into a couple of cars at Bladder Field in 1947. Bladder Field still remains just north of town on Crownhill Road, but it is no longer an active airport.

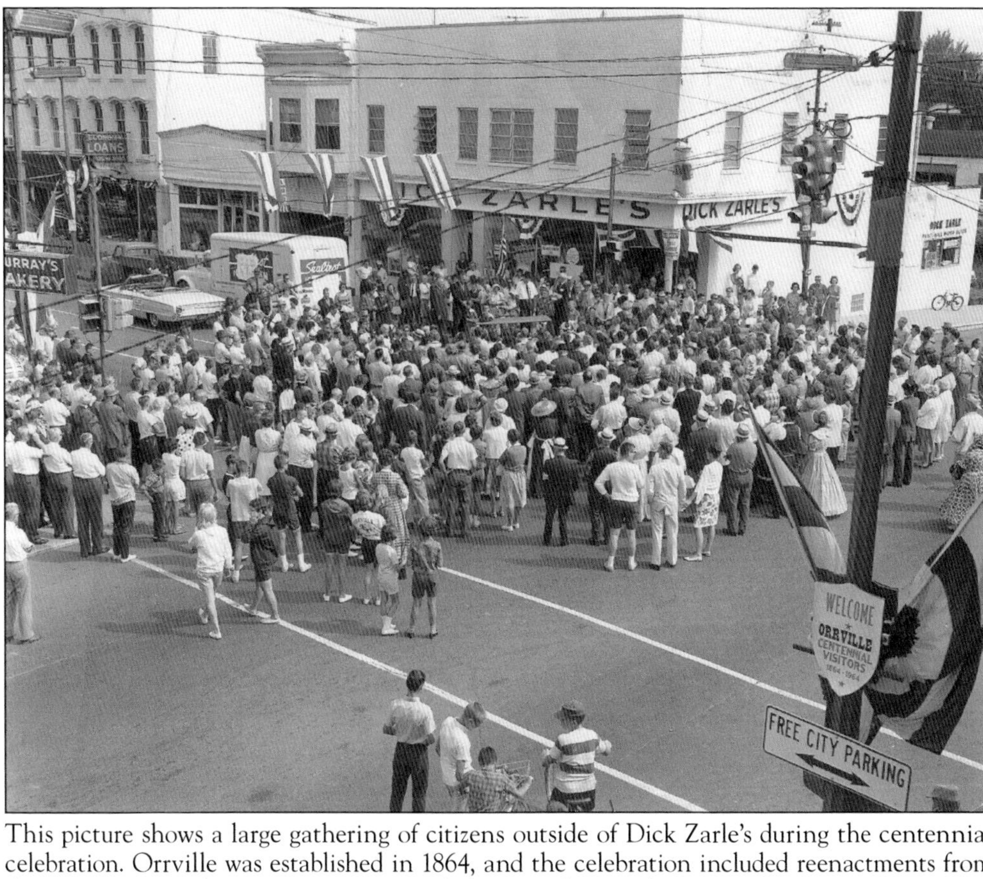

This picture shows a large gathering of citizens outside of Dick Zarle's during the centennial celebration. Orrville was established in 1864, and the celebration included reenactments from that time, citizens dressing up in pioneer clothing, and a parade.

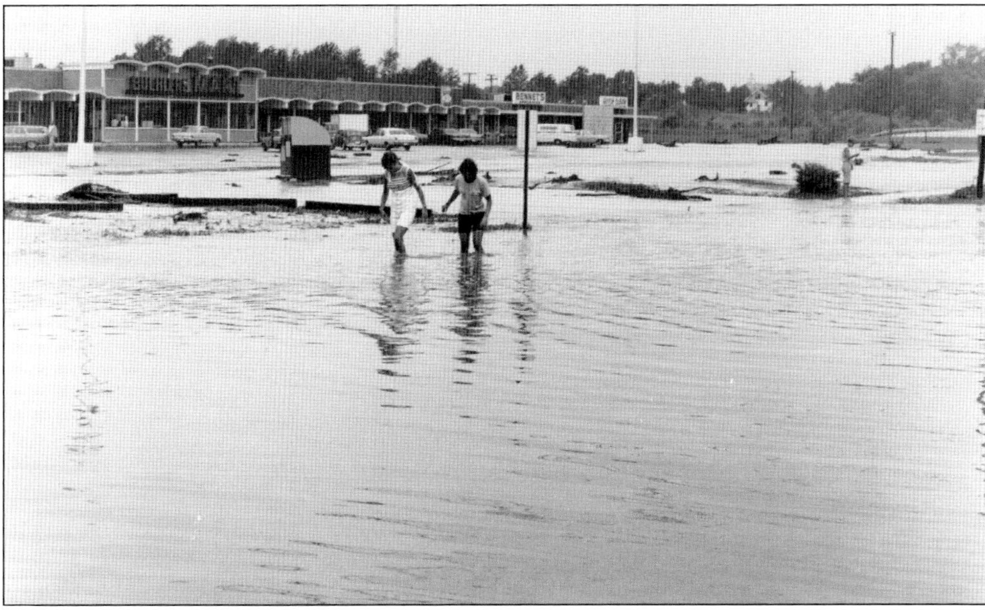

These unidentified women walk across High Street in front of Buehler's and Bennet's Appliances during the flood of 1969. The rain came on the Fourth of July, measuring 10 to 14 inches total and causing damage throughout Orrville, Wayne County, and many portions of northeastern Ohio.

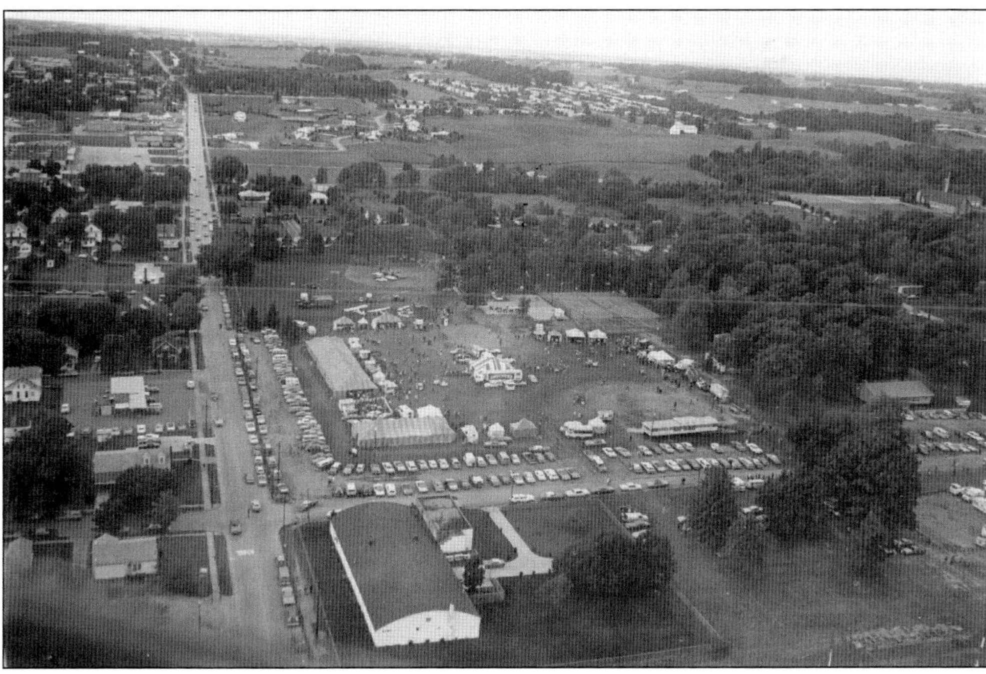

Here is an aerial photograph of the Jelly Jamboree held at Orr Park in 1974. The Jelly Jamboree was a trade show of sorts, allowing every business in Orrville to set up a booth or tent to showcase their products or services. The jamboree was hosted by the J.M. Smucker Company, which would feature a free sample of a different product annually. The celebration included the trade show, carnival, and a parade with floats from all the participating businesses.

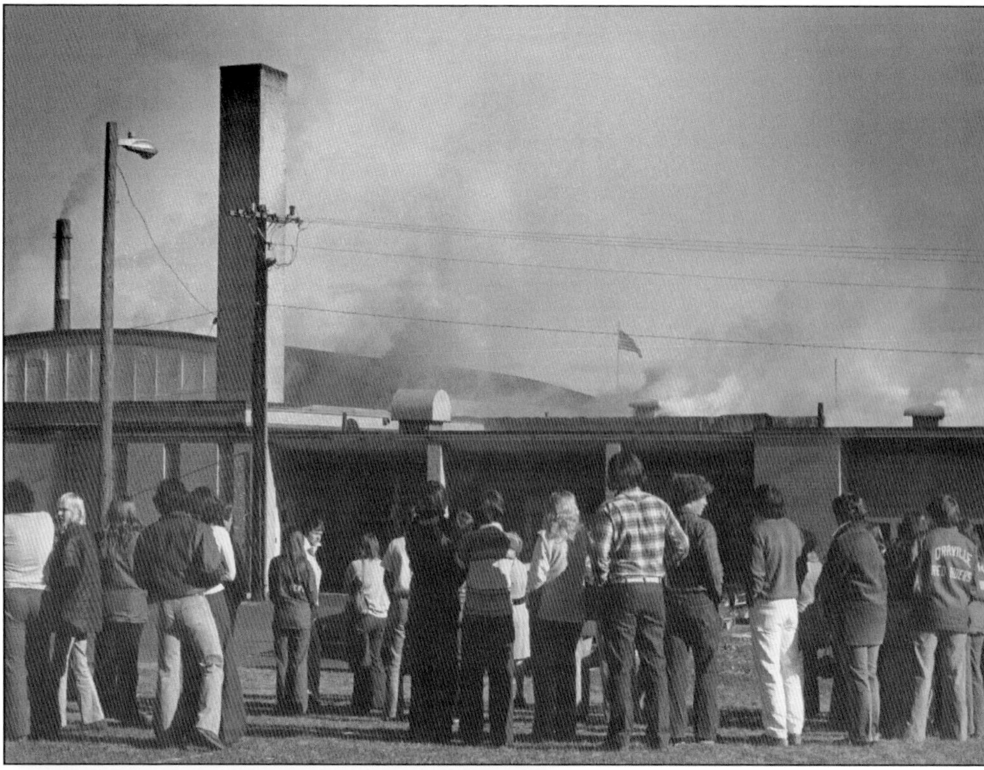

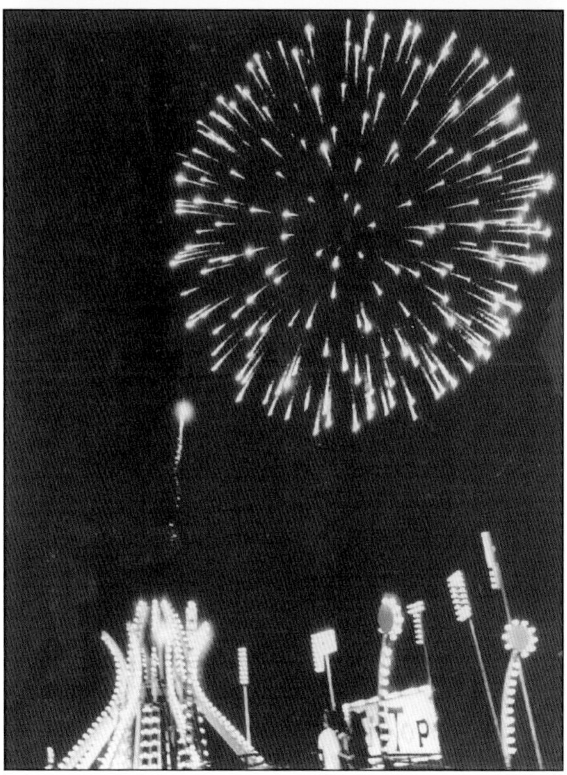

A fire in the auditorium at Orrville High School in 1977 leaves the student body outside as they witness that section of the building go up in flames.

The top of a carnival ride is seen here against the night sky with fireworks. This image was captured on the closing night of the yearly Forth of July celebration that takes place at Orr Park. The carnival is annually hosted by the Orrville Firefighters Association and ends with the Fire in the Sky fireworks show on the final night of the weeklong festivities at 10:15 p.m.

About the Organization

The following is the mission of Orrville Historical Society: "Bringing to Life, Life in the Past Lane—The Purpose of this organization is to collect, preserve, and share the Orrville area history and to be an active participant in community events. We shall lead in the education of the history of Orrville for our community and its visitors."

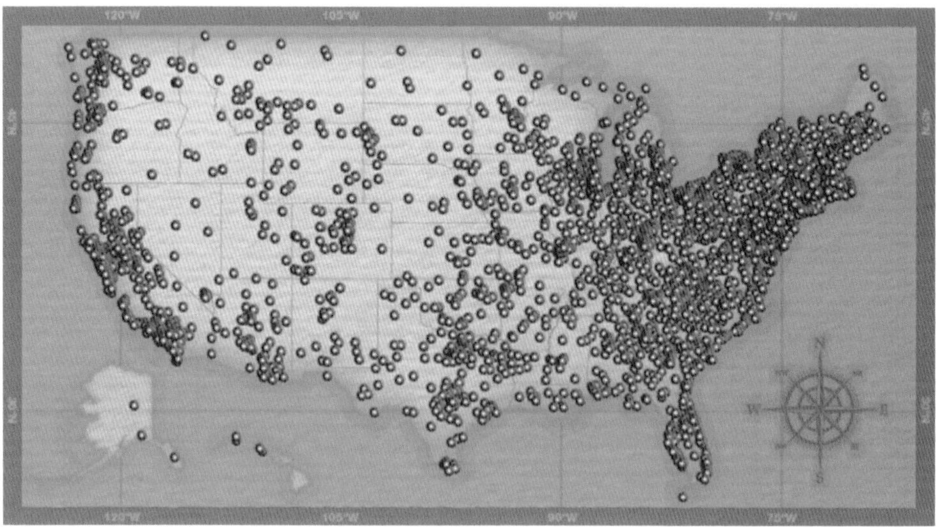

Consistent with our mission to preserve history on a local level, this book was printed in South Carolina on American-made paper and manufactured entirely in the United States. Products carrying the accredited Forest Stewardship Council (FSC) label are printed on 100 percent FSC-certified paper.

MADE IN THE USA